OXFORD
UNIVERSITY PRESS

OXFORD
UNIVERSITY PRESS

Oxford University Press, Inc., publishes works that
further Oxford University's objective of excellence
in research, scholarship, and education.

Oxford   New York
Auckland   Cape Town   Dar es Salaam   Hong Kong   Karachi
Kuala Lumpur   Madrid   Melbourne   Mexico City   Nairobi
New Delhi   Shanghai   Taipei   Toronto

With offices in
Argentina   Austria   Brazil   Chile   Czech Republic   France   Greece
Guatemala   Hungary   Italy   Japan   Poland   Portugal   Singapore
South Korea   Switzerland   Thailand   Turkey   Ukraine   Vietnam

First published by Oxford University Press, Inc., 2004
198 Madison Avenue, New York, New York 10016
www.oup.com

First issued as an Oxford University Press paperback, 2005
ISBN-13: 978-0-19-518911-7   ISBN-10: 0-19-518911-6

Oxford is a registered trademark of Oxford University Press

The Library of Congress has cataloged the cloth edition as follows:
Lazare, Aaron, 1936-
On apology / Aaron Lazare.
p. cm. Includes bibliographical references and index.
ISBN-13: 978-0-19-517343-7   ISBN-10: 0-19-517343-0
1. Apologizing. I. Title.
BF575.A75L39   2004

Design: planettheo.com

9 8 7 6 5 4 3 2 1
Printed in the United States of America on acid-free paper

To my wife, Louise,
and to the memory of my parents,
H. Benjamin Lazare and Anne Lazare

Contents

Acknowledgments

There is an oft-quoted African proverb: "It takes a village to raise a child." I found that it also takes a village to write a book. My village is the faculty and staff of the medical school campus at the University of Massachusetts, Worcester, my family, and friends outside the university.

I learned about apology on a daily basis from my wife Louise and my children Jacqueline (deceased), Sam, Sarah, Tom, Hien, Robert, David, and Naomi. My grandchildren, particularly Gabriel, taught me about the importance of apology in children. Sarah contributed to discussions of the law and apology.

From the very beginning of my interest in apology, over ten years ago, a psychologist colleague of mine, William Vogel, Ph.D., met with me regularly to encourage me, read and criticize my manuscripts, and assure me of the importance of my task. He brought to our discussions a vast knowledge of history. Marjorie Clay, Ph.D., director of ethics, did a masterful job of editing in the broadest sense. She understood what I was trying to communicate and did not rest until she felt I got it right. I believe I became a better writer under her tutelage. Both Bill and Marjorie ensured that I wrote logically and with precision. Both criticized my failings directly, with no holds barred, but with sensitivity and caring. Both are intellectuals who are committed to contributing to society. I will be forever grateful that they saw my work on apology as worthy of their tireless energy and their generosity of spirit.

Administrator Sandra Beling worked tirelessly beyond 9-5, and always in good spirits, to find original source material, review chapters, share ideas, and assemble the manuscript for publication. Administrative assistants Linda Boria and Diana Coppolino read manuscripts, offered ideas about apologies, and organized my work life to make it possible to complete the book while working in my role as the chancellor/dean. Paula MacDonald worked diligently as a research assistant.

Numerous people generously offered their advice, recommendations, encouragement, and personal apology stories. These people were coworkers, friends, relatives, and friends of my children: Mark Shelton, Andrea Badrigian, Lanny Hilgar, Robert Nemeth, Lee Hammel, Manuel Zax, Albert and Linda Sherman, Paul Appelbaum, Mai Lan Rogoff, Salah M. Hassanein, Jon Kabat-Zinn, Pat Loughery, Betsy Wright, Anastacia Wilson, Susan Wentz, Jim Wells, Will Sogg, Rabbi Leslie Gutterman, Rev. G. Truman Welch, Rev. John E. Brooks, S. J., Paul Miller, Myron Cummins, Mort and Vivian Sigel, Bob and Shirley Siff, John Goodson, Eileen Duhamel, Alan Preston, Virginia Preston (deceased), Nick Cannon, Loren Preston, Ben Preston, Jim Granger, Sandy Lazare, Sally Mason, Joan Lazare, Helen and Harold Perkel, Janet Cannon, Pat Cannon, Frances and James Cannon (deceased), Ken Rothwell, Brady Millican, Ed Hausman, Matt Gorman, Matt Tedrow, Billy Anderson, Gemma Sole, Meriwether Burruss, Burncoat High School in

Worcester, Massachusetts, and Carl Sandburg High School in Orland Park, Illinois.

My coworkers helped by carrying some of my workload to keep the medical school functioning at full speed: Rick Stanton, Cheryl Scheid, Michele Pugnaire, and Tom Manning.

Jack and Shelley Blais's selfless generosity and support inspired me in ways they may never comprehend.

My high school English teacher, Mrs. Beatrice Harelick, is always in my mind when I think about psychological matters and writing. She was an inspiration to many students at Bayonne High School in Bayonne, New Jersey.

Leon Eisenberg, M.D., my mentor and friend for 36 years, has always encouraged innovative inquiries into the human condition.

Bryan Hamlin was responsible for inviting me to present my ideas to an international audience at Caux, Switzerland, where I received the gift of meeting Professor Rajmohan Gandhi, who discussed my presentation.

I am deeply indebted to the Josiah Macy, Jr. Foundation, under the leadership of June Osborne, M.D., for its generous support in promoting communication skills in the medical encounter.

I am particularly grateful to Fiona Stevens, my editor, at Oxford University Press, for her encouragement and support throughout the entire process of publication.

On Apology

ONE

The Growing Importance of Apologies

One of the most profound human interactions is the offering and accepting of apologies. Apologies have the power to heal humiliations and grudges, remove the desire for vengeance, and generate forgiveness on the part of the offended parties. For the offender, they can diminish the fear of retaliation and relieve the guilt and shame that can grip the mind with a persistence and tenacity that are hard to ignore. The result of the apology process, ideally, is the reconciliation and restoration of broken relationships.

Most people, if asked, will tell you stories of grudges that have destroyed important relationships and, in some instances, have even torn families and friends apart. The offenses that lead to these grudges range from events such as failing to visit a friend in a hospital or not attending a wedding or funeral to betrayals of trust and public humiliations. An effective apology at the time might have prevented the grudge, and a belated apology, months, years, or even decades later, might have effected reconciliation.

Consider this story of an apology delivered 61 years after the triggering event. A 71-year-old man, Manuel, approached me one evening at a social event to thank me for helping him restore an important relationship through an apology. He kindly wrote me, shortly afterward, about the circumstances of the event and the apology itself. "When I attended your apology lecture sometime last year I was struck by the simplicity and importance of the concept of a true apology as you so ably described it. I stored it in my mind, told people about it, and then later it dawned on me that I had a personal use for it, and composed the following letter, addressed to a friend of mine with whom I had grown up from our ages of about four to seventeen. He is now 70 and I am 71. Both of us have been married over forty years and have children and grandchildren." Manuel delivered the letter four months after writing it, "having waited until I had the opportunity to give it to him, to watch him read it, and to talk to him about it."

"Dear Eddie," the letter began. "This is a letter of apology for an event that took place about sixty years ago. It has only been recently that I decided to write this letter, but thoughts about the event have been with me now and then since it occurred.

"I can see you standing on your rear porch, facing a ring of boys forming a crescent and facing you, shouting at you. I don't remember their words, but the meaning they carried had to do with your being a sissy because you threw a ball in the way a girl would. I was within the crescent, but I don't know if I was saying anything. I was stuck there and did not want to be there.

Finally, I advanced toward you and you said something like you knew I would stand by you.

"I did not stand by you. My vocal chords were paralyzed. I was struggling with the task of choosing between my two allegiances. I backed away from you and rejoined the other kids. My insides were churning and I remained there in the street forever.

"My memory has not allowed me to recall what took place in the days that followed that incident, and even though I know that time passed and our friendship was rekindled, that scene has revisited me at various times over the years.

"When you called me on the phone in the 1970s and asked me to think back to our Dorchester days together, I was truly happy to hear your voice, and then even happier to later see you again after the intervening thirty-odd years. But from a far away corner of my being, that scene of the taunting boys clicked open in my mind's eye, as it had at other times, but this time it was vivid. In that scene I saw your disappointment in me, as I inflicted such cruelty upon you.

"So now I am apologizing for my behavior then on Wildwood Street. Though I wanted to say these words to you, I felt that I couldn't. Typing these words has been difficult enough for me." The letter ended with, "Your loving friend, Manny."

"As Eddie read this letter," Manuel wrote to me, "I saw his face first register surprise, then a smile slowly spread over his features. We hugged and he said 'I love you.' He explained that he had a weak throwing arm throughout his life, which was the reason why he threw the way he did. He reminded me that he never took the position of quarterback when we played football because of that. Finally, Manuel told me that "one end result of my letter of apology is that I have been released of that haunting image of hurting Eddie." Manuel wrote me a second time, about two years later, to tell me that Eddie died 18 months after he received the written apology during their visit. He also shared these thoughts with me: "The fact that I delivered my letter of apology to Eddie before he died was important to me, because it was something that had been weighing on my mind for so long; and also, I was able to see Eddie's reaction, indicating how he felt about me, one of close friendship, which I shared. Had Eddie died before I delivered the letter, I would have been denied the satisfying resolution of the removal of a . . . mental burden."[1]

This moving story is not, to be sure, an everyday apology. Most apologies are communicated within a shorter time interval following the offense, and most apologies are not so emotionally evocative. Yet, as we shall see, this story has numerous characteristics of many apologies described in this book and experienced in daily living. These characteristics include the timelessness of the emotional pain on the part of one or both parties, the initial reluctance to apologize, the simplicity of the act of apologizing, the relief of guilt of the offender, the spontaneous generosity and forgiveness on the part of the offended, and the restoration of the relationship.

The importance of apologies in personal relationships has its parallel in national and international apologies. We read in the newspapers about Senator Trent Lott's serial apologies for comments widely thought to be supportive of segregation. His future as a congressional leader hung in the balance. We read about a protracted discussion over whether and how the U.S. government should apologize to the Chinese government for the loss of their fighter jet plane. Recovery of our reconnaissance plane with its crew hung in the balance. We learned with surprise that China apologized "to everyone" for withholding information about the SARS outbreak, an epidemic thought to have originated in China. We read about the ongoing debate over whether presidents William J. Clinton and George W. Bush should apologize for slavery. For more than a year, we read about Roman Catholic priests responding to demands of sexual abuse victims for apologies. We even read on the front page of the *New York Times* that the U.S. Supreme Court decision over gay sexual conduct could be regarded as an apology: "The Supreme Court issued a sweeping declaration of constitutional liberty for gay men and lesbians today, over-ruling a Texas sodomy law in the broadest possible terms and effectively apologizing for a contrary 1986 decision that the majority said 'demeans the lives of homosexual persons.'"[2] Of particular interest in a presidential election year (2004) was the apology of Richard A. Clarke, "counterterrorism czar" for presidents Clinton and G. W. Bush, apologizing for his role in the failure to prevent 9/11. Several times each week, we see public apologies reported in our national newspapers. The importance of these apologies and our attempts to understand them has clearly become a part of our everyday lives.

ARE APOLOGIES ON THE RISE?

When I began to study the apology process in 1992, only one book, published in 1991, offered a broad perspective on the field, *Mea Culpa: A Sociology of Apology and Reconciliation.*[3] I was interested to discover that the author of this influential and often-cited book, Nicholas Tavuchis, was motivated to study apologies because of his personal experience. My own motivation for studying apology, as I will describe later in this chapter, was also triggered by a personal experience.

Tavuchis opined that there was no increase in apologies in our culture at the time of his writing. "It is difficult to state with any certainty whether nowadays we show a lesser propensity to apologize than in past times or recognize fewer occasions that specifically call for apologies," he wrote.[4] He did suggest, however, the possibility that apologies might grow in importance. "As impersonal and legal systems of social control proliferate in our own culture and in other cultures, apologies may loom even larger than they have in the past as voluntary and humane means for reconciling personal and collective differences."[5] Only two years after the publication of Tavuchis's book, *Time* magazine published an article entitled, "Who's Sorry Now? Last Month Everybody Apologized for Past Horrors."[6] Clearly, something was changing in our culture, and I began to notice how frequently apologies appeared in the media.

I was curious to see whether my impression that apologies were on the rise could be quantified by data, so I compared the number of articles in two of the most influential U.S. newspapers, the *New York Times* and the *Washington Post*, containing the word "apology" or "apologize" during the five-year period of 1990-1994 with that of 1998-2002 (using LEXIS®-NEXIS®). The two newspapers combined had a total of 1,193 such articles during the first five-year period, compared to 2,003 articles during the latter five-year period. Analyzing the entire 13-year period from 1990-2002, I found that the frequency of apology articles reached its peak during the years 1997-1998 (the average for both newspapers combined was 456 per year) while decreasing somewhat and reaching plateau thereafter (392 for the year 2002 for the two newspapers combined).[7]

Others have noticed this "apology phenomenon" as well. Newspaper columnists covering the national and international scene have written about the growing importance of public apologies, while articles, cartoons, advice columns, and radio and television programs have similarly addressed the subject of private apologies. The topic of apology has even become material for comedic turns, with late-night television show hosts such as David Letterman and Jay Leno poking fun at celebrity apologies, and the popular sitcom *Seinfeld* devoting an entire episode to the issue of who is owed an apology and what counts as an offense.[8] In addition, a brisk market exists for "how-to" books and articles on apology, as evidenced by the numerous articles in *Family Circle* and similar publications, and books such as *The Power of Apology: Healing Steps to Transform All Your Relationships*[9] and *The One Minute Apology: A Powerful Way to Make Things Better.*[10] The professions of law and medicine have begun to write about apology as well. Beginning in the early 1990s, articles described the role of apology in both civil and criminal law, analyzing how it functions during trial and in pre-trial mediation.[11] Even the formerly forbidden idea that physicians should apologize to their patients for medical mistakes has become a subject of discussion in both the medical and legal literature.[12]

Another indicator of the growing international importance of apologies is the fact that China now boasts of several apology companies, as well as apology "call-in" shows on state radio. The Tianjin Apology and Gift Center, part of a psychological stress reduction center, has a staff of 20 who write letters, deliver gifts, and offer explanations.[13] The employees are middle-aged, educated, well-spoken men and women who have significant life experience, often as lawyers, teachers, and social workers. Most of the clients are involved in family or business disputes or are estranged lovers. This method of apology in China, through paid surrogates, illustrates not only the importance of apology in other cultures but also how delivering apologies differs according to culture. It seems to me unlikely that such a business would thrive in the United States, where the offended party expects to receive the apology directly from the offender or at least from a significant third party.

This increase in apologies might appear to be a positive trend, since most of us were taught that we should apologize when we have offended others and we should forgive others when they have apologized to us. Yet many of these apologies have been described as empty, shallow, hollow, cheap, insincere, fraudulent, or "just talk." I call them "failed" or "pseudo-apologies," and I believe they often do more harm than good. More than simply being ineffective, these pseudo-apologies commonly compound the offenses they were intended to heal.

Examples of failed apologies are everywhere. When an acquaintance says to you, "I apologize for whatever I may have done," he or she has failed to apologize adequately, because he or she has not acknowledged the offense and may not even believe an offense was committed. Another common example is the statement, "If you were hurt, I am sorry." Not only does this statement begin with a conditional acknowledgment of the offense (e.g., "I will be sorry only if you are hurt"), but it even suggests that your sensitivity may be the problem. When President Richard M. Nixon, in his resignation speech, stated that he deeply regretted "any injuries that may have been done," and when Senator Robert

W. Packwood apologized for the "alleged offenses" of sexually abusing female pages, both failed to acknowledge definitively what the public believed to be true, thus insulting the intelligence of their respective audiences. Similarly, when Senator Trent Lott apologized for his implied support for Senator Strom Thurmond's past racial policies by claiming "it was a poor choice of words," and then followed that apology with four additional apologies, each more fervent than the last, his audiences may have wondered whether he really believed that he had done anything wrong in the first place. Boston's Cardinal Bernard Law's repeated and varying apologies for his role in the clergy sexual abuse scandal is yet another example, giving the public reason to wonder whether each new apology was offered in anticipation of another public exposure of wrongdoing.

With failed apologies growing in prevalence and with so many trash confessional and forgiveness programs on television, it is no wonder that many observers of the American scene have grown cynical about apologies, seeing them either as efforts to manipulate others or as shallow attempts by the offenders to free themselves from guilt. But I have another view of this phenomenon. I see the proliferation of pseudo-apologies as eloquent testimony to the power of "real" apologies. In fact, I believe pseudo-apologies are parasitical on that power. With a pseudo-apology, the offender is trying to reap the benefits of apologizing without having actually earned them. People who offer a pseudo-apology are unwilling to take the steps necessary for a genuine apology; that is, they do not acknowledge the offense adequately, or express genuine remorse, or offer appropriate reparations, including a commitment to make changes in the future. These three actions are the price of an effective apology. To undertake them requires honesty, generosity, humility, commitment, courage, and sacrifice. In other words, the rewards of an effective apology can only be earned. They cannot be stolen.

WHY HAVE APOLOGIES GROWN IN IMPORTANCE?

I believe there are several overlapping explanations for the upsurge in apologies, especially in the public arena. One event that may have contributed to the increasing number of apologies in the decade of the 1990s was the dawn of the millennium. When not preoccupied with the "Y2K" phenomena, people tended to view the year 2000 as a time for new beginnings, using the years running up to it as an occasion for soul searching and moral reckoning, in the process giving themselves a "clean slate" for the new millennium. For example, South Korean Prime Minister Kim Dae Jung responded to a Japanese apology by saying, "We must settle the accounts of the 20th century . . . as we enter the 21st century."[14] In a 1997 article on apology, *New York Times* writer Karl E. Meyer commented, "So it seems only fitting that as the year 2000 approaches that countries less than people feel a need for a moral reckoning."[15] Michael Henderson of the *Christian Science Monitor* observed, "as we approach a new millennium, sincere attempts are being made to clean the slates,"[16] while Lance Morrow of *Time* magazine spoke of "millennial soul searching."[17]

In addition to the secular meaning of the millennium, the year 2000 had particular significance for Roman Catholics. It was a Jubilee or Holy Year and the first such Jubilee that fell on the turn of the millennium. (The first Jubilee was proclaimed by Pope Boniface VIII in 1300.) According to the 1994 encyclical letter *Tertio Millennio Adveniente,* Pope John Paul II stated, " . . . the Church should make this passage with a clear awareness of what has happened to her during the last ten centuries. She cannot cross the threshold of the new millennium without encouraging her children to purify themselves, through repentance of past errors."[18]

This impulse to apologize on the eve of the new millennium extended to all walks of life, even in the sports world. George Steinbrenner, owner of the New York Yankees, made a millennial apology to Yogi Berra, when he visited the former Yankee catcher and manager to apologize for his insensitivity in firing Berra nearly 14 years earlier. Berra's wife, Carmen, thought the visit was Steinbrenner's way of clearing his conscience in anticipation of the millennium. "With the year 2000 coming, everyone is thinking about the future, about peace, about making things right," she commented.[19] (See chapter 9 for a further discussion of this apology.)

Another explanation for the increase in the frequency of apologies is the rapidly increasing globalization of the world, enhanced by our exponentially increasing technology. High-speed travel, television, cell phones, faxes, e-mail, digital photography, the Internet, and international banking have indeed shrunk the world to a "global village" Marshall McLuhan described in 1967, " . . . a world of total involvement in which everybody is so profoundly involved with everybody else."[20] Thirty-six years later, Robert Wright, author of *Nonzero: The Logic of Human Destiny,*[21] offered similar words: "All along, technological evolution has been moving our species towards this nonzero-sum moment, when our welfare is crucially correlated with the welfare of the other, and our freedom depends on the sympathetic comprehension of the other."[22]

In such a global village, it would matter greatly to the Canadians if the United States were to spill oil or nuclear waste into waters near its borders, and vice versa. It mattered to most of Europe that Chernobyl was emitting nuclear debris, and many nations share a growing concern over the rusting of Russia's nuclear-powered submarines. It matters to the super-powers and to neighboring states whether there is peace or war in the Middle East or anywhere else in the world. Starvation in one country is of concern to its neighbors and beyond. Global warming and responsibility for it is of concern to most nations. In a global village, strong nations need their neighbors to succeed and share good will in order to develop and sustain markets. One need only to look at the aftermath of 9/11 to see how interconnected the world has become: A major tragedy in one country leaves a wide swath of disaster throughout the world, including restricted travel, fewer imported goods, damaged economies, and pandemic fear.

I believe the globalization of the world increases the importance of the apology process in two distinct ways. First, neighbors who interact on a continual basis have more disputes to settle than those who live, literally, "oceans apart." As neighbors in this global village, we use apology as an essential method of conflict resolution. Second, the very nature of our instant global communications, our being continually exposed to the world, diminishes the possibility of secret behaviors that others regard as offensive. These uncensored communications can reveal thoughts and attitudes that the originator would rather have kept secret, and for which an apology may now be expected.

One example of secretive behavior exposed by the Internet involved Chinese Prime Minister Zhu Rongji. A deadly explosion at a rural Chinese school killed 38 children between the ages of 9 and 11. Mr. Zhu initially confirmed government reports that a lone madman or a deranged suicidal bomber was responsible. The subsequent story, however, revealed that the children at the school had been forced to make fireworks to finance their under-funded school. The *New York Times* reported that the bereaved parents rejected the official explanation of a suicidal bomber, a statement that "caused a barrage of caustic criticism on Internet chat rooms and reactions ranging from outrage to resignation among people across the country," the article noted.[23] Following further reports in the Hong Kong and foreign media, Premier Zhu admitted that schools had illegally used student labor in the past. He added, "I believe that, no matter what the facts are, the State Council and I both bear an unshirkable responsibility. That is to say, we have not properly implemented the government and Chairman Jiang's instructions."[24] Premier Zhu's remarks appear to be a successful apology, one that might not have occurred without Internet publicity.

A second example illustrates how instant and uncensored communications can expose offensive behaviors and ideas that the originator may have preferred to keep private. North Carolina State Representative Donald S. Davis received an e-mail message from an Internet site that said, in part, "Two things made this country great: White men and Christianity."[25] The e-mail continued by observing that our country owed its origin and its early successes to the Christian Bible and the Ten Commandments. Davis did not consider the letter racist. Instead, he commented, "There's a lot to it that's truth, the way I see it. Who came to this country first—the white man, didn't he? That's who made this country great."[26] On a Monday evening following the Friday he received it, Davis forwarded the message to every member of the North Carolina House and Senate.

The result was predictable. After receiving complaints from his colleagues, Davis sent this apology: "I humbly want to apologize if the e-mail forwarded from my office . . . was offensive or disrespectful to any one in this General Assembly, state or nation." He said that he forwarded the e-mail for "information and to show the type of messages that come across the Internet" and claimed that the e-mail did not represent his personal belief and that he was not "a racist or white supremacist."[27]

Subsequent chapters will show why Davis's remarks failed as an apology. My point here is to illustrate how sending an e-mail, particularly during off-hours, can be a risky endeavor. Before the awesome speed of e-mail, a competent secretary would have advised against sending the communication.

The third example of the impact of instant and uncensored communication was the dissemination of photos of the humiliation of Iraqi prisoners by members of the United States military. World reaction forced apologies from President George Bush, Secretary of Defense Donald Rumsfeld, and others.

Another possible explanation for the increase in apologies is the enormous destruction of human life and the introduction and proliferation of nuclear weapons during the past century. These phenomena, coupled with the current emphasis on transnational interdependence, may have resulted in the increased attention given to morality and justice following World War II and the end of the Cold War. In other words, we are attempting to change our behavior in order to survive. Elazar Barkan, in his book *The Guilt of Nations: Restitution and*

Negotiating Historical Injustices, writes, " . . . beginning at the end of World War II, and quickening since the end of the Cold War, questions of morality and justice are receiving growing attention as political questions. As such, the need for restitution to past victims has become a major part of national politics and international diplomacy."[28] He points out that, particularly for democracies, "Admitting responsibility and guilt for historical injustices . . . " has become a marker for " . . . national political stability and strength rather than shame."[29] For example, the German government voluntarily made significant apologies and reparations to Jews and to others who suffered under Nazi rule, and the U.S. government similarly made apologies to Japanese Americans who were interned during World War II. In addition, there are ongoing important national debates, based (in part) on conceptions of justice, over the acceptance of responsibility for past offenses: slavery in the United States, the Armenian genocide, the destruction of Native American nations, the potato famine in Ireland, Australia's removal of Aborigine children from their families, Japanese atrocities during World War II, and apartheid in South Africa.

Another factor that may be contributing to the increased frequency of apologies is the balance of power that has been shifting among groups and nations over the past several decades. We have had many opportunities to watch formerly powerless groups assert their right to be treated equally by those who had previously devalued them. In the United States, for example, women and African Americans, having claimed the right to vote, have been striving to compete on an equal basis in the marketplace. South African blacks have gained power through inspired leadership, the strength of their religion, and the Afrikaners' fear of retaliatory violence. (Hope-

fully, the groups responsible for the oppressive behaviors—
men, whites, and Afrikaners—have also contributed to the shift
in power through positive changes in their own moral values.)
Previously disempowered groups are using their newly
acquired power to remind others of inequities—both past and
present—and to declare that devaluing behavior is unacceptable and that a new social contract must be negotiated. Apologies are a civilized way to redress these inequities.

The increasing power and influence of women in society
provides a final explanation for the growing importance of
apology in society. As women emerge as leaders in corporate
governance, the professions, the clergy, political office, and
other forms of leadership, they bring to society a perspective
on the apology process very different from that of men. As we
shall see in the next chapter, women, in contrast to men,
apologize more frequently, are more comfortable in admitting
culpability, and are more apt to use apology to decrease
interpersonal tension.

A PERSONAL PERSPECTIVE

My interest in the subject of apology was stimulated by an
unpleasant personal experience. Two friends betrayed my trust
over an important matter. Their lying about it only com-
pounded my hurt. For weeks after this discovery, I was dis-
traught and distracted from my daily activities. I felt I had lost
two friends, and, equally distressing, I began to question both
my trusting approach to relationships and my overall ability to
judge people. One day, it occurred to me that if these friends
would sincerely apologize, our relationships could be restored.
This idea, which may seem simple and obvious to many

readers, was an epiphany to me, a sudden, spontaneous realization of something I felt was important and perhaps even profound. I was intrigued that an apology, which appears to be such a simple event, could change so much.

This epiphany began my intellectual interest in the apology process. I found myself pondering a series of questions: Why do people apologize? Why is it so difficult to apologize? Why do some apologies heal while others fail? Why do some attempts at apologies offend, making matters worse? Do apologies have to be sincere to be effective? What do apologies mean to the offended parties? How is apology related to forgiveness? Is it ever too late to apologize? Is the ability to apologize a sign of strength or weakness? In what ways are public apologies different from private ones?

In order to seek answers to these questions, I read everything I could find on the subject in newspapers, magazines, and books. The material ranged from the "how to" variety to scholarly works by sociologists, psychologists, and theologians. I observed that major national newspapers as well as local newspapers contained several articles each week involving apologies. I studied historical apologies and apologies in novels. I observed and studied apologies involving my family, friends, colleagues, patients, and myself.

My family situation has provided unexpected insights into the psychology of apology. My wife and I adopted eight children over the 12-year period of 1966 to 1977.[30] At one point in time, seven of our children were teenagers. We tried to teach them the appropriate use of apologies as part of our desire to create an atmosphere of civility. It was an interesting challenge, to say the least, and taught me a great deal about the power of apology, as well as the reluctance to apologize.

One experience from my family illustrates how even an apparently simple apology can have a complexity that teaches many lessons. On a Saturday afternoon, my wife bought her favorite treat for dessert that evening, a gourmet, nut-filled brownie. But as dinnertime approached, my wife was unable to find it. Suspecting our youngest child, Naomi, then 16, who was the only child in the house at the time, my wife asked her whether she had taken the brownie. Naomi denied the accusation. But my wife was confident that Naomi was the culprit, and so she began to lecture her on the importance of telling the truth and of trust in relationships. Naomi continued her denial.

The next morning, my wife asked again. "Naomi, are you sure you did not take the brownie? I hate to think one of my children would do such a thing. There must be trust between a mother and daughter." (Notice that the level of the discussion had now escalated from taking a brownie to trust between mother and daughter.) Our daughter denied it even more emphatically. She then turned her gaze just over my wife's head and spotted the missing brownie on a shelf where my wife had originally placed it. My wife now remembered putting it there. Naomi's face turned smug and self-satisfied as she said, "Well, are you going to apologize?"

My wife then launched into a sincere, agonizing, and shame-filled apology. "I am so very sorry that I thought you or any of my children would have taken the brownie and would have lied about it," she said. "I feel so terrible . . . ," etc. My daughter castigated her by saying, "You should have known that I am allergic to nuts and would never have taken a brownie with nuts. Don't you know about my allergies?" My daughter was not presuming high moral principles, since taking candy or pastries from one another is not, according to family standards, a mortal sin. The mortal sin is lying about it. Naomi was now offended (or at least pretending to be offended) that she was being accused of taking a pastry with nuts when a good mother should know that her daughter is allergic to nuts.

Naomi let my wife continue with her apology until she felt she had seen her suffer enough. She then said with smug pleasure on her face, "I love it when you apologize, Mother, because it makes you feel so foolish." Several weeks later, my wife phoned me at work to tell me that Naomi apologized for something she had done. This event was remarkable because we could not recall Naomi ever apologizing for anything.

This simple story of a successful apology embodies the complexity and power of the apology process. It illustrates how the phenomenon of apology can be a window into the human emotions and behaviors that maintain and restore human dignity. In this apology, we see the interplay of shame, guilt, and humiliation; what motivates reconciliation; the role that negotiations play; the transfer of power and respect between two parties; the importance of the suffering of the offender; the overall contributions to the healing process; forgiveness; and the importance of teaching apologies by modeling them for others. These and other aspects of the apology process will be discussed in considerable detail in the chapters that follow.

My professional role and my intellectual interests gave me another useful perspective for the study of apology. As dean of a medical school and chancellor of an academic health center, I have mediated and adjudicated numerous interpersonal and organizational conflicts, some of which required meaningful apologies for their resolution. As a practicing psychiatrist and psychotherapist working with individuals, couples, families and groups, I have often seen the effect of apologies—or the conspicuous lack of them—in conflicts involving family members. A common theme in these conflicts is the humiliation of one member of the family by another. It is heart-wrenching to observe grudges in families, lasting from weeks to a lifetime, resulting from the unwillingness of individuals to apologize and to forgive. Finally, for two decades, I have been studying and teaching the medical interview and the psychology of shame and humiliation, particularly as these emotions result from interactions between physicians and patients.[31] Patients are often ashamed of their illness and sometimes humiliated by their physicians. Apologies, I have learned, are perhaps the only way to heal, or at least to minimize, the harm of humiliations. Unfortunately, in the past, physicians have been reluctant to apologize because of their pride and their fear that apologies, which usually contain admissions of guilt, might make them vulnerable to malpractice suits. Recently, however, a growing interest in medical errors on the part of the medical profession has prompted study of how physicians should acknowledge these errors and apologize for them.

As important as it is for family members, friends, and members of organizations to resolve conflicts, it is even more important for larger groups in conflict over territory and wealth as well as racial, ethnic, and religious differences to resolve their conflicts in civilized manners. As a speaker at the international convention "Peace Building Initiatives" in Caux, Switzerland,[32] I was deeply moved to witness the hunger of the audience, representing 60 nations, as they attempted to apply the apology process to resolve their national conflicts.

This book, based on my study of over 1,000 apologies, will present an analysis of the apology process that I believe will help readers understand why they and others experience apologies as successes or failures, both in personal relationships and in the public realm. I do not intend to tell readers how to feel or think, but I want to help them understand why they feel and think the way they do. The result, I hope, is that readers will learn the importance (and the limitations) of genuine apologies in restoring shattered relationships, understand the significance of the growing number of public apologies, and develop the skills to act on their knowledge.

I have often wondered what has sustained my interest in studying and teaching about apologies throughout the past decade. I believe it is more than a detached intellectual interest or an attempt to restore the broken relationships that launched my study of apology. It is a passion that derives from the excitement of developing and applying an old idea—apologizing for wrongs done—in order to make a positive difference in the lives of others as well as in the lives of those apologizing. It is also the deep satisfaction of interactive communication with the audiences who attend my lectures, as well as with friends and colleagues with whom I have discussed these ideas. Their newly awakened interests in the subject as well as the ideas they generate have been a gift to me. As we explore the subject of apology together, we discover valuable applications to our relationships at home, with relatives, with friends, and at work, as well as in our understanding of national and international conflicts and our hope for their resolution.

The Paradox of Apologies

In his letter to me describing the origin of a decision to apologize for an offense committed 61 years earlier, Manuel wrote that he had been "struck by the simplicity and importance of the concept of a true apology."[1] There is, to be sure, simplicity to an effective apology. When we read about or receive a good or effective apology, we intuitively know it is successful. We may even suspect that effective apologies will share common features, such as the offender's acknowledging a mistake and expressing remorse, or a healed relationship, as the outcome. Nicholas Tavuchis makes a similar observation as he describes apologies as "so simple and straightforward," but he prefaces these adjectives with the key phrase, "at first glance,"[2] leaving open the possibility that further scrutiny may yield a different result. Later he describes the process of apology as "mysterious,"[3] a description that is quite at odds with the ideas of simplicity and straightforwardness he had earlier advanced. What Tavuchis may be alluding to is the paradoxical nature of the apology process: the fact that an apology is remarkably complex and yet simple and straightforward at the same time. In this and subsequent chapters, we will explore the structures, purposes, and processes that produce this paradox.

I believe it will be useful to begin with an exploration of the definitions of apology and the words that we use and misuse in offering apologies. Next we will consider whether and how gender, culture, and language influence the construction and expression of apologies. Looking at the apology process itself, we then examine why people apologize, the psychological needs the offending party must meet, and the methods that can be used to achieve effective apologies. Finally, we will consider the similarities and differences between public and private apologies.

THE MEANING OF APOLOGY

"Apology" refers to an encounter between two parties in which one party, the offender, acknowledges responsibility for an offense or grievance and expresses regret or remorse to a second party, the aggrieved. Each party may be a person or a larger group such as a family, a business, an ethnic group, a race, or a nation. The apology may be private or public, written or verbal, and even, at times, nonverbal.

Some scholars suggest additional criteria for apology, such as an explanation for the offense, an expression of shame and/ or guilt, the intention not to commit the offense again, and reparations to the offended party.[4] Whether and when these additional criteria are necessary and what they contribute to the apology process will be discussed throughout the book. I will show in subsequent chapters that an apology often involves more than a unilateral offering of one party to another but can be a dialogue and even a negotiation between two parties.

An alternative and earlier meaning of "apology" in English is derived from the Greek word *apologia*, meaning justification, explanation, defense, or excuse. A speech in defense of an idea or person is called an *apologia* and the person making such a speech an "apologist." Apology in this sense does not involve an acknowledgment of transgression and, thus, needs no request for pardon or forgiveness.[5]

Many early church and Greek writings are referred to as *apologias*. The term "Christian apologetics," for instance, refers to a branch of theology concerned with the defense of Christian beliefs, usually against criticism by others. Plato's dialogue describing Socrates' death, titled *Apologia*, is an explanation of why Socrates did not leave Athens when threatened with execution. Richard M. Nixon's "Checkers" speech, Douglas MacArthur's "Old Soldiers Never Die" speech, and President Jimmy Carter's statement about the failed rescue of American hostages in Iran are modern examples of such apologias.[6] These speeches are explanations and defenses, not acknowledgments of mistakes and expressions of remorse.

A contemporary illustration of this original meaning of apology is offered by Peter J. Gomes in his *The Good Book: Reading the Bible with Mind and Heart.*[7] He replaces the traditional section heading "Foreword" with "Apologia," and explains that he is using the word in the early sense, " . . . as a formal argument to speak in defense of anything that may cause dissatisfaction. It is more explanation than excuse. It does not ask for pardon but rather seeks to offer light to those who may need it but may not want it."[8]

People associate the expression "I am sorry" with apologies, often with confusing results. If I say "I am sorry to hear that your aunt is ill," or "I am sorry your recovery from illness was so difficult," I am not apologizing. I call this the compassionate or empathic "I am sorry." These statements are not apologies, since they do not contain acknowledgments of grievances, acceptance of responsibility for causing them, and expressions of personal remorse.

If, on the other hand, I lose an item that someone loaned me, I may say, "I am so sorry for losing the item. I feel terrible. I should have been more careful. I will replace it before we meet again." This use of "sorry" is part of an apology because I am acknowledging an offense, accepting responsibility for it, expressing remorse, and offering reparation. Similarly, if I bump into someone out of my carelessness and knock the person's grocery bags to the ground, my saying "I am sorry," together with my chagrin and attempt to pick up the bundles, is an apology. Confusion arises when it is not clear whether the person who says "I am sorry" is being apologetic or compassionate. Sometimes people say, "I am sorry" in the compassionate sense hoping that the other will perceive it as an apology. I will discuss this use in greater detail in chapter 4. The word "sorry" may also be used, usually by adolescents, as a sarcastic apology in the form of "SorrEE!" or "sooooo sorry." A talk show host from Australia informed me that this form of expression is common not only in the United States but in her country.

In addition to the fact that "I am sorry" does not always convey an apology, it also appears that the word "apology" is replacing the polite or compassionate use of the word "sorry." Examples of this trend include apologies people make when they leave a meeting or a dinner before it is over because of a prearranged appointment ("I apologize for leaving"); apologies hotels write on signs next to renovations ("We apologize for the inconvenience"); apologies some museums write on signs listing their rules ("We apologize that we cannot allow smoking, littering, and pets"); and apologies offered by parking garages when their space is filled ("Our lot is filled. We apologize"). In all of these examples, the parties offering the apology are expressing concern or sympathy for limits or inconveniences placed on others. Instead of using the word "apology" in such circumstances, the person who must leave early can say "excuse me," or "I am sorry, but I must leave early," or "I regret I must leave." The hotel can "regret" or be "sorry for the inconvenience." The museum can also "regret" or be "sorry" for its restrictions. These are all polite, caring, sympathetic, and empathic statements, but they are not apologies.

One result of this dual meaning of "apologize" is that when your friend simply says, "I apologize," you have no idea whether you have received an apology or a perfunctory "sorry about that" with no acknowledgment that an offense was committed or that remorse was offered. A simple test for determining whether "I apologize" is an apology in the formal sense of the word is to ask whether the person making the statement would repeat the behavior if a similar situation arose. Certainly, the hotel apologizing for renovations and the museum setting its rules about smoking and pets are not about to change their behaviors or rules. Nor are parking garage owners remorseful when their spaces are full.

An editorial in the *Boston Herald*, in which the publisher apologizes for an article written by one of its columnists, illustrates this misuse of the word "apologize:"[9]

The *Boston Herald* has always taken pride in its ability to keep in touch with and respond to the needs of the community we serve. That remains our mission today.

Recently, however, members of the Latino community have taken offense at some language used in a Nov. 30 column by Don Feder on Puerto Rican statehood. *To those who took offense at his words I offer my personal apology.*

They were not the words I would have chosen. Should we have been more sensitive to the feelings of the Latino community? Yes. But all of our columnists are given wide latitude to express their opinions in their own way. We stand by their right to do so.

We hope we will be judged by the Latino community, and by all our readers, not on one column, but on the totality of our contributions to this city and our coverage of its people.

We recognize that we live in a rapidly changing community, and we hope to reflect in our editorial pages and in our coverage of the news the richness of that diversity. At the *Boston Herald, diversity will continue to mean not just ethnic and racial diversity, but a diversity of views and opinions.* (Emphasis added.)

Although the editor regrets and is sorry that the community was offended by the article, he nonetheless argues that publishing the article was justified because it was consistent with the newspaper's policy of diversity of views and opinions. This editorial is not an apology.

GENDER AND APOLOGY

When I lecture on the topic of apology, I often ask the audience, "Who apologizes more: men or women?" The response is striking: The men remain silent, while the women wave their hands and say, with conviction and even pride, "Women!" I have also noticed that women attending my lectures on apology outnumber men by a ratio of approximately 3:1. They seem more interested, more engaged, and more interactive than their male counterparts. In addition, the newspaper reporters and columnists who phone me for background comments for articles they are writing on apology are usually women.

I experienced this gender disparity in Indian culture in a direct and powerful way when I was invited by a female physician of Indian heritage to speak on apology at an annual meeting of a medical society for Indian physicians. As I made my remarks, I noticed that the women physicians and the nonphysician wives of the male physicians seemed very responsive and enthusiastic: Their affirmative head nodding and body language spoke volumes. The male physicians and nonphysician husbands of the female physicians, on the other hand, were silent and even dour. Clearly, they were not happy with me. As I was leaving the hall, I walked past a group of U.S.-born college-age children of the Indian physicians chatting among each other with great amusement. I asked them what was happening. What was I missing? They informed me, smirking all the while, that the hidden agenda of my being selected to speak on this topic was to help their fathers learn to apologize to their mothers. These students fully understood the game that was being played and my naïve participation in it.

In my psychiatric practice, I have observed a particular kind of apology style in some women who regard their apologizing as excessive and even shameful. These women appear to have been intimidated by their parents—particularly their fathers—during childhood. This observation has been corroborated to some extent by several women who approached me after my lectures to talk about their self-admitted excessive need to apologize. (They do not raise the subject during the public question period.) They discussed this behavior including its familial antecedents with considerable shame and inquired about ways of changing. I infer from these discussions, as well as from my patients in psychotherapy, that these apologies are meant to placate the threatening parent of their childhood: "I'm sorry. I'm sorry. Please do not hurt me."

The greater frequency of apologies in women as compared to men ("real" apologies, not coerced by intimidation) is corroborated by several areas of scholarly analyses. Noted sociolinguist and author Deborah Tannen observes that "women tend to focus more on the question, 'Is this conversation bringing us closer or pushing us further apart?' Men, on the other hand, tend to focus more on the question 'Is this conversation putting me in a one-up or a one-down position?'"[10] A study by Janet Holmes, cited by Tannen in *Talking from 9 to 5*,[11] provides additional evidence that women apologize more frequently than men.[12]

Another group of studies that help explain women's proclivity to apologize more than men comes from research on guilt, a common precursor of apologies. Jane Bybee, in her review of gender differences in the experience of guilt, concludes that "women compared to men have a higher proclivity for guilt," "are more likely than males to mention feeling guilty about inconsiderate and dishonest behavior," "compared to males, females more frequently mention guilt arising in the context of close interpersonal relationships," and, compared to males, "are more likely to admit culpability" and "offer more numerous and complex concessions for wrongdoing."[13]

The conclusion that women apologize more than men is consistent with pioneering work by Carol Gilligan on the development of women and the voices of women not commonly taken into account in theories of psychology. She makes the convincing case that women are different from men in their "ethic of care," the "tie between relationship and responsibility," and the importance of "the experience of interconnection." Although Gilligan does not speak of apologies, her work helps us understand why apologies are particularly meaningful to women who, more than men, are committed to restoring relationships.[14]

From a literary perspective, Elaine Showalter, a professor of English literature at Princeton University, argues that male authors allow their male characters to mistreat women and escape without an apology. She cites Shakespeare, Henrik Ibsen, Thomas Wolfe, and Arthur Miller to illustrate her point. She writes, "Allowing a hero to humiliate himself before a wronged woman would render him awkward, wimpish, embarrassing, and lacking in sex appeal—in a word, unmanned." Showalter argues that "if literary heroes never apologize and rarely explain . . . it must be because male authors regard such actions as dishonorable."[15]

Showalter cites Ibsen's *A Doll's House* to support her argument. Torvald, in refusing to apologize to his wife Nora, explains that he "would gladly work day and night" for her, but "no man would sacrifice his honor" [apologize] even for his loved one. Nora responds, "It is a thing hundreds of thousands of women have done." Showalter adds that, in contrast, female writers make men live up to their misdeeds, "forgiveness comes the hard way: You have to earn it."[16]

It is important for us to continue to develop our understanding of the differences between men and women in their frequency and manner of apologizing. After all, women constitute half of the human race and will continue to achieve more equality of opportunity, including places of leadership in society. I believe their overall style of interaction and management of grievances through apologies can be expected to enhance group cohesiveness and facilitate conflict resolution.

CULTURE AND APOLOGY

Similarities and differences in apologies between cultures and their languages have become the subject of increasing interest as relationships and dialogue between nations intensify in our ever-shrinking global village. Many U.S. newspapers attempted to educate the American public about the vocabulary of apology in China following the collision between the U.S. reconnaissance plane and the Chinese jet. The study of such phenomena belongs to the fields known as sociolinguistics or psycholinguistics, and although a review of this field is well beyond the scope of this book, I offer several observations to illustrate how apologies are influenced by culture.

A profound difference exists between the word "apologize" in English and the words used for apology in other languages. Because the English word "apology" has no root that acknowledges guilt or blame (it comes from the Greek word *apologia*—to justify or defend), "apology" by itself has little emotional power. As noted earlier, it also has lost much of its precise meaning by being confused with the compassionate "sorry." The result is that the simple phrase "I apologize" is seldom effective. If you accuse another of an offense and that person answers with those two words—"I apologize"—you receive little satisfaction, expecting other expressions, such as

"I feel so terrible. It was wrong of me to do this. How can I make this up to you?" In contrast, the Spanish word *disculpa* contains the root word that means blame or culpability. A common German phrase for "I apologize" is *entschuldige bitte* in which the core word, *schuldig*, means guilty. (The whole phrase translates roughly to "Please take away my guilt.") Even in languages where the key word conveys blame or guilt, verbal modifiers and nonverbal behaviors such as pounding the chest and using other body gestures that amplify the apology are frequently used.

The Japanese language treats the concept of apology quite differently than does the English language. Much has been written in both Japanese and English about Japanese apologies. This interest, I surmise, is a reflection of the importance of apologies in Japanese culture and the interactions between Japanese- and English-speaking people during World War II, the U.S. post-war occupation, the subsequent economic growth of Japan, and the importance of Japan as an ally of Western democratic nations.

In general, the Japanese differ culturally from Americans in that "Within a group, maintenance of harmonious and smooth interpersonal relations, interdependence, and mutual trust are of utmost importance."[17] Thus, Japanese apologies are focused primarily on restoring the relationship with the offended party, rather than on relieving an internal state of mind, such as guilt, which is more characteristic of person-to-person American apologies. It follows from the basic premise of the importance of maintaining harmony that the Japanese use a wider variety of apologies to suit the social status of offenders, while Americans tend to use similar apologies for everyone. The Japanese are also more likely to offer and receive apologies than Americans and will often apologize even when the other is at fault.

The Japanese language has a wide range of apology words such as *gomen nasai, sumimasen, shituree, hansei,* and many others. The use of these words depends on the formality of the situation, whether women or men are more apt to use the phrase, the relative power in the offended/offender relationship, and the amount of responsibility the person assumes. Japanese apologies are more likely to include expressions of self-denigration and submission than do English apologies. For example, they often contain modifiers that can be translated "humbly," "in humility," "profusely," "abjectly," and "unconditionally." As these words suggest, Japanese apologies are more apt to communicate sub-missiveness, humility, and meekness, whereas Americans are more apt to communicate sincerity, at least in personal apologies. In addition, the Japanese discourage explanations and excuses for behaviors, a practice they regard as disgraceful, while in English, explanations are usually regarded as honest and legitimate aspects of the apology. The Japanese apologize for a wider range of people for whom they feel responsible, such as members of their university, their school teachers, and friends from work, whereas Americans are apt to apologize only for their spouses, children, parents, and pets.[18]

Some might take issue with the point that the Japanese apologize more than Americans. After all, they might point out, the Japanese were reluctant to apologize to America's World War II allies and neighboring nations in the Pacific Rim for atrocities and human indignities they caused during the war. Although these observations are correct, they do not contradict my point that the Japanese generously and frequently use apologies to maintain the harmony and social cohesion of the group. Rather, the Japanese regard other nations and those of lesser social status as outside of their group and, thus, as unworthy of receiving an apology. The Japanese reluctance to apologize for what we call "war crimes" is also attributed to the unacceptable behavior of blaming their ancestors or Emperor Hirohito.[19]

The point of this brief analysis is not to present a comprehensive analysis of Japanese apology but rather to illustrate that communicating and receiving effective apologies to and from people of different cultures and languages is a complex and challenging process that requires an understanding of a culture as well as the precise use of language. Although there are linguistic analyses of apologies in various languages, there is, to my knowledge, no comprehensive book on comparative apologies. In our ever-shrinking global village, it is only a matter of time before we see such a publication.

THE APOLOGY PROCESS

When we observe one party apologizing to another, we may wonder what are the needs of the offended party who is receiving the apology and what is the motivation of the offender who is apologizing? The answers to these apparently simple questions are so complex and so important that I devote two chapters (chapter 3 and chapter 6) to explore the answers in considerable detail. The short answers I offer now are that the parties who have been offended have one or more of the following needs they hope will be addressed: the restoration of respect and dignity, assurances that they and the offender have shared values, assurances that they were not at fault, assurances that they are safe from further harm by the offender, knowledge that the offender has suffered as a result of their offense, a promise of adequate reparations, and the opportunity to communicate their suffering and other feelings about the offense. On the other hand, people are motivated to apologize for two general reasons. The first reason is their response to shame, guilt, and empathic regard for those they have offended. The second reason is their attempt to restore the relationship and to avoid further damage to the relationship, abandonment, retaliation, or other punishments. Since the offender and the offended are often unaware of each other's needs, it is understandable that many apologies end up not satisfying either party.

The next apparently simple question that is actually quite complex is: "How does one apologize?" or alternatively, "How do apologies satisfy the needs of the offended parties?" We will explore this process further in chapter 4 and chapter 5. The short answer to these questions is that the apology process can be divided into four parts: 1) the acknowledgment of the offense; 2) the explanation; 3) various attitudes and behaviors including remorse, shame, humility, and sincerity; and 4) reparations. The importance of each part—even the necessity of each part—varies from apology to apology depending on the situation.

BRIEF VERBAL AND NONVERBAL APOLOGIES

One might get the idea from the earlier analysis of apologies that the process of apologizing must be long and cumbersome. Although this idea may be true for particular situations when a comprehensive acknowledgment of the offense and a detailed commitment of reparations are necessary, many effective apologies can be brief and some may even be nonverbal. Three brief apologies and three nonverbal apologies illustrate this point.

In the first brief apology, a pedestrian accidentally bumps into another person, or a waiter brings the wrong dish. The apology can be simply "I am terribly sorry," accompanied by appropriate body gestures, with no explicit acknowledgment of the offense. Both parties know that a minor offense was committed and that the offender is remorseful. The implicit message is, "I did something wrong. It was my fault. It was not deliberate. It was not personal. I was clumsy. I will be more careful next time." The reparation by the pedestrian offender may involve helping the other pick up the package he dropped, while the reparation by the waiter may be providing especially fast service, correcting the order, or even providing some (or all) of the meal free.

In the second illustration, a lawyer failed to deliver a document at the time he promised. He phoned his client to say, "I am late in delivering the document. I am shamefaced and I have just placed the letter in the overnight mail." Such an apology might be satisfactory as long as the delay was the first such grievance and led to no serious consequences. The lawyer has acknowledged the offense and explicitly expressed shame as an equivalent of remorse. In this case, no explanation or reparation is needed.

In the third illustration, a professor and member of a church gave a seminar series at the church's adult forum. During the seminar, the professor loaned each member of the group a copy of a book that he believed would be useful. One of the parishoners returned the book six months after the conclusion of the seminar. She left the book on the professor's pew with the following note of apology. "I'm truly embarrassed how long I've had this," she wrote. "Thank you for a wonderful series." This apology acknowledges the offense, expresses embarrassment (a variant of shame), and offers reparation by means of the compliment. No explanation was given, and none was needed.

Not everyone would agree that an apology can be nonverbal. To those reluctant to accept this position, I offer three stories of nonverbal interactions. In the first illustration, a driver fails to see a red traffic signal until the last minute. He applies the brakes to avoid hitting a pedestrian, then grimaces, covers his face with his hands, and makes other body gestures. The pedestrian perceives these gestures to be an apology in which the driver has nonverbally acknowledged fault and shame and indicated that he had no intent to harm. The pedestrian responds with a hand gesture indicating that the apology was accepted.

The second illustration of a nonverbal apology involves President Harry S. Truman's trip to Mexico in 1947. During his travels, he made an unscheduled stop at Chapultepec Castle to place a floral wreath at the foot of a monument bearing the names of six teenage cadets who died in the Mexican-American War in 1847. Truman placed the wreath, bowed his head briefly, and returned to the car. A cab driver said to an American reporter, according to historian David McCullough, "To think that the most powerful man in the world would come and apologize."[20] One newspaper described the gesture as paying respect and healing national wounds. Its headline read, "Rendering Homage to the Heroes of '47, Truman Heals an Old National Wound Forever."[21]

In the final illustration, columnist, author, and former priest James Carroll described a papal apology made during a visit to

Jerusalem. "In Jerusalem, John Paul II left his wheeled convey-
ance to walk haltingly across the vast plaza before the Western
Wall. For two thousand years, beginning with the Gospels,
Christian theology has depended on the destruction of the
Temple as a proof for claims made in the name of Jesus, the new
Temple. Nothing signifies Christian anti-Judaism more fully than
this attachment to the Temple in ruins. . . . So when John Paul II
devotedly approached the last vestige of that Temple, and when
he placed in a crevice of that wall a piece of paper containing
words from his previously offered prayer for forgiveness—'We
are deeply saddened by the behavior of those who in the course
of history have caused these children of yours to suffer'—more
than an apology occurred."[22] One could argue that the pope
delivered a written apology. I believe that the pope's visit to the
Western Wall—even without the note—was in itself an apology.

These six stories, which I have called "brief apologies" and
"nonverbal apologies," meet the basic definition of an apology:
an acknowledgment of an offense and an expression of
remorse. Furthermore, they satisfy some of the needs of the
offended parties, such as restoration of dignity and respect,
acknowledgment of shared values, assurances of safety in the
relationship, and assurances that the offended party was not
guilty. These stories illustrate yet another dimension of the
complexity of apologies, their simplicity and even nonverbal
nature, in contrast to others (which we shall explore in subsequent chapters) that take the form of extended speeches.

PRIVATE AND PUBLIC APOLOGIES

Apologies can be classified as either public or private. By private
apologies, I refer to apologies solely between two individuals,

without an external audience. By public apologies, I refer to apologies between two individuals in the presence of a broader audience, such as apologies between the leaders of two nations that are covered by national and international press. Public apologies also include those Nicholas Tavuchis describes as being from "One to Many," from the "Many to One," and from "Many to Many."[23] Examples of public apologies from the "one to the many" are President William Clinton's apology to the nation for his inappropriate sexual behaviors and Senator Trent Lott's apology to the nation for alleged racial remarks. Examples of apologies from the "many to the one" include apologies from the justice system to convicted criminals who eventually have been found innocent or from companies whose product or operations damage an individual. The most common examples of apologies from the "many to the many" are apologies from nation to nation or from nation to offended groups within a nation.

Public and private apologies, in my opinion, are more alike than different. Both meet similar needs in offended parties and both apply the same structure of acknowledging the offense, offering explanations, expressing shame and remorse, and making reparations. There are, nevertheless, significant differences that are worth noting. For private apologies to be effective, the offended parties usually need to feel that the offenders are sincere in their remorse. Public apologies, in contrast, require public declarations of the offense "for the record," and the restoration of public dignity (or "face") in order to be effective. If these ends are achieved, the question of sincerity may never arise. Private apologies can often be characterized by spontaneity, emotionality, flexibility, and responsiveness to the reactions of the offended parties, and may be extended over long periods of time. Public apologies, in contrast, are carefully prepared in advance with the help of others and are subject to the influence of third parties; thus they may be less spontaneous and less emotional and are often offered in response to public pressure. The precise written statement of the apology for the public record is essential to public apologies.

With private apologies, it is easy to identify the offender and the offended. In public apologies in which a group is the offender, who speaks for the group is not so easily identified and may need to be determined by authority, by vote, or by strategic decision making. When the United States is the offending party, for example, the question arises: Should the apology be offered by the president, the secretary of state, or the U.S. ambassador to the offended nation? If a corporation or a university is the offender, should the apology be offered by the university president or by the specific individual or group responsible for the offense? When celebrities apologize to a larger group, should they offer the apology personally or ask their agents or lawyers to assume this role? When a nation's leader decides to offer an apology to a person or a group, does that leader have the standing to declare on behalf of the nation that an offense was committed and that the nation is remorseful? Such a situation could arise if a U.S president decided to apologize to Vietnam War veterans for the way they were treated on their return home. Could a president who has never served in the military successfully apologize on behalf of the nation? Does a sitting Roman Catholic pope have the standing to apologize for the mistakes of the church's priests and parishioners from earlier centuries?

The matter of who should receive the apology is equally complex in public apologies when the offended persons or groups are not easily identified. If the United States apologized for slavery, which African Americans are the offended parties? Should all African Americans, including recent immigrants from Africa, receive the apology, or only the descendants of slaves? While it is clear that people who suffered in concentration camps or who worked as slave laborers in Nazi Germany are offended parties, what about their children and grandchildren? How does one determine appropriate reparations for different categories of offended parties?

Public apologies for historical events that occurred generations ago raise the question of who committed the offense. In other words, are we guilty for acts we did not personally commit, many of which occurred before we were born? We might ask, "How can I be guilty for slavery or the internment of the Japanese Americans during World War II if I was not even born at the time of the offense? Why should I apologize?" Should Germans born after World War II be held responsible for Nazi atrocities? My answer to these questions is two-fold. First, people are not guilty for actions in which they did not participate. But just as people take pride in things for which they had no responsibility (such as famous ancestors, national championships of their sports teams, and great accomplishments of their nation), so, too, must these people accept the shame (but not guilt) of their family, their athletic teams, and their nations. Accepting national pride must include willingness to accept national shame when one's country has not measured up to reasonable standards. I believe that this accountability is what we mean when we speak of having a national identity, or a sense of national belonging, or a national soul. A second and related rationale for people apologizing for actions they did not directly commit is that those people have profited from these actions. Imperialistic acquisition of land and the use of slave labor by a nation, for example, may continue to benefit future generations of citizens. Such beneficiaries, while not guilty, may feel a moral responsibility to those who suffered as a result of the offense.

THE PARADOX OF APOLOGIES

Despite all the rules about apology and advice about how to apologize, which seem to treat all apologies as if they were the same, I believe that each apology should be viewed as a unique event. Many factors combine and interact to create this uniqueness: variables that precede and influence the apology itself, as well as characteristics and conditions that affect how the apology process unfolds. For example, one important condition that precedes the apology is the nature of the grievance. These range from minor offenses, such as lost tempers, slights, and trivial unintentional damage to property, to serious betrayals of trust and wholesale assaults (including murder) against the rights of large populations over long periods of time. In addition, each grievance may be perceived as personal or nonpersonal. Grievances may be committed by individuals or groups against other individuals or groups. The meaning of the grievance, both intended and perceived, may vary according to the culture of each party. Furthermore, the nature of the damage experienced by the offended party, what they want and need from the apology process, as well as the motives of the offending party, may differ widely from situation to situation. Finally, the offended parties can differ according to their willingness to accept apologies and to forgive, or their propensities to harbor or nurse grudges.

The apology itself varies along many dimensions. As I will explain in chapter 3, a variety of needs may be met by an effective apology, and these needs themselves may be satisfied to greater or lesser degrees of completeness. Acknowledging the offense spans a spectrum that extends from nonverbal to written to comprehensive, detailed descriptions of the offense. Expressions of remorse, shame, and humility can vary according to their presence or absence, clarity and sincerity. Explanations may be nonexistent, meaningful, or even insulting. Reparations extend from none or symbolic gestures to total restoration of damage caused by the offense, including future reparative commitments. As we will see in chapter 10, a successful apology may be the result of a complex negotiation between the offended and the aggrieved over many variables.

Given the basic structure of apologies and their myriad differences, I believe that apologies, like human beings, are both simple and complex, fundamentally the same, but also individually unique. Despite this double-barreled paradox of simplicity and complexity, sameness and uniqueness, it is my hope and intention to bring order, meaning, and rationale to the common human interaction we call "apology."

THREE

How Apologies Heal

One of the most important questions we can ask about the apology process is how do apologies heal damaged relationships? Another way to approach this question is to ask what psychological needs do successful apologies satisfy, and, conversely, what psychological needs do unsuccessful apologies fail to meet for the offended parties? After studying a wide range of apologies drawn from both personal and public contexts, I am proposing that successful apologies heal because they satisfy at least one—and sometimes several—distinct psychological needs of the offended party. These needs are:

- restoration of self-respect and dignity
- assurance that both parties have shared values
- assurance that the offenses were not their fault
- assurance of safety in their relationships
- seeing the offender suffer
- reparation for the harm caused by the offense
- having meaningful dialogues with the offenders

In order to characterize each of these needs in detail, I will use examples of apologies in which a single need appears to dominate. However, as I intend to show later in this chapter, in many situations these psychological needs are so inter-meshed that it becomes difficult, if not impossible, to distin-guish them. In chapter 11, we will explore how meeting these needs facilitates the process of forgiveness.

RESTORATION OF SELF-RESPECT AND DIGNITY

Many offenses are experienced as assaults on the offended party's self-respect or dignity, and so a successful apology must some-how restore these vital aspects of the self in order to heal. We commonly refer to such offenses as insults or humiliations. I use the term "humiliation" to include a broad range of experiences, ranging from feeling slighted or offended, the least serious, to feeling devastated or "annihilated," the most serious. Humilia-tion is the emotional response of people to their perception that they have been unfairly lowered, debased, degraded, "dissed," or reduced to inferior positions in situations in which they feel powerless.[1] In fact, the etymological root of "humiliation" comes from the Latin *humus*, which means soil or ground. During World War II, the Nazis took humiliation to an extreme in their treatment of selected ethnic and national groups, whom they referred to as *untermenschen*; literally translated as "under-people" but meaning subhuman, or lower than human.

Reactions of individuals, groups, or nations to humiliations may be particularly destructive and can include hostile behaviors including murder and war as well as desires for vengeance and holding grudges. Anyone who has ever experienced humiliation can easily identify the components of the reaction that follow.

First, immediately following the offense, one often feels stunned or "blindsided" for several minutes. Then, thoughts about the event seem to multiply, intensify, and persist for hours or even days, leaving the individual annoyed and perplexed: "Why can't I get this out of my mind?" Sleep may be disturbed for several days. One often experiences a sense of powerlessness, the feeling that there is little or nothing one can do to change the situation. The anger that follows humiliating offenses—humiliating rage— can be intense and distressing. Behaviors motivated by such rage (sending off a nasty e-mail, having an outburst of anger, termi- nating a relationship, threatening suit or physical harm) seem rational and appropriate at the time, but as days and weeks pass and inner distress calms down, their irrationality and inappropri- ateness become evident to us: We realize that rage had impaired our earlier judgment. Finally, grudges can form.

I consider grudges to be a form of residual or dormant anger, a combination of resentment and memory that contin- ues long after the offense has occurred and perhaps even been forgotten. A characteristic of grudges is that it takes very little to return residual anger and memory into the full-blown rage that ensued from the original event. I believe that such grudges are quite common in everyday life, and that it is possible to find several long-standing grudges in most extended families. The offenses that initiated the grudges may appear to an outsider to be relatively trivial, such as forgetting someone's birthday, making an insulting comment about someone's appearance (or their spouse's appearance), failing to attend a funeral, or not being invited to a family event. Many serious grudges between siblings are caused by the belief that one received preferential treatment from their parents, particularly in the settling of any estate that may be involved. Another cause of sibling grudges is the belief that responsibility for the care of the elderly and dying parent was not evenly shared. In such cases, siblings may be estranged for the remainder of their lives.

Nor are grudges limited to relationships between individuals. Some scholars have suggested that an important cause of World War I was France's grudge toward Germany, a result of France's humiliation at the hands of the Germans in the Franco-Prussian War of 1871.[2] Similarly, an important cause of World War II was Germany's grudge toward France and other allied nations for having humiliated them with the Versailles Treaty, a document many Germans referred to as the "Treaty of Shame."[3] Thucydides, the Greek historian who, in the fifth century B.C.E. wrote the history of the Peloponnesian wars, tells us, according to historian Donald Kagan, that the three causes of war are honor, fear, and interest. Kagan goes on to suggest that if we understand honor to mean "deference, esteem, just due, regard, respect, or prestige we will find it an important motive of nations in the modern world as well."[4] Assaults on honor can be understood as humiliations. The *New York Times* columnist Thomas L. Friedman, in commenting on the speech of Maylasia's prime minister Mahathir Mohamad, suggests an understanding of humiliation that goes beyond specific wars: "If I've learned one thing covering world affairs," he writes, "it's this: the single most underappreciated force in international relations is humiliation."[5]

Identifying who has been humiliated is difficult because, among other things, it is even humiliating to acknowledge one's humiliation. People are reluctant to admit to a loss of standing, or their powerlessness, at the hands of others. Someone who has been humiliated might rather want to appear strong and unaffected by the offense, meanwhile seething with anger and waiting for an opportunity to get even. Because it is so important to be aware of the situations that can cause others to feel humiliated, I have compiled a list of common situations that create a high risk of causing offense.

PERSON-TO-PERSON

- Overlooked or taken for granted
- Rejected
- Denied basic social amenities
- Manipulated or treated like an object
- Treated unfairly
- Verbally abused
- Reduced in status or role
- Betrayed
- Falsely accused
- Psychologically or physically threatened
- Physically or sexually abused
- Publicly shamed
- Beliefs or affiliations denigrated
- Boundaries or privacy violated

NATION-TO-NATION

- Excluded from important councils
- Receiving unfair trade restrictions
- Having borders violated
- Being the victim of unprovoked attacks, war
- Civilians and prisoners receiving inhumane treatment during wartime
- Occupied by an invading country

- Being the victim of espionage
- Having unfair reparations imposed for prior offenses

Using this list might help a person (or group or nation) understand when they have insulted or humiliated another party, in the process explaining the tension in the air and giving them an opportunity to consider an appropriate response. One such response might be an apology.

A complementary list of similar offenses is presented by Roy L. Brooks, editor of *When Sorry Isn't Enough: The Controversy over Apologies and Reparations for Human Injustice,* in his description of assaults on human dignity. He writes, " . . . a human injustice is the violation or suppression of human rights or fundamental freedoms recognized by international law, including but not limited to genocide; slavery; extrajudicial killings; torture and other cruel or degrading treatment; arbitrary detention; rape; the denial of due process of law; forced refugee movements; the deprivation of a means of subsistence; the denial of universal suffrage; and discrimination, distinction, exclusion, or preference based on race, sex, descent, religion, or other identifying factor with the purpose or effect of impairing the recognition, enjoyment, or exercise, on an equal footing, of human rights and fundamental freedoms in the political, social, economic, cultural, or any other field of public life. In sum, a human injustice is simply the violation or suppression of human rights or fundamental freedoms recognized by international law."[6]

The apologies that follow illustrate situations in which the dominant need of the offended party is the restoration of dignity and respect. One example is the story in chapter 1 describing the interchange between my wife, Louise, and our 16-year-old daughter, Naomi, over a missing brownie. My wife offended my daughter, first by accusing her of taking the brownie and lying about it; and second, by accusing her of violating trust in the mother-daughter relationship. Naomi, in response, felt hurt that her mother could believe her capable of stealing and felt diminished by her mother's assessment. Louise's apology was successful because it diminished her own dignity while restoring Naomi's. By saying, in effect, "I am the culprit, not you. I misplaced the brownie and blamed you when I should have known better," Louise was admitting that in this instance, her child had demonstrated better judgment and more dignity than she had. After my wife apologized, Naomi said: "I love it when you apologize, Mother, because it makes you feel so foolish." Her comment reflects an important insight into how many apologies heal: They transfer the negative evaluation from the victim (Naomi) to the offender (Louise). The victim, previously powerless to defend herself, now has the power to forgive or not to forgive. Naomi was triumphant and let her mother suffer until the score was even. Only then was she ready to accept the apology and forgive.

Another example of a situation in which an apology restored a person's sense of self-worth occurred in an interaction I had with a former patient. Several years after the patient had completed psychotherapy, she left a message for me to phone her. I misplaced the message and consequently failed to phone her. Later, she wrote me a scathing letter informing me that by not returning her phone call, I had failed to respond to her need for me to visit her when she was hospitalized for a potentially serious condition. (I did not know from the message that she was ill or in the hospital.) She experienced my lapse as both "abandonment and humiliation." I was mortified by my lapse and asked to meet with her (of course without charge) to offer my heartfelt apology.

At the end of our interchange, she looked relieved. I asked how she understood our current interaction. She told me that my failure to phone her made her feel she was not as important as I was. My apology, she said, made us equals.

A third illustration, taken from a BBC news story, describes a U.K. pilot of Muslim heritage who was falsely accused of training the September 11 hijackers. After being arrested at the request of the FBI, the man spent five months in a London prison before a British court ruled that there was no evidence against him. He is suing the FBI and the U.S. Department of Justice for $20 million. The pilot initially asked for compensation and an apology. Since his release he has been blacklisted and unable to fly planes because of emotional distress. He said that if an apology had been given, he would not have resorted to legal action. "It's not for the money, it's the principle," he said, "My family doesn't deserve to be labeled as terrorists and I didn't deserve five months in prison."[7] The man wanted his dignity restored and was willing to accept an apology as the mode of that restoration. However, when the government refused to apologize, he was forced to seek a different remedy. Ultimately, the restoration of his dignity may come as a monetary award imposed by the court.

We see a similar psychological process at work in group-to-group and international relations. One example is President Clinton's apology to the African Americans who were the subjects of the infamous syphilis experiments at Tuskegee. (The men believed they were being treated for "bad blood" when in fact they were part of experiments studying the natural progression of untreated syphilis.) By means of the apology, people who had been treated as nonhuman experimental subjects were now acknowledged as humans with rights like any others. Simultaneously, a proud and powerful nation acknowledged its disgraceful and immoral behavior.[8] A second example is the U.S. government's apology to Japanese Americans interned during World War II. Many of the former internees experienced the apology as restoration of their dignity or "face." (In the Tuskegee apology, financial reparations had been made many years before the apology. In the apology for the internment of Japanese Americans, financial reparations accompanied the apology.)

A visual illustration of the restoration of dignity through apology emerged in response to a question I raised during a presentation on apology. I asked the audience members what psychological need is met when they receive a very satisfying apology. One man rose and said, "After someone offends me, he is here [extending an arm parallel to the ground] and I am here [extending the other arm about 12 inches lower than the first]. After the apology, we are like this [extending both arms at the same height]." Others have responded to the same question with similar imagery such as, "It levels the playing field."

In these stories of humiliation followed by restoration of dignity, a recurring theme is the exchange of humiliation and power. The offenders initially humiliate the victims and render them powerless to avoid the humiliation. The apology process reverses the situation by transferring the humiliation from the victims to the offenders, who then become the "stupid," insensitive, or immoral ones. Originally having had the power to hurt, the offender now gives the power to forgive or not to forgive to the offended party. This exchange of humiliation and power between the offender and the offended may be the clearest way of explaining how some apologies heal by restoring dignity and self-respect.

ASSURANCE THAT BOTH
PARTIES HAVE SHARED VALUES

A second fundamental need of the offended party that an apology may address is the affirmation of shared values by the offender's acknowledgment that he or she made a mistake, regrets it, and offers assurance that it will not happen again. By apologizing, the offending party reaffirms his or her commitment to the rules and values implicit in the relationship by saying, in essence, "I really am the person you thought I was." Trust is thus reestablished, making the relationship safe and predictable once again. Such apologies remind us that people can make mistakes and recover from them, that values once ignored can be reestablished, that relationships once damaged can be healed. We breathe easier knowing that our original estimation of the offending party was correct after all: Our trust was not misplaced. This restoration of trust and goodwill through the affirmation of shared values also applies to groups or nations.

When those who have offended us refuse to acknowledge their behaviors as unacceptable, we may feel we can no longer count on the trustworthiness, predictability, and support that we always took for granted. This uneasiness is especially upsetting if the parties have a close relationship. Because a natural reaction is to distance ourselves from the offending party, the result may be estrangement rather than forgiveness. "How can I ever trust him again? He doesn't even know that what he did was wrong. Maybe I never really knew him."

Worse than the failure to apologize are situations in which the offender repeats the offensive behavior and then offers serial apologies or pseudo-apologies that are fraudulent, misleading, and offensive. Under these circumstances, we not only feel that the offenders are not worthy of our trust but that they have treated us as fools, thus humiliating us. We will discuss several examples of these so-called apologies in chapter 4.

In cases where the offended party is not a single person but a group or nation, the offending party may have violated a social boundary that the group has tacitly agreed marks the line between "acceptable" and "unacceptable" behavior. Sometimes referred to as a "social contract," these boundaries and limitations represent the sum of all of the "give-and-take" negotiations that balance the freedoms, rights, and responsibilities of the group's members. Examples of social contract violations include students who cheat on examinations, athletes who take strength-enhancing drugs or use nonregulation equipment, corporations that defraud the public, businesses that discriminate because of race or gender, newspaper reporters who write fraudulent stories, and media that make disparaging comments about a person's sex, race, or religion. Some social contract offenses are of such magnitude that the offended party demands and receives not only a verbal apology but also written documentation—a memorialization—that the offended party has made a mistake and is remorseful.

Depending on the severity of the offense, people who violate the social contract in public settings are considered "outcasts," literally cast out of relationships with individuals, their group, or society as a whole. To be accepted back into the group, these offenders must offer an apology that explicitly and publicly reaffirms the contract violated ("What I did was wrong"), expresses remorse ("I feel terrible for what I did"), and promises forbearance ("It will not happen again.") The social group needs reassurance that the offender will not repeat the proscribed behavior. People such as Timothy McVeigh, the Oklahoma City bomber who dismissed the 19 slain children as "collateral damage,"[9] frighten us because they do not hold sacred the same values we do. By refusing to admit that what he did was wrong, McVeigh embraced his standing as an outsider. His refusal to apologize says in effect, "I stand by my actions. I do not live by your rules. I do not feel remorse. I might do it again." Any group that seeks to offer its members security, predictability, and cohesiveness cannot tolerate such an explicit—and ongoing—rejection of the social contract.

In chapter 1, I attributed the increase in national, and even international, apologies, in part to the fact that formerly powerless groups are now demanding respect and denouncing behaviors that devalue them. But we can also understand this phenomenon as the expression of an evolving social contract that expands to include the rights and needs of these groups. Consider the following two public apologies, one involving Seiichi Ota, a Liberal Democratic Party lawmaker in Japan, and Bob Ryan, a widely respected sports writer for the *Boston Globe*. Both stories demonstrate how the social contract changes over time: Behaviors that were, at times, tacitly accepted in the past are now rejected explicitly, publicly, and vigorously. Both stories provoked widespread media attention, Ota on an international level, and Ryan in the United States.

In a discussion of Japan's declining birth rate, Liberal Democrat Ota referred to an alleged gang rape by five university students, saying, "Gang rape shows the people who do it are still vigorous. I think that might make them close to normal."[10] According to Kyodo News Service, " . . . eight members of a group of female lawmakers of the lower house and the House of Councilors submitted a letter of protest to

Ota at his office. The letter said, 'The remark denigrates women and approves of such a crime. It degrades not only the victim but all women,' and urged Ota to seriously reflect on his remark and give an apology."[11] Prime Minister Junichiro Koizumi joined the criticism by saying, "rape is an unforgivable, heinous act and has nothing to do with whether you are healthy or not."[12] Prime Minister Koizumi added that, "[Ota] deserves to be raped. Rape is an atrocious act of cowardice and has nothing to do with 'virile' qualities."[13]

Trying to contain the firestorm of criticism his remark had provoked, Mr. Ota later told reporters, "I want to reconsider and express my apologies."[14] At another time, he remarked, "I used inappropriate and exaggerated words. I am deeply disappointed with myself. My remarks have caused great distress to many people. I offer my apologies to the victim . . . and many other women."[15] He continued, "I wanted to add that rape is a serious crime and must be severely punished, but I didn't have time."[16] Still, in a later apology, he said his remarks were "truly inappropriate as a Diet member representing the public."[17] At a news conference, he added that he regarded his remarks as a "fatal mistake" and that he would make amends by actively addressing rape-related issues.[18]

The second story involves a comment made by Bob Ryan, noted *Boston Globe* sports columnist, during a television interview with sports commentator Bob Lobel. In the pre-game show before the playoff series between the New Jersey Nets and the Boston Celtics, Ryan began to discuss what he considered obnoxious behavior on the part of Joumana Kidd, the wife of Nets star Jason Kidd. Ryan said, "I got theories with this woman, this Joumana Kidd who wants to be a star . . . wants face time on camera. The great way to get face time is to bring the cute, precocious kid. [Mrs. Kidd frequently brought her 6-year-old son to the games.] Oh, great. I'd like to smack her."[19] What was public knowledge at the time was that Jason Kidd, as a result of striking his wife in a domestic dispute, had been fined and required to participate in domestic violence and anger counseling. Lobel immediately recognized Ryan's error and asked him if he wished to retract his statement, but Ryan said he would stand by his comments. However, during a subsequent interview, he said that he realized his "colossal error" on his drive home from the TV studio.

The *Boston Globe* suspended Ryan for one month without pay, and he was forbidden from participating in radio and television broadcasts during that time. His editor, Martin Baron, commented that Bob Ryan's comments were "offensive and unacceptable" and violated the newspaper's standards.[20] Ryan apologized to Mrs. Kidd, the newspapers, its readers, and the TV station: "I hyperbolically stated that Mrs. Kidd should be 'smacked' for her general behavior. It was, of course, atrocious judgment on my part. I wish to state clearly that I am aware of the very real problem of violence against women in our society, and that in no way is it a joking matter. I apologize to Mrs. Kidd, and to all women, for my remark."[21]

At the center of both stories are comments about appropriate male behavior toward women: Ota suggesting that gang rapists might be "close to normal," and Ryan implying that physical abuse of women might be justifiable. Whether or not the rape or physical abuse of women was ever considered acceptable behavior in the past, the demand for apologies makes it clear that the community will not condone even public *talk* that appears to legitimize or accept these behaviors now. The issue was not whether or not they were sincere in their apologies. What mattered was that their respective apologies indicated that they understood the nature of the offense and expressed remorse. Their willingness to make these sentiments public can be seen as a reaffirmation of the values shared by the group, just as their offenses had been a public violation of those same values. These reaffirmations of shared values in public apologies are commonly recorded in great detail to ensure precision of agreement and for posterity.

ASSURANCE THAT THE OFFENSES
WERE NOT THEIR FAULT

In some situations, offended parties find themselves questioning whether they were somehow responsible for the offense. They ask themselves, "Was I being too thin-skinned?" "Was I asking for it?" "Was it my fault?" They want to hear something in the apology that assures them they are blameless. They need to know that their conduct was not the reason for the attack or humiliation, and that their view of the world is essentially reliable. The following two examples illustrate apologies that were able to relieve this concern over misplaced culpability.

United Press International reported that abuse survivor Colm O'Gorman received an apology from the Irish Catholic Church for the sexual abuse committed by the late Father Sean Fortune during the years 1981–1983. Speaking of the abuse, Mr. O'Gorman said, "From the very first moment I made my decision to report what I had experienced, I wanted above all *to have the burden of responsibility for that abuse to be taken from me.*"[22] (Italics added.)

In another case, two sisters, ages 27 and 24, were awarded $1 million and received an apology from the Vermont Social and Rehabilitation Department for "failing to protect them from being repeatedly raped by their stepfather."[23] The cases were first reported when the older sister became pregnant with her stepfather's child when she was 14. An article in the *Boston Globe* describes how the sisters were psychologically damaged from childhood. The commissioner of social services acknowledged the abuse the girls had suffered and that the district's response was "inadequate, that it failed to protect the girls." The sisters said that money could not erase their problems with intimacy, their hypervigilance with their own children, their ongoing fears, and their ruptured relationship with their mother. After the settlement, the older sister said, "We're smiling today but it's not because we won, it's because we've been heard." One of the sisters said, *"It's getting over the feeling that I was the bad girl."* [24] (Italics added.)

The need to exonerate responsibility for the offense is especially important for people who have been victims of sexual abuse. But this sense of culpability is not limited to such offenses. Even victims who are reasonably sure of their innocence can experience apprehension that they somehow contributed to the offense. Thus, when offenders accept full responsibility, their victims commonly declare, "I feel validated." Other times, the victims are so grateful for validation that they shoulder some responsibility in order to diminish the humiliation felt by the offending parties.

ASSURANCE OF SAFETY IN THEIR RELATIONSHIP

In addition to needing affirmation of shared values and exoneration of responsibility for causing the offense, the offended party may also need to feel physically or psychologically safe.

In these situations, the apology must answer questions such as: What were the motives for the offense? Was the offense purposeful and personal? Was it some misplaced sense of revenge? What are the chances the offense will recur? Can I let myself be vulnerable? Can I trust this relationship?

A hypothetical example would be an apology offered by a burglar who invaded someone's home, assaulted a member of the family, and was later apprehended. The family needs more than an admission of the offense and an expression of regret to regain its sense of safety. The family wants to know how the burglar selected the home: Was the family known to be wealthy? Was the burglary an act of revenge for some past misdeed by one of the victims? Was there something in particular the burglar wanted? Was this home and its family a random choice? Does the burglar have a criminal record? In order to be effective, the apology must fully clarify the nature of the offense, which will hopefully restore a sense of control over physical and psychological safety to the offended parties.

Similarly, spouses betrayed by adultery need more than a simple acknowledgment of shared values to meet their needs. They will need to know the nature of their spouses' adulterous relationships, the history of previous adulterous relationships, an understanding of the spouses' beliefs about marital fidelity, and an understanding of why their marriage apparently failed. Can the spouse be trusted? Was the affair private or do others know? Do the victims have the power to change the relationship or are they powerless? This additional information gives the offended parties the knowledge necessary to make a well-grounded decision either to terminate or repair the relationship.

A public example of this need for safety involved a confrontation between Temple University basketball coach John

Cheney and University of Massachusetts coach John Calipari, in which Cheney threatened Calipari in an obscenity-filled outburst during a post-game press conference. The alleged reason for the outburst was Cheney's distress over Calipari's "riding the officials" and berating them after the game. During the outburst, Cheney threatened to kill Calipari and have his players beat up the UMass team. Part of the impact of the threat was the distress of Calipari's family. Calipari said, "My wife was upset. The thing that got me mad was when my daughter said, 'Dad, are you going to get hurt in Philadelphia?'"[25] In this case, Coach Calipari needed more than an acknowledgment of the offense to ensure the safety of his team, his family, and himself. He needed to know whether Coach Cheney had a past record of violence, whether there was something unique about the circumstances surrounding the threat that would make acting on the threat likely, and whether there was some personal animosity between the two coaches that needed to be addressed. To be effective, any apology Cheney offered had to resolve these issues. Only then would it be possible for Calipari and his family to feel safe. As it turned out, the two coaches spoke and resolved the issues between them to the satisfaction of both. There were no subsequent repercussions.

SEEING THE OFFENDER SUFFER

For some apologies to be effective, the offended party needs to see the offender suffer. The attitude is, "You hurt me and now it is your turn to get what you deserve." In many effective apologies, the offender's suffering is evident as they express their remorse, guilt, shame, and humiliation for what they have done. Offended parties usually regard this expression of suffering as evidence of the sincerity of the offenders. Even when the offended parties intend to forgive, they may wait for seconds, minutes, hours, days, and even weeks until they perceive that the suffering of the offender has been sufficient to ensure that "justice is served." This kind of exchange is technically referred to as "retributive justice," and expressed colloquially as "a tit-for-tat," or "an eye for an eye."

Sometimes suffering is neither imposed by the offended party nor self-imposed, but instead comes at the hands of a third party. In these cases, retributive justice assumes its more punitive aspect, in which the offended party is ordered or forced to apologize. Consider, for example, the case of Roy E. Frankhouser, a "self-described chaplain to the Ku Klux Klan," who was accused of harassing a woman. He took photographs of his victim through her office window, broadcasted images of an explosion destroying her office, made threatening phone calls, and distributed threatening fliers. The victim, a social worker whose job was to assist people filing discrimination complaints, was so fearful that she left her job and her home and moved with her daughter repeatedly.[26]

Part of Frankhouser's punishment, according to the *New York Times,* was to read aloud a televised apology to the victim on *White Forum,* his public access show. He was also ordered to submit written copies of the apology to the victim for publication in the *Philadelphia Inquirer.* Additional punishments were imposed, including community service, efforts to promote anti-discrimination campaigns, and the contribution of a percentage of his salary to the victim and her daughter.[27]

Another illustration of an apology whose function was to satisfy the need for retribution and whose implementation required a third party involved General George S. Patton, Jr., a three-star U.S. Army general. (This example is also discussed in chapter 10 as it relates to apology as a negotiation.)

Following his military victory in Sicily during World War II, Patton slapped and threatened two U.S. soldiers who were patients in field hospitals and who had no visible wounds.[28] He assumed the men were suffering from psychiatric (nonmedical) conditions. Patton's physical abuse was an offense that could have led to a court martial. The media and members of the U.S. Congress who disliked Patton pressured his superior, four-star general Dwight D. Eisenhower, to force his resignation from the military. However, Eisenhower did not want to lose his most effective field general, and so he demanded that Patton apologize to all personnel in several field hospitals as well as to the two offended soldiers. The apology was intended as a punishment to appease those who regarded Patton as an arrogant, insensitive individual. Patton, however, believed the only thing he did wrong was to displease Eisenhower. He felt his behavior toward the two soldiers would "make men of them" and perhaps save their lives in future combat. His apologies were therefore insincere, but they effectively satisfied the needs of the various offended parties. Eisenhower's son, John S. D. Eisenhower, wrote in a recent biography of his father that in order to save Patton, General Eisenhower had to "exact a heavy price by way of retribution."[29]

Even when the dominant need of the offended party appears to be seeing the offender suffer, usually other needs are met in these apologies. One such need is the restoration of self-respect that is enhanced by the offended party's power to make the offender suffer. Another need that is satisfied is the need to believe that important values are in fact shared and that the offender feels bound by the social contract.

When I talk about the importance of the offender's suffering in the healing of some apologies, friends and colleagues, mostly in the helping professions, become noticeably uncomfortable. They would like to think that good people like themselves are above such desires and passions. Perhaps, they might concede, it is acceptable to think about punishing behaviors, but one should not act on them. In any case, by including punishment and suffering as important components of some apologies, I am offering an observation rather than describing an ideal or making a recommendation. Whether we like or not, at times and in some cases, if the apology is to succeed, people need to know that "the other guy" suffered, too.

REPARATION FOR THE
HARM CAUSED BY THE OFFENSE

Reparation refers to repairing, undoing the damage, making amends, or giving satisfaction for an acknowledged wrong or injury. (When the party makes redress without acknowledging remorse, we tend to refer to this process as a "settlement," not reparation.)[30] I discuss reparations in greater detail in chapter 5 along with other aspects of the apology process. The point I am making here is that for some apologies, both private and public, reparation is the central or dominating feature of the apology. All other functions of the apology take a back seat. The following example, a common situation that many people have experienced, illustrates the centrality of reparations.

A couple arrives at their favorite restaurant at 8:00 P.M. after a tense day at work, with the children, or with each other. They have looked forward to their weekly night out. On this occasion, a busy time at the restaurant, they enjoy a drink and place their food order with the waiter. Time goes by and their order does not arrive, nor do they see the waiter. They nearly empty the bread basket while their irritation intensifies and their appetites diminish. At 9:00 P.M., the waiter arrives, contrite with an apology and an explanation. The order had been placed improperly, he says, and would not be ready for another 10-15 minutes. Despite the apology, the couple is now tired, irritated, and irate. They feel the restaurant has ruined their evening, and they consider walking out and not returning. Although the apology seemed genuine, the couple is unimpressed. The waiter walks away, only to return several minutes later with the meal. He announces that the meal and the drinks are "on the house." The couple relaxes and now feels the waiter has made a wonderful apology. Of course the waiter accepted responsibility on behalf of the restaurant. Of course he was regretful. But such communications were meaningless until he offered reparation, which—without question—was the dominant healing force in this particular apology.

Reparations can also be the dominant healing force in public apologies. Illustrations include the accidental damage caused by an oil spill or a collision of naval vessels. In such cases, formal expressions of regret and investigations are quick to appear. But in the end, it is reparations—or the lack of them—that determine the success of the official apology. In some situations, the offender offers reparations in order to avoid addressing other more important aspects of the apology, such as restoring self-respect and dignity, affirming shared values, or assuring the victim that the offense was not the latter's fault. Such was the case in the clergy sex abuse scandal, in which it appeared that reparations were offered to buy the silence of the victims. Even though the church paid out significant sums of money to the victims of pedophile priests, some victims demanded a more complete apology. For these people, monetary acknowledgment of their suffering was insufficient. Other psychological needs were also important. I will discuss a particularly poignant example later in this chapter, involving a situation in which a survivor who had earlier received reparations still wanted his abuser to understand how much he had been harmed.

Because the importance of reparations seems to vary from case to case, I offer this generalization as a way of assessing their role in specific situations. If an offense results in unintentional damage to or loss of a person's possessions, and no preexisting ill will exists between the parties, reparation (perhaps by replacing the item or paying for it) may be sufficient to heal the relationship. On the other hand, if the damage is perceived as intentional, if the damaged or lost possession is irreplaceable or not remediable as is the case with a loss of life, or if the relationship had been strained before the offense, then reparation by itself may not suffice. In such situations, the victim may need to understand the motives of the offender, estimate the probability of continued danger, or seek restoration of dignity and respect.

HAVING MEANINGFUL DIALOGUES
WITH THE OFFENDERS

Apologies are not always unilateral communications that an offender offers to the offended. They are often dialogues, interactive processes, or negotiations, in some cases initiated by the offender and in other cases by the offended. In such interactive processes, the victims often need to express their distress to the offender (and perhaps to other witnesses), including details such as the meaning of the distress and the nature and severity of the suffering. I offer three stories to illustrate the importance of these offender-offended interactions.

The first illustration involves Reva Shefer, a 75-year-old Holocaust survivor and the first person to receive payment, $400, from the Swiss government as partial reparations for Swiss complicity with the Nazis during World War II. When she received her payment, Shefer commented, "The amount means nothing. I care about the fact of it. No matter what it took, finally, after all these decades, somebody is saying, 'You suffered and we know it.'"[31]

Martha Minow, author of *Between Vengeance and Forgiveness*, illustrates how important it can be to the victims to be able to tell their stories. She reports that a commissioner of the United Nations Truth Commission for El Salvador made the following observation: "For some, ten years or more had gone by in silence and pent-up anger. Finally, someone listened to them, and there would be a record of what they had endured. They came by the thousands, still afraid and not a little skeptical, and they talked, many for the first time. One could not listen to them without recognizing that the mere act of telling what had happened was a healing emotional release, and that they were more interested in recounting their story and being heard than in retribution. It is as if they felt some shame that they had not dared to speak out before and, now that they had done so, they could go home and focus on the future less encumbered by the past."[32]

In the third illustration, Pumla Gobodo-Madikizela, a psychologist and member of the Truth and Reconciliation

Commission in South Africa, offers a particularly poignant story in *A Human Being Died That Night*. Gobodo-Madikizela quotes a widow whose husband had been murdered by de Kock, an Apartheid criminal. The woman explains, "De Kock is the only one who helped us retrace the steps of what really happened. You have no idea how much of a relief knowing the truth about my husband was. De Kock brought us the truth so that we can be with our husbands, understand what happened to them and then release them again . . . Now I can mourn properly because this has helped me retrace his steps in life in order to let him go in death."[33]

We can only speculate about the many ways in which the victims' participation in the dialogue, including their communication to others even beyond the offender, has a healing or therapeutic impact. First, the victim is assured that the offender, and sometimes a broader audience, knows the nature of the offense. Second, the victim receives validation that the offense really happened, that he or she did not distort reality or memory. Third, the victim may be moved by the offender's willingness to listen and understand the full impact of the offense. Fourth, the shame of the offense can often turn into pride of survival. Fifth, the victim puts emotional pain into words, which results in a kind of catharsis. Sixth, the victim may experience some retributive justice in seeing the offender suffer through stating the offense. Seventh, the victim may be able to grieve, perhaps for the first time, what has been lost. Eighth, the victim, particularly in private apologies, can experience feelings of caring and sorrow from the offender.

Some of the healing functions that result from the apology process can occur in other settings. One example is a criminal trial in which the offended party has the opportunity to present a victim impact statement in the presence of the offender and others in the court room. Another example is the psychotherapy session (individual or group) in which the offended party can describe his or her suffering to an attentive and empathic therapist or group of other patients.

SOME APOLOGIES MEET MULTIPLE NEEDS

The previous discussion described situations in which the healing nature of a specific apology depended largely on how successfully it met a dominant psychological need. But more often than not, apologies address multiple needs. The next three apologies (or requested apologies) are public. The first involves the Armenians' request for an apology for what they regard as genocide. Beginning in 1915, more than 1.5 million Armenians—Christians living under Turkish rule—were exterminated through direct killing, starvation, torture, and forced marches into the desert. Armenians from around the world have continuously requested an apology from the Turks, who in turn deny that genocide occurred. What do the Armenians want from such an apology?

A group of 150 distinguished scholars and writers signed a statement honoring the fiftieth anniversary of the U.N. genocide convention and condemning the Armenian genocide. In the statement they affirm the importance of acknowledging this tragic event. "Denial of genocide strives to reshape history in order to demonize the victims and rehabilitate the perpetrators," the announcement explains. "Denial murders the dignity of the survivors and seeks to destroy remembrance of the crime. In a century plagued by genocide, we affirm the moral necessity of remembering."[34] This eloquent statement describes several of the needs that an apology from the Turks would satisfy: restoration of dignity, reaffirmation of the shared value that genocide is morally reprehensible, retributive justice, and the incorporation of these memories into Armenian history and identity. Every American-born Armenian with whom I have met and spoken is acutely aware of and pained by their history and the lack of acknowledgment of their genocide. Their stories are passed from one generation to another.

The next story involves an 82-year-old man, the son of Holocaust victims, who is seeking an apology from the French National Railroad Service for offenses committed during World War II. According to the *New York Times*, Kurt Werner Schaechter is suing the railroad service for its role in the deportation of 76,000 Jews from France to concentration camps in the east during World War II. In addition to compensation of one euro, he asked that the court require the company to acknowledge it played an active role in the deportation. Out of the 76,000, only 2,500 survived the death camps.[35]

Mr. Schaechter began his quest in 1991 while searching the French National Archives in Toulouse for knowledge about his parents. He discovered the dates and destinations of the convoys that transported his father and mother to concentration camps and learned that both were immediately killed, his father at Sobibor and his mother at Auschwitz. He was shocked to find evidence of the French National Railroad Service's willful collaboration with the Germans.

Since the compensation requested—one euro—is so trivial, we might wonder why Mr. Schaechter bothered with the expense and effort of a lawsuit. Why does he want the railroad service to acknowledge its role in such immoral behaviors? Mr. Schaechter explains, "I am doing this out of a responsibility to history. What distinguishes us from animals is our memory. Humanity cannot forget its history."[36] I believe that the requested apology would meet the need for achieving a shared understanding that a nation's railroad may not deport innocent citizens for profit. The work he has already accomplished meets other needs: First, his detective work over the years may have relieved Mr. Schaechter of emotional distress from believing he may have somehow been responsible for his parent's death, since he was an adult when they were captured. Second, learning some of the details of what happened to his parents may facilitate his grieving over their death. Third, by publicly incriminating the railroad, he extracts suffering from them by attracting publicity that portrays them in a shameful and humiliating light. Finally, by asking for only one euro he calls attention to the importance of the other needs by lessening the emphasis on reparations. Eliminating financial compensation as the motivating force behind the request effectively blocks the possibility for someone to say, "all he cared about was the money."

The final illustration of an apology that was demanded in order to satisfy several psychological needs involves Curtis Oathout, a 39-year-old man who was sexually abused by a priest, Father Bentley, when he was between seven and nine years old. The priest had previously acknowledged the abuse, and Mr. Oathout had received a $225,000 settlement. However, the acknowledgment and reparation apparently did not meet Mr. Oathout's psychological needs, because he tracked down the priest for a face-to-face meeting. He tape-recorded his conversation with Bentley, and the *New York Times* later published a transcript.[37]

In the conversation, Mr. Oathout tells Bentley that he wants to be dead and that he feels angry. "You harmed me so bad, it hurts, to my core. I demand you talk to me."[38] Later in the meeting, Oathout demands to know whether Bentley realizes how much pain he has caused him throughout his life and then demands that the priest provide a list of his offenses. After the priest offers a feeble response, Oathout continues his angry interrogation with a question as to whether the priest knew that what he did was wrong. The priest answers in the affirmative, but Oathout contradicts him and tells Bentley that he (Bentley) did not know that what he did was wrong. The priest further offends Oathout by telling him that he had apologized repeatedly by saying he was sorry each morning following the abuse. Bentley then explained that he suffered from "immature sexual development," a condition that made it easier for him "to relate to young people."[39] Further enraged, Oathout threatens Bentley by telling him that he better not ever hurt another child, " . . . don't you ever, you'd better not. You better not, you'll be seeing me . . . if I ever hear of you hurting another kid . . . I mean that, Bentley, you just look in my eyes and see that."[40]

Before this meeting Oathout had already received financial reparation, which failed to provide him adequate satisfaction. He then pursued his need to have the priest be aware of the grievance and to learn whether the offended party knew that what he did was wrong. In our terminology, Oathout needed to know whether Father Bentley shared important values (protection of children, priests' obligations to their parishioners, etc.). At the same time, he probably wanted some affirmation that the abuse was not his fault (or, more accurately, the fault of the child that he was). By trying to elicit more of the story, he may have been attempting to experience some catharsis and to grieve his lost relationship to his church or religion, and to a priest toward whom, at an earlier time, he most likely had positive feelings. He also wanted reassurance that other boys will be safe from this priest in the future. Thwarted at every turn to have his needs met, this previously powerless seven-year-old becomes enraged, threatens the priest, and refers to him by his last name, thus symbolically defrocking him. We might say that his humiliation of the priest inflicts punishment, takes power, and possibly lessens his own humiliation.

Father Bentley may have thought he had apologized, but on his own account, all he offered was a pathetic "I'm sorry" the morning after the abuse, all the while continuing his abusive behavior. His explanation of the offense was similarly weak: a self-diagnosis of "immature sexual development." Oathout wanted an apology that would meet the needs we have identified in this chapter. Aside from financial reparation, he received nothing of value to him. Worse than that, what he received was a complete lack of understanding. What this story demonstrates is that an apology that fails is potentially more destructive than no apology at all. With no apology, one can hope for a future apology, but with a failed apology, one often concludes the matter is hopeless. Oathout's rage gives testimony to the effects of this devastating conclusion.

COMMENTS

I have attempted to make the case that a successful apology must meet one or more of several distinct psychological needs of the offended party. Although I have described seven such needs, others who study and write about apologies will undoubtedly offer alternative and perhaps more useful ways of characterizing the process. My point is that one way to increase the chances of offering a successful apology is by understanding the various psychological needs that apologies meet. Then, if an apology fails, whether we are the offender or the offended, we can ask ourselves which of these needs was not met and take steps to remedy that deficiency.

Identifying the various needs of offended parties is not the same as successfully meeting these needs. For example, it is well and good to agree that restoring self-respect and dignity is an important psychological need met by many effective apologies. However, it is another matter altogether to determine how apologies restore self-respect and dignity. Similarly, it is well and good for apologies to assure the offended parties that they share important values with the offender, but another matter altogether to determine how apologies accomplish this task. I think of these dichotomies as differences between needs, on the one hand, and methods or processes, on the other. Consider what is involved in building a house or preparing a meal: A house may serve one or more of several needs, such as functional use, economy, or beauty. But the methods used to build a house include consideration of other factors such as location, architectural design, materials, and workmanship. Similarly, a meal may serve one or more needs such as taste, presentation, economy, or nutrition, while the methods include the ingredients and the skill of the cook. In like manner, this chapter suggests apologies heal by meeting one or more of the seven needs described earlier. The next several chapters will focus on the methods used in the apology process: acknowledging the offense, offering an explanation, communicating certain attitudes and behaviors (remorse, shame, humility, sincerity), offering reparations, using proper timing, and negotiating differences between parties.

FOUR

Acknowledging
the Offense

The most essential part of an effective apology is acknowledging the offense. Clearly, without such a foundation, the apology process cannot even begin. As self-evident as that statement may seem, we should not assume that acknowledging an offense is a simple task. The reason that this part of the apology can be so challenging is that the acknowledgment may involve as many as four parts: 1) correctly identifying the party or parties responsible for the grievance, as well as the party or parties to whom the apology is owed; 2) acknowledging the offending behaviors in adequate detail; 3) recognizing the impact these behaviors had on the victim(s); and 4) confirming that the grievance was a violation of the social or moral contract between the parties. An effective apology requires that the parties reach agreement on all four parts, although it is common for one or more of the parts to be implicit—that is, not verbally stated. In a simple apology between two people, for example, the offender does not have to state in so many words that the party to whom he is apologizing is the offended party. An inability to reach agreement on these matters is, in my view, the most common cause of failed apologies. I shall illustrate this point in the pages ahead with numerous apologies, both successful and failed.

Even when the offense seems obvious the offender still needs to explore what the offense means to the offended party. For example, if I accidentally break your vase, I need to understand the value you attach to it, and how you feel about my handling it without your permission. Similarly, if I embarrass you in front of others, I need to understand your sensitivity to my words and your relationship to the people who witnessed your embarrassment. In both cases, the possibility of offering a meaningful apology may depend on how well I grasp the full nature of the offense from your perspective.

An example of the importance of acknowledging the correct offense in a simple personal apology occurred during some rather vigorous roughhousing between my six-year-old grandson and myself. In the middle of our play, I squirted instant whipped cream on his cheek near his mouth. He began to cry and told me he was angry with me. I responded immediately that I was very sorry. He answered that it was too late to say "sorry." An hour later while he was playing in my office, I turned to him and repeated how sorry I was for squirting the whipped cream, explicitly naming the offense for the first time. To my surprise, he told me he liked my squirting the whipped cream. It was fun. What he was upset about was bumping his head against the sofa, an event of which I was unaware and for which he blamed me. I could then make a heartfelt apology (a massage and a kiss on the head) for having inadvertently caused his collision with the sofa. (In truth, I had not felt terribly remorseful about the whipped cream.) After he seemed comforted, I asked if he forgave me. "Yes," he said. I asked him why he forgave me. He responded, "because you kissed my head and because I know you will make pancakes for breakfast." For all its apparent insignificance, I believe this encounter with a six-year-old child provides an excellent illustration of the importance of identifying the offense. If the goal is an effective apology that restores a damaged relationship, the best way to begin is by accurately understanding how the offended parties feel they were wronged.

Clarifying the details of the offense assumes particular importance in public apologies because the parties offering the apology and/or the parties receiving the apology may consist of many, sometimes even millions of people. If the offense is not described in enough detail, conflicting interpretations may result, often with destructive consequences. Because these apologies are frequently codified in written form and then become part of the history of both parties, the offending party must "get it right" the first time, with no ambiguity and no need for later attempts to restate the original understanding.

Lack of forthrightness at the outset can prolong the acknowledgment stage, leading people to question the validity of the subsequent apology. Consider the various apologies Boston's Cardinal Bernard Law offered during the Catholic Church's pedophile crisis. Acknowledgment of the cardinal's responsibility for the offense increased in scope and seriousness as the legal proceedings continued throughout the year. Another example was Senator Trent Lott's serial apologies for remarks praising Senator Strom Thurmond that many interpreted as racist. As with Cardinal Law, Lott's apologies contained different and increasingly serious descriptions of the wrong he had committed. Multiple varying restatements of the offense in each case led to public skepticism about the credibility of both men. (I will discuss Senator Lott's widely publicized apology in more detail in chapter 10.)

An effective acknowledgment of the offense can make significant contributions toward meeting several of the needs we discussed in the previous chapter. First, acknowledgment says to the offended party, "I was wrong," thus assuring that both parties still share important values. In addition, by acknowledging the offense, the offender says, in effect, "it was not your fault." Finally, if the offenders are to understand the extent of the offenses they have committed, they may need to engage the offended parties in a dialogue, assuring the latter that they have been heard.

I offer the next three stories as striking examples of acknowledgments that eloquently and completely describe the offense, accept responsibility for the offending behaviors, and recognize the violation of a social contract as well as the resulting harm. These acknowledgments are part of apologies of national or international significance: Two are from the United States, and one is from Germany.

EFFECTIVE PUBLIC ACKNOWLEDGMENTS

The first example of a complete acknowledgment is U.S. President Abraham Lincoln's second inaugural address, generally regarded as his second greatest speech, surpassed only by the Gettysburg Address.[1] I believe, along with others, that this 703-word document is, without question, an apology for American slavery.[2] Although the speech could be considered an exemplar of the apology process itself, containing as it does all four parts of the apology process—acknowledgment, remorse, explanation, and reparation—I want to focus on the acknowledgment stage: Lincoln's understanding of slavery as a "national offense."

Lincoln's description of slavery is stark and unsparing: "One eighth of the whole population" whose "two hundred and fifty years of unrequited toil," enforced by "blood drawn with the lash," enabled some to wring "their bread from the sweat of other men's faces."[3] Speaking as a representative of an entire nation, including himself, that must now accept full responsibility for slavery, he suggested that the offense was not simply a violation of the social contract but a violation of God's will as well: "Woe unto the world because of offences! For it must needs be that offences come; but woe to that man by whom the offence cometh!"[4] Later he suggested that God "gives to both North and South, this terrible war, as the woe due to those by whom the offence came."[5]

Interestingly, although this acknowledgment describes the offense as viewed from the perspective of the slaves (" . . . unrequited toil, blood drawn from the lash, . . . from the sweat of other men's faces"), the meaning attached to the offense seems to refer to the nation as a whole. "Both parties [the North and the South] deprecated war," Lincoln noted, "but one of them would make war rather than let the nation survive; and the other would accept war rather than let it perish. And the war came."[6] Later Lincoln added, "These slaves constituted a peculiar and powerful interest. All knew that this interest was, somehow, the cause of the war. To strengthen, perpetuate, and extend this interest was the object for which the insurgents would rend the Union."[7] I believe this passage suggests that Lincoln had two "victims" in mind: slaves, as direct recipients of the pain, humiliation, and abuse that slavery entailed, and the nation, whose very existence was imperiled by the pursuit of this "peculiar and powerful interest."

The second illustration of an effective acknowledgment is from Richard von Weizsacker, president of the Federal Republic of Germany. During a speech to the Bundestag commemorating the fortieth anniversary of the end of the war in Europe, von Weizsacker detailed the grievances inflicted on the victims of Germany during World War II, in a manner somewhat reminiscent of Lincoln's painful candor. He began by emphasizing the importance of such honesty, "We need and we have the strength to look truth straight in the eye—without embellishment and without distortion," he said. Later, he repeated the point, "Remembering means recalling an occurrence honestly and undistortedly so that it becomes a part of our very beings. This places high demands on our truthfulness."[8]

His description of the offending behaviors with its long list of victims is specific and unflinching. "Today we mourn all the dead of the war and the tyranny," he said. "In particular we commemorate the six million Jews who were murdered in German concentration camps . . . all nations who suffered in the war, especially the countless citizens of the Soviet Union and Poland who lost their lives . . . the Sinti and Romany Gypsies, the homosexuals and the mentally ill . . . the people who had to die for their religious or political beliefs . . . the hostages who were executed. We recall the victims of the resistance movements in all countries occupied by us. As Germans, we pay homage to the victims of the German resistance—among the public, the military, the churches, the workers and trade unions, and the Communists."[9]

He also describes the impact offending behaviors had on victims who survived. "Alongside the endless army of the dead, mountains of human suffering arise," he observed, "grief over the dead, suffering from injury or crippling or barbarous compulsory sterilization, suffering during the air raids, during flight and expulsion, suffering because of rape and pillage, forced labor, injustice and torture, hunger and hardship, suffering because of fear of arrest and death. . . . Today we sorrowfully recall all this human suffering. . . . There can be no reconciliation without remembrance."[10]

This painful acknowledgment of Germany's multiple offenses is complete in every detail: It enumerates the many victims of Nazi Germany (Jews, Gypsies, homosexuals, the mentally ill, Poles, Soviets, among others), the reasons for their victimization (religious and political beliefs, among others), and the nature of their suffering (rape, pillage, forced labor, torture, hunger, and death, among others). Von Weizsacker does not try to diminish the enormity of the offense by offering rationalizations or excuses. He clearly identifies the responsible parties, as he admonishes all Germans "to face the consequences with due responsibility."[11] Remembering and acknowledging, he emphasizes, is the only path to reconciliation. It must, he declares, become "part of our very being."[12]

The third example of a successful acknowledgment of offenses comes from Kevin Gover's remarks at a ceremony celebrating the one hundred seventy fifth anniversary of the establishment of the Bureau of Indian Affairs (BIA). At the time, Gover was assistant secretary of Indian Affairs for the U.S. Department of Interior. In his remarks, he explicitly accepted responsibility on behalf of the BIA: "We must first reconcile ourselves to the fact that the works of this agency have at various times profoundly harmed the communities it was meant to serve."[13] He then gave an exhaustive account of the offenses committed against the Native American people, beginning with the forced removal of the southeastern tribal nations. "By threat, deceit, and force," Gover said, "these great tribal nations were made to march 1,000 miles to the west, leaving thousands of their old, their young and their infirm in hasty graves along the Trail of Tears."[14]

However, Gover pointed out, removing Indians from their ancestral homes did not satisfy the country's greed. "As the nation looked to the West for more land," he said, "this agency participated in the ethnic cleansing that befell the western tribes."[15] He described the various means used: "the deliberate spread of disease, the decimation of the mighty bison herds, the use of the poison alcohol to destroy mind and body, and the cowardly killing of women and children."[16] What resulted was a "tragedy on a scale so ghastly that it cannot be dismissed as merely the inevitable consequence of the clash of competing ways of life."[17] The BIA contributed to the tragedy by "failing in the mission to prevent the devastation," Gover asserted, with the result that "we will never push aside the memory of unnecessary and violent death at places such as Sand Creek, the banks of the Washita River, and Wounded Knee."[18]

Gover did not limit his description of the offense to the consequences of war alone. "After the devastation of tribal economies and the deliberate creation of tribal dependence on the services provided by this agency," he said, "this agency set out to destroy all things Indian."[19] Once again, Gover's list of offensive behaviors is extensive and concrete: "This agency forbade the speaking of Indian languages, prohibited the conduct of traditional religious activities, outlawed traditional government, and made Indian people ashamed of whom they were," he reported. "Worst of all, the Bureau of Indian Affairs committed these acts against the children entrusted to its boarding schools, brutalizing them emotionally, psychologically, physically, and spiritually."[20] The consequences of these practices have led to ongoing harm, he said, "the trauma of shame, fear, and anger has passed from one generation to the next, and manifests itself in the rampant alcoholism, drug abuse, and domestic violence that plague Indian country."[21] He asserted that the BIA was responsible for these continued harms. "So many of the maladies suffered today in Indian country result from the failures of this agency. Poverty, ignorance, and disease have been the product of this agency's work," he concluded.[22]

With these remarks, Gover faithfully and thoroughly acknowledges the many offenses of the BIA. Specifically, he identifies the responsible party (the BIA); describes the offending behaviors (the many ways Indians were harmed); recognizes the impact of the offending behaviors (in this case, past, present, and future); and confirms that the grievance violated a shared understanding of how "competing ways of life" should be handled. It is easy to see how such a thorough acknowledgment of the offense could pave the way for a successful apology.

PERSONAL REFLECTIONS

I find the apologies from Lincoln and Gover to be heartwrenching, the most difficult of all those I describe in this book to read without tears. I suspect that the quality and specificity of the narratives contribute to that response, but I also experience a feeling of profound shame when I read them, because it is my country and my people who are the culprits, not the Nazis. As a boy growing up in the United States I enjoyed "cowboy and Indian" movies and rooted for the destruction of the "bad Indians." The implicit racism of the forties and fifties was so pervasive that it seeped into the American psyche with hardly a ripple. Even though I have never personally harmed an African American or Native American, I feel shame for what happened to these populations, because they reflect (and should reflect) very badly on every citizen of the United States. As I mentioned in chapter 2, if we can be proud of national accomplishments not of our making, so, too, must we accept shame for national misdeeds not of our making. Accepting these responsibilities is part of what we mean when we speak of having a national identity.

There are interesting stories behind Gover and von Weizsacker's apologies. Von Weizsacker's father held important positions in the Nazi Reich, was found guilty at the Nuremberg trials for crimes against peace and humanity, and was sentenced to seven years in prison (he was released after eighteen months). Perhaps his son was apologizing, in part, for the sins of his father. Gover, too, had an ambiguous role in offering an apology for the activities of the Bureau of Indian Affairs. Himself a Native American whose father had suffered from alcoholism, Gover's understanding of the offenses committed against Native Americans was rooted in personal experience. His position at the BIA placed him in the unique position of apologizing to his own people on behalf of and as a member of the U.S. government.

Lincoln's apology is extraordinary, in my judgment. Recently elected to a second term and as president of a nation on the verge of winning the Civil War, he could have justifiably spoken with pride about the accomplishments of the nation and himself. Instead, he offered an apology full of humility and remorse for the offense of slavery. He spoke as an Old Testament prophet whose role was to call the people to return to God's way. Frederick Douglass, a former slave and the only "colored man" to attend the inaugural reception, told Lincoln that he thought "it was a sacred effort."[23] Although his speech received mixed reviews at the time, Lincoln was personally confident that it would "wear as well—perhaps better than anything I have produced; but I believe is not immediately popular."[24] As it turned out, despite his determination "to finish the work we are in, to bind up the nation's wounds . . . to do all which may achieve and cherish a just, and a lasting peace, among ourselves, and with all nations,"[25] Lincoln was assassinated 41 days after delivering the speech.

FAILURE TO
ADEQUATELY ACKNOWLEDGE OFFENSES

Moving from examples of extraordinary acknowledgments of offenses to the more common phenomena of failed acknowledgments, I find it both remarkable and disturbing that offenders so frequently try to manipulate the acknowledgment stage of an apology in order to reduce or avoid responsibility for the offense. The results are failed or pseudo-apologies: apologies that, at best, do not heal the damaged relationship and, at worse, further offend the aggrieved party. I believe that there are at least eight different ways that statements of the offense can fail, some of which may overlap. I offer these categories to help readers understand why they sometimes experience apologies as disappointing, annoying, insulting, and occasionally amusing. These categories include: 1) offering a vague and incomplete acknowledgment; 2) using the passive voice; 3) making the offense conditional; 4) questioning whether the victim was damaged; 5) minimizing the offense; 6) using the empathic "I'm sorry"; 7) apologizing to the wrong party; and 8) apologizing for the wrong offense.

OFFERING A VAGUE

AND INCOMPLETE ACKNOWLEDGMENT:

"I APOLOGIZE FOR WHATEVER I DID"

A common reason why an apology fails is that the wrongdoer states the offense in a vague and incomplete manner, such as saying, "I am sorry," or, "I apologize," with no further comment. Examples of slightly more detailed but still inadequate apologies include statements such as, "I am sorry for anything (or everything) that I did," or, "I am sorry for what happened," or, "I am sorry for all I have done to upset you," or, "I apologize for what happened yesterday."

Sometimes offenders will offer a vague "I'm sorry" statement of the offense because they are so intimidated by the prospects of the victim's response that they blurt out, "I am sorry, I am sorry, I am sorry," just to placate the unpleasantness of the situation. This apology is meaningless, because the offenders may not even know what offenses they committed or even whether offenses were committed. The offended parties often receive limited satisfaction from such apologies because they usually know the offender does not even understand the grievances and because they have not had the opportunity to express the grievances. (See chapter 8 for a further discussion of such apologies.) These apologies often occur between superiors and subordinates at work, between husbands and wives, or between parents and children, situations in which intimidation, whether real or perceived, may play a role.

Arnold Schwarzenegger's apology for mistreating women—offered just days before the California recall election in which he was elected governor— illustrates a vague and incomplete apology. The specific offenses, alleged by six women and dating from the 1970s to 2000, included grabbing a woman's breast, reaching under a woman's skirt and grabbing her buttock, trying to remove a woman's bathing suit in a hotel elevator, and pulling a woman onto his lap. When asked whether he had touched them in a sexual manner, he acknowledged unspecified wrongdoing.[26] What he said was: "A lot of [what] you see in the stories is not true, but at the same time . . . I have behaved badly sometimes . . . I have done things which were not right which I thought was playful . . . now I recognize that I have offended people. . . . I apologize because this is not what I tried to do."[27] In a later interview, he said he could not remember what he did. He offered no apologies to any individual woman who claimed to have been the victim of his sexual advances. The executive director of the California chapter of the National Organization for Women, Helen Grieco, voiced the reaction of many when she said, "Your explanation is appalling, insults our intelligence and shows that you just don't get it. Your behavior was not playful; it was illegal."[28] In my opinion, Grieco's response was exactly right.

Pop singer Janet Jackson offered a failed apology for her behavior during a halftime show at the 2004 Super Bowl. During a duet with Justin Timberlake, which was seen by 89 million viewers, he sang, "gonna have you naked by the end of this song."[29] Timberlake pulled off a part of Jackson's costume revealing her breast with a partially concealed nipple. After the event Jackson issued a public apology: ". . . I am really sorry if I offended anyone. That was truly not my intention."[30] Timberlake told friends he was duped by Jackson and his friends suggested that her goal was to promote her new recording.[31]

In the apology, she never acknowledges what she did and therefore never said it was wrong, inappropriate, or in bad taste. This failed apology was aggravated by Jackson's conditional acknowledgment . . . "if I offended anyone."

USING THE PASSIVE VOICE:
"MISTAKES MAY HAVE BEEN MADE"

Another common way of avoiding responsibility for committing an offense is to use the impersonal or passive voice, saying, "it happened," or "mistakes were made," rather than, "I did it." For example, when President William Clinton, in one of his apologies, simply said, "mistakes were made," the *New York Times* contrasted his remark with General Robert E. Lee's admission following the failure of Pickett's Charge at the battle of Gettysburg: "It is all my fault."[32]

President Ulysses S. Grant provided another example of using the passive voice, in one of his annual messages to Congress. He began his speech by citing his lack of training for political life. "It was my fortune, or misfortune, to be called to the office of chief executive without any previous political training," he said.[33] He continued by noting that he had only witnessed two previous presidential campaigns before launching his own candidacy, and at only one of them had he been eligible to vote. Having thus established his impoverished training for the presidency, he argued, "Under such circumstances it is but reasonable to suppose that *errors of judgment must have occurred*. Even had they not, differences of opinion between the Executive bound by an oath to the strict performance of his duties, and writers and debaters must have arisen. It is not necessarily evidence of blunder on the part of the Executive because there are these differences of views."[34] (Italics added.) Even though "errors of judgment must have occurred," Grant is suggesting that it may be difficult to distinguish between errors and mere differences of opinion between himself and his critics, adding that these differences of opinion do not necessarily mean that the "Executive" was wrong.

Finally, Grant gets to the section that he may have intended to be an apology. "*Mistakes have been made*, as all can see and I admit," he writes, "but it seems to me oftener in the selections made of the assistants appointed to aid in carrying out the various duties of administering the Government—in nearly every case selected without a personal acquaintance with the appointee, but upon recommendations of the representatives chosen directly by the people. It is impossible, where so many trusts are to be allotted, that the right parties should be chosen in every instance. History shows that no Administration from the time of Washington to the present has been free from these mistakes. But I leave comparisons to history, claiming only that I have acted in every instance from conscientious desire to do what was right, constitutional, within the law, and for the best interests of the whole people. Failures have been errors of judgment, not of intent. . . ."[35](Italics added.)

I believe this speech fails as an apology in at least three ways. First, Grant deflects responsibility by using the passive voice (". . . errors of judgment must have occurred" and "mistakes have been made, as all can see, and I admit.") Nowhere does he "own" the offense; instead, he tries to give the blame to others—to the assistants appointed to aid in carrying out the duties of government or to the representatives who had selected them. Next, he tries to "normalize" his actions by suggesting that presidential administrations have always made mistakes and that his is no exception. Finally, he justifies his choices by claiming that "in every instance" he had acted from "conscientious desire to do what was right, constitutional, within the law, and for the best interests of the whole people." For these reasons, I believe that Grant's speech is not an apology at all but is rather an *apologia*—a justification or defense of his administration's actions and decisions.

MAKING THE OFFENSE CONDITIONAL:
"IF MISTAKES MAY HAVE BEEN MADE . . . "

In a speech addressing the Roman Catholic Church's pedophile crisis, Cardinal Edward M. Egan, the leader of the New York Archdiocese, illustrates the conditional apology. He commented, "If in hindsight we also discover that mistakes may have been made as regards prompt removal of priests and assistance to victims, I am deeply sorry."[36] Although he may have thought he was apologizing, Egan in fact manages to qualify his apology three times in a single sentence. First, he suggests that only in hindsight would people think it wrong to reassign pedophile priests (a suggestion that in itself is insulting). Then, he makes the offense conditional (only if hindsight reveals any mistakes), and finally, he seems unwilling to admit responsibility ("if . . . mistakes may have been made"). How much more effective would this so-called apology have been had the cardinal said, "We made a terrible mistake. We should have known it was wrong to ignore victims and to reassign pedophile priests to new parishes. We are very sorry and deeply troubled that innocent children were hurt as a result of our failure to remove these priests from the parishes."

Commenting on the conditional nature of the cardinal's remarks, Clyde Haberman wrote in the *New York Times*, "You don't need to read Kipling to be reminded what a big word 'if' can be. It is a favorite of politicians after they have done something especially dumb, and want to give the appearance of apologizing without actually apologizing. . . . How many times have you heard politicians wrap themselves in that cloak of conditionality?"[37]

President Richard Nixon's resignation speech provides yet another example of this "cloak of conditionality" when he remarked, "I regret deeply any injuries that *may have been done* in the course of events that led to this decision. I would say only that if some of my judgments were wrong, and some were wrong, they were made in what I believed at the time to be in the best interests of the nation."[38] (Italics added.) Once again, we have an example of a compound reduction of the effectiveness of an apology. Nixon's use of a conditional phrase ("if some of my judgments were wrong") suggests the possibility that none of them were wrong. By also using the passive voice ("injuries that may have been done"), he makes his acknowledgment of the offense conditional on whether anyone has been injured, leaving open the possibility that either the injuries never occurred or that someone else may have done them. Even when he finally, reluctantly, admits that his judgments were wrong, he quickly adds that he believed they were justified ("they were made in what I believed at the time to be in the best interests of the nation").[39]

It is no wonder that U.S. citizens, the primary recipients of this "apology," were disappointed. The president does not fully accept that he has injured the nation, he barely acknowledges that some of his judgments were wrong, and he asks the public to accept the claim that he was serving the best interests of the nation, rather than his own self-interests. By his distortion of the truth and his condescension to the American public, Nixon not only fails to offer a meaningful apology but also commits the additional offense of insulting or humiliating the listening audience.

If Nixon had been honest with himself and with the nation, he might have said, "I regret deeply the injuries I caused the nation as a result of my poor judgment. Although at the time, I believed that what I did was in the best interest of the nation, I now realize that I was terribly mistaken." Had Nixon apologized properly on this and other occasions, he might have been spared the wrath of the nation that his attitudes and actions provoked.[40]

QUESTIONING WHETHER THE VICTIM IS DAMAGED: "IF ANYONE WAS HURT . . . "

Another way of avoiding responsibility for the offense is to question whether the victim was or should have been damaged in the first place. The most common forms of acknowledgments use phrases such as, "if you were offended . . . " or "to the degree that you were offended . . . ." In such situations, the wrongdoer is saying, in effect, "Not everyone would be offended by my behavior. If you have a problem with being so thin-skinned, I will apologize to you because of your need (your weakness) and my generosity. I hope this makes you happy." Notice how the form of this apology transforms the victim into the cause of the offense and the offender into a blameless and generous benefactor. One readily sees that this failed apology, which is supposed to undo an insult and restore dignity, in fact only inflicts more damage—or as we might say colloquially, it "adds insult to injury."

A student-run newspaper at Spokane Community College published a letter that was offensive to women, minorities, and gay students and was signed by "Whitey." The alleged purpose of the letter was to "raise awareness about racism on campus" and not to cause racial tension or sensationalism.[41] However, students discovered that "Whitey" was fictitious and that newspaper staff members had, in fact, written the letter. Predictably, the students were upset at being manipulated, and the writers and editors eventually apologized in an editorial. They offered their "deepest and most sincere apologies to *anyone who may have been hurt* by the racist letter."[42] (Italics added.)

This "apology" suggests that the problem was not the newspaper's publication of the letter but rather the reader's vulnerability to being hurt. Some students said that the apology was inadequate because "it did not admit that its decision to fabricate and print the racist letter was a mistake."[43] In my view, these students were correct. The "apology" failed to acknowledge the role the editorial played in causing people to be hurt.

A more appropriate acknowledgment of the offense would have been, "We offer our deepest and most sincere apologies for writing this racist letter. Although we thought it could raise awareness about racism on campus, we were clearly mistaken. What we did was unequivocally wrong and misguided. We are currently engaged in serious soul searching. We deeply regret hurting so many people and are committed to restoring your confidence in us in the future." Such an apology would have acknowledged the offense and reestablished the moral contract by admitting that the editors' judgment was wrong.

Another example of this kind of inadequate apology is the response made by Carlos Jagmetti, Swiss ambassador to the United States, to the publication of a diplomatic cable he had written. (Jagmetti had been advising the Swiss government about its response to accusations that Switzerland acted as banker to Nazi Germany during World War II.) In the cable, he referred to Holocaust victims as "opponents" and as "people who cannot be trusted." Although Jagmetti apologized, saying he regretted "having offended the sensibilities of Jewish groups and the public with some expressions in the report . . . ," [44] he never admitted that what he did was wrong. Instead, he suggested that Jewish and public "sensibilities" were the problem. A more appropriate apology would have said, "What I said in the cable was both incorrect and inappropriate. I deeply regret making these comments." Perhaps Jagmetti would not convince many people that his apology was sincere, particularly in light of the morally questionable relationships between certain Swiss bankers and the Nazi government. However, the apology would affirm the judgment that anti-Semitic comments violate the social contract, at least among democratic nations.

As defending golf champion in the Masters Tournament, Tiger Woods had the privilege of selecting the menu for the following year's Champions Dinner. Fuzzy Zoeller, another golfer in the tournament, made the following observation during a CNN interview: "That little boy is driving well and he's putting well," Zoeller said. "He's doing everything it takes to win. So, you know what you guys do when he gets in here? You pat him on the back and say 'congratulations and enjoy it' and tell him not to serve fried chicken next year. Got it? . . . or collard greens or whatever the hell they serve."[45]

Public outrage at Zoeller's remarks was swift and ferocious. In his own defense, Zoeller explained, "My comments were not intended to be racially derogatory, and I apologize for the fact that they were misconstrued in that fashion. . . . I've been on the tour for 23 years and anybody who knows me knows that I am a jokester. It's too bad that something I said in jest *was turned into something it's not*, but I didn't mean anything by it and *I'm sorry if I offended anybody. If Tiger is offended by it*, I apologize to him too."[46] (Italics added.)

This apology fails for many reasons. First, Zoeller never acknowledges the nature of the offense he had committed (referring to Woods as a "little boy," a term that would be particularly offensive to African Americans, as well as making fun of supposed African American dietary preferences). Second, by saying, "If Tiger is offended by it, I apologize to him," he blames the victim for being offended. Third, he apologizes not for what he said but for the fact that his words were "misconstrued in that fashion" and that people did not realize that much of what he says is in jest. Fourth, at the time of the apology, he had never discussed the matter directly with Woods to learn his view of the offensive behavior. (Tiger Woods's father is African American and his mother is of Asian descent.)

For an effective apology, Zoeller could have said, "I am sorry for my insensitive (or thoughtless, or hurtful) remarks. I was wrong. It will not happen again. Be assured that I will ask for a private meeting with Tiger so I can directly apologize to him." In fairness to Zoeller, he made a better apology several days later after he had been fired by K-Mart and had withdrawn from the Greater Greensboro Classic. He said he wanted to talk to Woods about the remarks before picking up another golf club. He withdrew from the $1.9 million tournament because of "my respect for the game of golf, ladies and gentlemen, and my love for my fellow pros."[47] According to the Associated Press story, "Zoeller choked back tears as he read a brief statement to reporters, at one point straying from his prepared text to say 'it hurts. . . . I am the one who screwed up and I will pay the price. . . . I started this and I feel strongly that I have to make things right with Tiger first before anything else. . . . I also regret the distraction this has caused the world of golf. What I said is distracting people at this tournament. And that's not fair to the other people on this course trying to play this tournament.'"[48]

In this apology, Zoeller shifted the blame to himself and identified the offended parties as Woods, the world of golf, and the professional golfers playing in the tournament. He also appeared to show genuine remorse and punished himself by withdrawing from a potentially lucrative tournament. But the apology is still incomplete, because he failed to acknowledge that what he said was wrong or inappropriate, saying instead that he "screwed up" and caused a "distraction" to the world of golf. He seemed more concerned with hurting the "world of golf" than hurting Tiger Woods or other African Americans.

MINIMIZING THE OFFENSE: "THERE'S REALLY NOTHING (OR VERY LITTLE) TO APOLOGIZE FOR . . . "

Minimizing or questioning whether an offense was even committed is another way to derail an intended apology. A good example of this kind of aborted acknowledgment involved Air Canada, which canceled 46 flights over a two-day period because of a contract dispute with its pilots. Thousands of passengers were affected. An airline spokeswoman said, "You have to remember that's out of 650 flights. I know quite a lot of people have been inconvenienced by this and we apologize but it's really minimal. All customers affected have been rebooked."[49] By using statistics to minimize the damage, the spokeswoman overlooks the fact that each person who was inconvenienced had a grievance. Her apology would be similar to telling the news media that minimal damage occurred in a plane crash since only two people out of 300 were killed.

Another way to limit the offense is to directly challenge the offended parties' judgment about the importance of the offense and their reactions to it. U.S. Col. Kassem Saleh was under investigation for "allegations that he simultaneously romanced dozens of women on the Internet and by phone and proposed to them."[50] Saleh's lawyer said on his behalf, "He is sincerely apologetic. He didn't intend to harm them in any way. But enough is enough." The lawyer added that he did not believe that Saleh committed a crime. Not surprisingly, his alleged victims were unconvinced by this so-called apology. "It's too little, too late," declared one. "That's definitely not sufficient for the betrayal, the deceit. He stole my heart."[51] Had Saleh genuinely wanted to demonstrate his concern for the victims, he should have offered the apology himself, not through an intermediary. Furthermore, he should not have told the victims how they should feel because that practice almost universally generates anger, not acceptance.

Another way to minimize the offense is to limit its scope. The Irish Republican Army (IRA) made an important but carefully circumscribed apology when it released a statement on the anniversary of one of its operations. "Sunday, July 21 marks the 30th anniversary of an IRA operation in Belfast in 1972 which resulted in nine people being killed and many more injured," the statement read. "While it was not our intention to injure or kill noncombatants, the reality is that on this and on a number of other occasions, that was the consequence of our actions. It is, therefore, appropriate on the anniversary of this tragic event, that we address all of the deaths and injuries of noncombatants caused by us. We offer our sincere apologies and condolences to their families. There have been fatalities amongst combatants on all sides. We also acknowledge the grief and pain of their relatives."[52]

This apology carefully distinguishes between the families of noncombatants and combatants, making it clear that the IRA is offering its "sincere apologies and condolences" only to the families of noncombatants killed in the operation. The families of combatants, on the other hand, received neither apologies nor condolences. They were offered instead a reminder that fatalities occurred on all sides of the dispute, and then a simple acknowledgment of their "grief and pain." The IRA's statement seems to suggest that the combatants had forfeited any claims to an apology because of their actions during the confrontation, and thus, that their families should get no special attention from the IRA.

USING THE EMPATHIC
"I'M SORRY" OR "I REGRET . . . "

One way to avoid taking responsibility for an offense is to use the phrase "I am sorry" or "I regret" in the empathic sense.

Examples of this use of "sorry" would be statements such as "I am sorry that you suffered so much damage," or "I am sorry you are so upset/angry with me," or "I am sorry you had to respond this way," or "I am sorry we had to bomb your village."

None of these expressions by itself communicates responsibility for making a mistake. Depending on the tone, these expressions may be meaningful communications of caring and regret, or they may be condescending, patronizing statements of superiority. They can be used as a devious means to elicit forgiveness without acknowledging responsibility, or even as attempts to blame others by accusing them of being overly emotional. But they are not apologies.

An example of this use of the word "sorry" occurred in a speech made by the U.S. ambassador to Japan, Walter Mondale, on the occasion of the fiftieth anniversary of the U.S. bombing of Tokyo, during which 100,000 people were killed. "I wanted to come here to say how sorry we are for how people had to suffer," Mondale said. "For 50 years now, the United States and Japan have been working together building the peace, building a strong relationship, and because of that the world is much safer and much more hopeful. For all the tragedy, I think we've learned our lesson and we're doing better."[53]

A careful reading of these remarks shows that despite using the word "sorry" and naming what the United States was sorry about ("... how people had to suffer"), Mondale never said that the United States accepted responsibility for the suffering. Although his speech may have expressed genuine empathy for what happened ("for all the tragedy"), it was not an apology, nor was it intended to be.

A similar empathic "non-apology" was offered by Commander Scott D. Waddle, following his submarine's ramming of a Japanese fishing boat that resulted in the loss of nine lives. Waddle sent a letter of regret to the Japanese national television network. "It is with a heavy heart that I express my most sincere regret to the Japanese people and most importantly, to the families of those lost . . . no words can adequately express my condolences and concern. . . . I too grieve for the families and the catastrophic losses that the families have endured."[54]

The Japanese were not appeased by Waddle's expression of regret and condolences. One family member said, "It's not an apology until he says it to each one of us in person."[55] They wanted an acknowledgment and acceptance of responsibility for the incident. After being relieved of his command, Waddle made subsequent apologies to Japan that corrected this failing. A detailed analysis of this apology appears in chapter 10.

These "pseudo-apologies" can even be a source of humor, as demonstrated by a *Blondie* cartoon in which Mr. Dithers decides to apologize to Dagwood for calling him a "dimwitted noodle brain." Dithers then apologizes by saying, "Dagwood, I'm sorry you're a dimwitted noodle brain" and declares that his conscience is clear because of his "heartfelt apology."[56] Instead of apologizing for what he said, Mr. Dithers expresses compassion for Dagwood's condition (being a dimwitted noodle brain). The humor comes from the fact that, although he intended to apologize, and his statement sounds like an apology ("I'm sorry"), and it even feels as if he had apologized ("there is nothing like a heartfelt apology . . ."), he did not actually offer an apology at all. We chuckle because the comic strip shows how easy it is to be misled by the empathic use of "I'm sorry."

APOLOGIZING TO THE WRONG PARTY

Misdirected apologies are another common occurrence. Mike Tyson's apology for biting Evander Holyfield's ear during a boxing match was not directed to Holyfield or to the public but to those who had the power to deprive him of his livelihood as a prize fighter. (See chapter 6 for an extended discussion of this apology.) Golfer Fuzzy Zoeller initially apologized to the media, not to Tiger Woods, the object of the alleged offense. When offenders direct apologies to the "wrong" people, it is instructive to consider what they gain from the interaction. In many cases, the person to whom the apology is directed has the power to limit the offender's future options. The purpose of the apology, then, is to manipulate the situation to protect themselves rather than to reconcile with the victim.

A shocking example of this kind of misdirected apology occurred after Justin A.Volpe, a New York City police officer, rammed a stick into the rectum of a handcuffed Haitian immigrant and then thrust the stick in the man's face. Aware of the mounting evidence against him, Volpe confessed to this crime and acknowledged that he intended to humiliate and intimidate the victim. When the judge vigorously pursued why he felt the need to humiliate his victim, Volpe's excuse was that he "was in shock at the time."[57] At the end of the hearing, the defendant said to the judge, "Your honor, if I could just let the record reflect I'm sorry for hurting my family."[58] Volpe did not ask to apologize to the victim. His lawyer, realizing his client's mistake, stated that Volpe was clearly remorseful and explained, "When you plead guilty, I think that's a sufficient apology."[59]

Volpe's apology to his family may have been genuine. However, his failure to direct his apology to the proper victim of his actions is quite disturbing. It is easy to be skeptical about whether Volpe is genuinely remorseful for what he did, and to consider the possibility that he might repeat the behavior again in similar circumstances. Perhaps he regards the victim as somehow beneath him, undeserving of respect, or he blames the victim for his troubles. The absence of remorse for such a violent and serious offense is shocking. People expect some kind of statement of regret, even though it may appear to be insincere. Volpe's lawyer recognized how important it was for his client to offer such a statement, and he tried to argue that the guilty plea was both an expression of remorse and an apology. However, pleading guilty is not the same as offering an apology. In fact, a person can be found guilty in a court of law and never feel guilty for his or her crime. Properly acknowledging the offense requires that the offending party accept responsibility for having acted in a manner that caused harm to the victims of the offense. By acknowledging harm to his family, but not his victim, Volpe failed to meet this requirement.

APOLOGIZING FOR THE WRONG OFFENSE

At times, the wrongdoer will apologize for a different offense than the one experienced by the offended party. Apologizing for the wrong offense can be a very self-serving tactic. The offenders choose offenses for which they will share the blame and which may even make them look good. This verbal "sleight of hand" tactic may satisfy some people, but it offends many more. For example, a man is discovered by his wife to be having an extramarital affair. He acknowledges as his offense the emotional pain he caused his wife. His distress over the possible termination of his marriage seems genuine. At some point in their discussion, however, the husband says that he does not think having extramarital affairs is such a terrible thing and that he would not be offended if she did the same. This point of view is the beginning of the end of the marriage. The husband only acknowledges his wife's distress and not the affair that actually caused the offense.

The next apology is an example of apologizing for the wrong offense in the public arena. Robert S. McNamara's 1995 book, *In Retrospect: The Tragedy and Lessons of Vietnam*,[60] generated much public controversy, anger, and outrage when it was published. Many newspaper reporters and commentators regarded this book as McNamara's apology for his role as secretary of defense during the Vietnam War. Paul Hendrickson, author of *The Living and the Dead,* commented, "The memoir, billed as a *mea culpa*, inspired such instant rage in America, and really in the world, that it was hard not to think that some part of [McNamara] wished it exactly that way— though surely the more conscious part of him had to be hoping, no, dying, for forgiveness."[61] In a lead editorial on the third day following publication, the *New York Times* commented, "His [McNamara's] regret cannot be huge enough to balance the books for our dead soldiers. . . . What he took from them cannot be repaid by prime-time apology and stale tears, three decades later."[62] McNamara insisted that the book was not an apology but was about "mostly honest mistakes . . . we made an error not of values and intentions but of judgment and capabilities."[63] Despite McNamara's disclaimer, I believe that most readers and commentators saw the book as an apology (albeit a failed one) because they wanted an apology, hoped for an apology, and needed an apology. They also saw it as offensive because of its lack of candor and betrayal of values.

If we start with the assumption that many people did regard the book as an apology, what are the offenses for which it is offered? McNamara admits to several strategic mistakes in the Vietnam War, such as misjudgments, offering status reports that were too optimistic, and preoccupation with other world events. However, his descriptions of these mistakes read more like justifications than apologies: He continually blames others and explains in great detail the difficulties that led to his mistakes. But the chief offense, the one that distressed so many, myself included, is that McNamara realized, at least by 1965, that the war could not be won. When he resigned in 1967 from his position as secretary of defense, nearly 16,000 American soldiers and about 1 million Vietnamese were dead. By the end of the war five years later, the number had risen to 58,000 American soldiers and about 3 million Vietnamese.[64] Despite knowing that the war was doomed to failure, he uttered not a word to the American public. David Halberstam, author of *The Best and the Brightest,* a highly regarded history of the Vietnam War, offers a clear picture of the offenses for which McNamara is responsible. He writes, ". . . in truth, McNamara lied and deceived the Senate and the press and the public. . . . He consistently lied to the nation about the levels of increment of troops. . . . But his greatest crime . . . was the crime of silence."[65] In my judgment, McNamara's offenses were not failed strategic decisions but a failure to tell the truth and speak up when it mattered.

What might an apology for the U.S. role in the Vietnam War achieve for our country? I believe that a meaningful apology could heal a number of very important old wounds. For example, such an apology could restore to U.S. military veterans the respect they never received. The view that government officials should not lie and should not be silent, particularly on important issues such as war, could be reaffirmed as values shared by both the government and its citizens. Confidence could be restored in the belief that it is safe for U.S. citizens to dissent from the government's policies and choices. Perhaps most important of all, such an apology could open a dialogue among citizens and between government and citizens that would offer a catharsis for the complex and contradictory feelings we have about the war, in the process providing an opportunity for grieving the loss of lives and for preserving national honor.

COMMENTS

As the apologies in this chapter show, when called on to make an apology, we can be quite determined and innovative in our attempts to avoid acknowledging the offense, with the result that the eventual apology is undermined. We may even think that we have convinced the offended parties, and perhaps even ourselves, that we have adequately acknowledged the offense, even though our attempts are transparent failures. This resistance speaks to the interesting duality in most of us: We can simultaneously feel that we should acknowledge the offense and yet we avoid doing so at all costs. (We will explore this conflict in chapter 6 as we consider the motives for apologizing and in chapter 7 as we examine the resistance to apologizing.)

The apologies in this chapter also suggest reasons why wrongdoers find it so difficult to acknowledge their offenses. The offenses in these failed apologies were often some kind of failure of performance or behavior that resulted in harm to others (as in the cases of Arnold Schwarzenegger, President

Nixon, President Grant, Col. Saleh, Robert McNamara, Admiral Waddle, Fuzzy Zoeller, police officer Volpe, the IRA, and Air Canada). To apologize effectively for these failures would require an accurate and complete acknowledgment of them. Instead, the offenders in these situations offered apologies in which the so-called acknowledgment was actually a denial or minimization of the offense. Rather than accepting responsibility and telling the truth—behaviors that could have restored relationships with offended parties—the offenders chose to preserve their view of themselves and to avoid punishment. It should not surprise us that such apologies fail.

FIVE

Remorse, Explanations, and Reparation

This chapter continues to explore the structure of the four-part apology process that is necessary to meet the needs of the offended party. The previous chapter examined the most important part of the apology, the acknowledgment of the offense. In the present chapter we will consider the remaining three parts of the apology: 1) communicating remorse and the related attitudes of forbearance, sincerity, and honesty; 2) explanations; and 3) reparations. In any given apology, any one or combination of these components can contribute to its success or failure.

REMORSE AND RELATED ATTITUDES

By "remorse" I mean the deep, painful regret that is part of the guilt people experience when they have done something wrong. To feel remorse for an action is to accept responsibility for the harm caused by it. Thomas Moore, a psychotherapist and writer, describes remorse as a necessary and valuable psychological experience that "helps a person take events of the past to heart, to be affected by them. . . . Remorse is an attack of conscience, an inner voice that might be heard and attended."[1] Following Moore, we can see how remorse serves as a form of self-punishment, an internal scolding that says, "Don't ever do that again." In fact, if someone repeats an offense for which he or she has apologized, we tend to look back on the apology with skepticism, perhaps seeing it as an attempt by the offender to manipulate the situation in order to avoid censure or punishment. Even if a person never repeats the offending behavior for which the apology was offered, an absence of remorse will often distract from the value of this and subsequent apologies. It is as if remorse must accompany an apology as a sign of its authenticity.

One healthy result of remorse is forbearance, a resolve to abstain or refrain from such behavior in the future. If remorse is a kind of promissory note, forbearance is partial payment of the debt. Forbearance says, "I realize that what I did was wrong because it violated values I (and others) believe are important. I realize that my action caused harm. I feel deep remorse about my behavior, and by never doing anything like that again, I will prove that I am not the kind of person who disregards values and wantonly causes harm." Remorse and forbearance are like the proverbial "horse and carriage": They work best together. Or, in a more literary vein, we can understand them as being like Janus, the Roman god with two faces. In this case, backward-facing remorse identifies the offense and acknowledges the resultant harm, while forward-facing forbearance promises a different future.

The following three examples each contain expressions of this connection between remorse and forbearance. James Kartell, a plastic surgeon, fatally shot his wife's lover, Janos Vajda, a computer programmer, during a brawl in his wife's hospital room. (Kartell's wife, Dr. Susan Kamm, was being treated for pneumonia at the time.) Kamm had left her husband for Vajda six months before the shooting. After his conviction for voluntary manslaughter, Kartell apologized to the Vajda family. "Words fail to express the depth of the sorrow I feel and how sorry I am about this very tragic incident and my responsibility," he said. "Would that life would be like a computer and there would be an 'undo' button and I could press that button and make everything right. But life isn't that way." His eyes simultaneously welled with tears.[2]

In an apology for his National Party's imposition of Apartheid, South African President F. W. de Klerk said, "It was not our intention to deprive people of their rights and to cause misery, but eventually Apartheid led to just that. Insofar as that occurred, we deeply regret it."[3] But de Klerk did not stop with this statement of regret. "Deep regret goes much further than just saying you are sorry," de Klerk explained. "Deep regret says that if I could turn the clock back, and if I could do anything about it, I would have liked to have avoided it."[4] Later in the speech, he described the new National Party logo as "a statement that we have broken with that which was wrong in the past and are not afraid to say we are deeply sorry that our past policies were wrong."[5]

Kevin Gover, assistant secretary of the Bureau of Indian Affairs for the U.S. Department of Interior eloquently expressed his remorse for grievances committed against Native Americans, previously discussed in chapter 4. "Let us begin by expressing our profound sorrow for what this agency has done in the past. Just like you, when we think of these misdeeds and their tragic consequences, our hearts break and our grief is as pure and complete as yours. We desperately wish we could change history, but of course we cannot. . . ."[6] He continued, "Never again will this agency stand silent when hate and violence are committed against Indians. Never again will we allow policy to proceed from the assumption that Indians possess less human genius than the other races. Never again will we be complicit in the theft of Indian property. Never again will we appoint false leaders who serve purposes other than those of the tribes. Never again will we allow unflattering and stereotypical images of Indian people to deface the halls of government or lead the American people to shallow and ignorant beliefs about Indians. Never again will we attack your religions, your languages, your rituals, or any of your tribal ways. Never again will we seize your children, nor teach them to be ashamed of who they are. Never again."[7]

These three expressions of remorse and forbearance go well beyond a simple statement and acknowledgment of the offense committed. Not only do they accept responsibility for the harm produced by the offense, they also use strikingly similar language to express the backward-facing nature of remorse: Kartell wishes life were like a computer with an "undo" button, while de Klerk wants to turn the clock back and Gover desperately wishes to change history. Unable to undo the wrong that was committed, each pledges to bring about a different future: Gover with his dramatic repetition of the phrase "never again," and de Klerk with his description of the National Party logo as "a statement that we have broken with that which was wrong in the past."

In contrast, the lack of remorse and forbearance indicates that the wrongdoer may not share the moral standards of the rest of society and, thus, is at risk to repeat the wrongful act. These behaviors engage the interest of the media, which in turn reflects the interests and responses of the public. Judges, juries, and probation boards also take notice of an offender's lack of remorse and sometimes factor it into their determination of the length of a sentence or their decision about whether it is safe to return an offender to society. Examples of how people react to unrepentant offenders include the following seven vignettes.

A baseball player who felt he had been deliberately hit in the head by a pitch from New York Yankees ace Roger Clemens said he lost respect for Clemens because he failed to show remorse.[8] According to the *New York Times,* Judge William K. Nelson told a woman who had beaten, suffocated, and strangled her husband, "You are a severely disturbed woman. You never said you were sorry."[9] Another *New York Times* story chronicled how John J. Royster beat four people, one of whom died. The headline read, "Lack of Regret in Confessions by the Suspect in 4 Beatings," and the continuation headline said, "Suspect Pleads Not Guilty to Strings of Beatings and Expresses Lack of Regret."[10] A 31-year-old man pleaded guilty to felony charges of sexual assault involving a 13-year-old girl. He suggested that the sex was consensual, asked forgiveness of the victim, and expressed the hope that she would "someday let him in her life."[11] The judge was enraged over "one of the most incredible things I have ever heard in a courtroom." He added that the man's statement "showed his lack of remorse."[12] Timothy McVeigh, responsible for the bomb blast in an Oklahoma federal building that killed 168 people, including children in daycare, flaunted his lack of remorse by referring to the slain children as "collateral damage."[13] His sentiment captured the attention of headline writers in newspapers around the nation. As his execution approached, newspaper writers focused on his lack of remorse.[14] The Associated Press, for example, began its story: "Offering no trace of remorse, Timothy McVeigh went to his death Monday with the same flinty look he showed the world when he was arrested for killing 168 people in the bombing of the Oklahoma City federal building." The headline of the story read, "McVeigh executed for Oklahoma City bombing; dies with no trace of remorse."[15]

Three young Germans in Halle, Germany, admitted in closed-door testimony (according to the lawyer for the victim's family) that they beat and kicked an African immigrant until he died. The lawyer said "they neither showed remorse nor apologized."[16] "Their failure to show remorse so shocked the victim's widow"[17] that she could not remain in the courtroom. In commenting on this story, the Associated Press remarked, "Prosecutors had the indictment translated into English, an unusual move responding to the international attention focused on how the country deals with hatred towards foreigners."[18]

Raymond Jameson, 41, and his 12-year-old son, Bobby, were bow hunting in camouflage clothing with Raymond's 47-year-old half-brother, Michael, in a rural New England town. Suddenly and unexpectedly, Raymond was shot in the leg. He calmed his son and asked him to seek help. His half-brother then approached, knelt down, and asked, "How bad are you wounded?"[19] Raymond asked him to seek help before he bled to death. Through the efforts of his son help arrived in time to save Raymond's life. Michael later told officials that his 12-year-old nephew had shot his father. The police initially charged Michael with hunting while intoxicated. Although this charge was later dropped, Michael was subsequently charged with the shooting and pleaded guilty to second-degree assault with an agreement to undergo treatment for alcohol abuse. He was sentenced to seven years in prison. Raymond underwent ten operations and eventually had his leg amputated below the knee.[20]

Raymond said that prior to the shooting, he and Michael had gotten along well, sometimes hunting together and dining at each other's homes. Following the shooting, they have not spoken, and Raymond says he never wants to see Michael again. "He kept changing his story, one stupid lie after another. . . . I probably would have had a different opinion if he'd come clean at the start, but he blamed it on my son. . . . When he walked out of the courtroom, *he didn't show any remorse at all.* He's never once said he was sorry."[21] (Italics added.)

Boston Globe columnist Scot Lehigh eloquently sums up the impact of the failure to express remorse by describing his own fury—how his blood boils—when murderers fail to express "some small human gesture" of remorse. It is, he says, "a rejection of societal morality." The signal given is that "your sorrow, your rules, your code, your morals, mean nothing to me."[22] In referring to one mass murderer, Lehigh notes, "he was unable even to display the simple humanity of acknowledging the devastation he had caused. In some way, that callousness is one final dehumanizing insult."[23] Lehigh's phrase, "dehumanizing insult," expresses the belief most of us share when faced with such an explicit rejection of the beliefs, attitudes, and values that serve as cornerstones for our existence together. As a result, we extrude them from our midst by labeling them as "inhumane," "sociopathic," or even "insane." We are so disturbed by the lack of remorse, in fact, that we may find fraudulent expressions of remorse more acceptable than its absence, as if we are somehow comforted by believing that wrongdoers know the rules of society, even if they choose not to honor them.

SHAME

Some apologies contain a verbal or nonverbal expression of shame in addition to or in place of remorse. People feel the emotion of shame when they have failed to live up to their aspirations or ideals. The expression of shame in an apology says, "My action is not a reflection of the person I am. This is not my true self, how I want to see myself, how I aspire to be." Shame, therefore, is complementary to remorse. Verbal expressions of shame include comments such as "I feel so ashamed of myself" or "I am red-faced or shame-faced," "I cannot live with myself" or "I feel like disappearing from the face of the earth." Characteristic nonverbal expressions of shame are a bowed head and eye aversion.

Many of the apologies in this book contain the word "shame." Of historical interest is an apology offered by Samuel Sewall in 1697 for his role in the Salem, Massachusetts, witch-craft trials of 1692. Standing before the South Church congregation, he accepted "blame and shame"[24] for his role in the trials. According to his biographer, this apology was motivated by his attempt to make peace with God after the death of his two-year-old daughter and a stillborn son. He believed, perhaps, that his tragedies were punishment for his judicial activities at the trials.[25]

In 1994, the Japanese government apologized to the Japanese people, not to the United States, for its "shame" about failing to break off diplomatic relations with the United States before attacking Pearl Harbor. The apology was precipitated by the declassification of official documents.[26]

Columnists David Brooks and Ellen Goodman both noted the absence of shame and remorse in Monica Lewinsky's failure to apologize for her role in her extramarital relationship with President Clinton. Brooks, in his op-ed piece for the *New York Times*, suggested that Lewinsky lived in a world of entertainment values in which there are no rights and wrongs, and thus the language of shame and regret does not exist. Because Clinton was her "sensual soul mate," she could not honestly express shame over what happened, just disappointment that the affair did not continue.[27] She was, quite literally, *shameless*. In this case, Monica did live up to her self-image of someone who always gets her way. Apologizing for her behavior would have been meaningless.

Similarly, syndicated columnist Ellen Goodman suggested that what was missing in all the testimony and interviews with Ms. Lewinsky was remorse, the recognition that she hurt others and that what she did was wrong. Goodman writes, ". . . I would also like to hear this young woman say that she is sorry for someone other than herself."[28]

Both Brooks and Goodman are suggesting that Lewinsky's self-concept was too narrow and self-absorbed, that she lacked awareness of the interconnectedness of human beings—the great network of relationships that constitute human society. A person whose "best self" is focused almost exclusively on his or her own self-interest will neither notice nor care that others have been harmed in the process. Such people believe they have nothing to be ashamed of and little, if any, reason to apologize.

HUMILITY

Apologizing is an act of humility since it is an acknowledgment of making a mistake and expressing remorse. Such humility contributes to restoring the dignity of the offended party. Apologizing without humility, and even worse, by expressing arrogance or *hubris,* transforms the intended apology into an insult. Communicating arrogance suggests a lack of remorse and a belief that the person making the apology is superior to the person receiving it. For example, consider the case of history professor Joseph J. Ellis of Mount Holyoke College, who lied to his students and colleagues for years by claiming service during the Vietnam War as a platoon leader and paratrooper, as well as participation in both the antiwar and civil rights movements. After being confronted by a reporter from the *Boston Globe*, Ellis responded by expressing regret and apologizing for "having let stand" his lies about his Vietnam experiences. He added, "Even in the best of lives, mistakes are made. . . , " and then remarked, "For this and any other distortions about my personal life, I want to apologize."[29]

By suggesting that his is one of "the best of lives," Ellis shows arrogance at a time when he should have shown humility. The apology further fails because of the nonspecific acknowledgment of his misdeed ("For this and any other distortions about my personal life"). Such a request for blanket forgiveness raises the question about what else he may have done that has so far escaped detection.

In chapter 3, we examined the various needs that may be met through the apology process. Now we can ask what roles do remorse, forbearance, shame, and humility play in the process? I believe that these attitudes emphasize how seriously the offender regards the offense, thus affirming that the offender and offended do, in fact, share important values. In addition, since these attitudes are states of distress, I believe they demonstrate how much the offender is suffering from having committed the offense. Shame and humility are also signs that the offender has "been brought down" from his or her place of power over the offended, while forbearance offers the promise of a different kind of future between the two parties.

It would seem to be a truism that apologies must be sincere in order to be effective. However, I believe that reality is not quite so clear. While ideally apologies are sincere, some apologies can be effective even without being sincere. Sincerity is most important when the apology is private, in a one-to-one situation. Insincerity in these cases would include deliberately withholding or lying about any or all of the components of apology: acknowledging the offense, expressing remorse, or offering an explanation. Since the original offense is often a betrayal of trust, deception in any of these parts could render the entire apology suspect. Thus, by giving the victim additional reasons for distrust, insincerity can subvert even the most carefully articulated apology.

In some cases, however, insincere apologies can partially succeed, because they may address one or more of the victim's psychological needs. For instance, if the acknowledgment of the offense is valid even though the remorse is fraudulent, the victim may value knowing exactly what happened. Or perhaps the acknowledgment is accurate and the reparations are meaningful. In such cases, I believe, a fraudulent expression of remorse or a bogus explanation may not totally invalidate the impact of the apology.

The role of sincerity in expressing remorse seems to be generally less important in public apologies, in which proper acknowledgments that a social or moral contract was violated has great social value regardless of sincerity. Examples include a criminal who insincerely acknowledges the wrongs of his action and whose expressions of contrition and remorse are fraudulent, or a company apologizing for racially prejudicial policies even when it is well known that the president of the organization is a racial bigot. In such cases, society wants to be reassured that offenders understand first the "terms" of the social contract and, second, that consequences follow when those terms are violated. Actions that provide these reassurances—such as acknowledging the offense, using remorse as a way of emphasizing the consequences of the offense, and offering reparations to repair the damage caused by the offense—are usually enough to restore the offender to "good standing" in society, even if sincerity is feigned or wanting. Offenders may not like the terms of the social contract, but as long as they accept them—even grudgingly and even after the fact—social order prevails.

In another example of an insincere apology with social value, an executive humiliates a subordinate at a public meeting. The executive is reprimanded by his superior and then, realizing that he has now compromised his position, apologizes to the subordinate at the next meeting. Everyone in the room may know that the apology is in fact insincere but its public character makes the respective power relationships and expectations quite clear: Although the offending executive had the power to humiliate his subordinates, limits were placed on that power by *his* superior, and thus, the company's values still remain in place. The humiliator was humiliated, and the offended subordinate enjoys restoration of respect and the retributive justice that has been served.

Similarly, insincere apologies can be exchanged at a national or international level. If one nation violates another's boundaries, or damages another's property, or is responsible for harming that nation's citizens, the offending nation may apologize publicly before the entire world. That these apologies are sometimes insincere does not detract from their social value as public endorsements of the rules of conduct between nations. This reaffirmation of acceptable behavior is especially important when the victim is a weaker nation, because international rules of conduct exist to ensure fair treatment regardless of size, wealth, or political power. In such situations, weaker nations restore their dignity and stature on the world stage.

OFFERING AND RECEIVING EXPLANATIONS

Offended parties often regard an apology as unsatisfactory if it does not include an explanation. They view the explanation as part of the debt owed to them. They will make comments such as, "You owe me an explanation," or, "Please tell me why you did this," or, "You could at least have had the decency to explain yourself." These statements suggest that the failure to offer an explanation is often perceived as an inadequate apology or even a further insult. Newspapers often call attention to the connection between apology and explanation by including the presence or absence of the explanation in their headlines.

Many people who have been the object of a personal offense would rather have an unpleasant explanation than none at all. We see this reaction in families in which a member has been murdered or is missing. Such events represent two separate challenges to the bereaved: first, the loss itself, which under any circumstances would be difficult to accept; but also, the unexpectedness of the event, the fact that the family does not understand why their loved one was murdered or abducted. An explanation relieves one of these burdens even though it does nothing to lessen the other: By hearing the offender's reason for his or her behavior, family members can stop endlessly speculating about what happened and can begin to grieve the loss they have suffered.

Examples of this need for explanations abound. "Why did you lie to me?" "Why did you fail to meet me for dinner?" "Why did you break your marriage vows?" "Why did you humiliate me?" "Why did you break into my house?" "Why did you kidnap my child?" "Why did you violate our nation's air space?" "Why are you killing innocent civilians?" "Why did you bomb our embassy?" The various explanations received in response to these questions help us regain our sense that the world is predictable after all, that there are reasons for such behavior even if we do not accept their validity. These explanations demystify offenses committed against us by telling us whether an offense was a random act of violence or an act of revenge. We learn how much responsibility we share for the offense and whether we should expect similar offenses in the future. The net result is that we gain a means of assessing our safety and taking appropriate actions to forestall future attacks.

The following examples illustrate how an explanation can diminish the apparent seriousness of an offense by providing information about the context in which it occurred. A person was invited to dinner at 6:00 P.M. Since she had been without sleep for 24 hours due to the illness of her daughter, she lay down for a brief nap at 5:00 P.M. and inadvertently slept through the evening. Her subsequent apology, which included the reason why she had failed to attend the dinner, diminished the seriousness of the offense. The host and hostess learned that it was not a lack of consideration, insensitivity, or hostility that precipitated the offense. Rather, she did not attend the dinner because she was exhausted and no one awakened her from her nap.

Another example followed the tragedy of a lost Russian nuclear submarine. When a reporter questioned the father of one of the servicemen who died on the sub, the father responded abruptly and rudely with the concluding remark, "I don't want to talk. Talk to the mothers."[30] The mother of the serviceman apologized for her husband: "He is just suffering so much over Lyosha."[31] By being reminded of the context of the interview, the reporter undoubtedly understood her explanation.

Explanations that diminish the seriousness of the offense communicate one or more of four things: 1) the grievance was not intentional and therefore not personal; 2) the behavior is not indicative of the "real self" of the offender; 3) the victim is blameless; and 4) similar grievances are unlikely to recur because of the uniqueness of the circumstances. Victims assess these matters in considering whether they will accept the apology, forgive the offender, and reconcile the relationship.

If the reasons given for an offense seem dishonest, arrogant, manipulative, or an insult to the intelligence of the victim, the explanation may escalate the offense. For example, during an interview with Capitol Hill radio reporters, House Majority Leader Dick Armey was asked about a book he was writing and his plans to donate the profits to charity. He responded, "I like peace and quiet and I don't need to listen to Barney Fag [pause]

Barney Frank, haranguing in my ear because I made a few bucks off a book I worked on. I just wouldn't want to listen to it."[32] The previous week, Barney Frank, an openly gay representative from Massachusetts, criticized House Speaker Newt Gingrich for his $4.5 million book deal. Armey apologized for his "Barney Fag" remark, publicly saying that he had misspoken, and then met with Frank, presumably to offer a personal apology. He later told reporters, "I do not want Barney Frank to believe for one moment I would use a slur against him. *I had trouble with alliteration.* I was stumbling, mumbling . . . I don't use the word in personal conversation . . . and I don't approve of anyone who does . . . *It was a mispronunciation.*"[33] (Italics added.)

Armey said he resented armchair psychologists drawing any conclusion about him from the remark, insisting he did not need any psychoanalysis about any subliminal or Freudian predilections. He added, "To have my five children or anybody else's five children turn on their television today and see a transcript of a mispronunciation on the air, as if I had no sense of decency, cordiality, respect or even good manners, is unacceptable."[34] An editorial in the *New York Times* suggested that this gaffe was part of a "pattern of accumulating incidents."[35] It also reported that Democrats and Independents were concerned that Armey's comment might be evidence that "the new Republican Congressional leadership has coarsened American political discourse to a remarkable degree in a very short time."[36]

The problem with Armey's apology was the explanation. It is not convincing to argue that substituting "Barney Fag" for Barney Frank is merely a mispronunciation. Could Representative Armey have made a more convincing apology? I believe that the answer, of course, is "yes." Such an apology would have acknowledged the violation of the generally accepted value that derogatory language should not be used when discussing homosexual individuals. Armey could have said, "I have given considerable thought to the recent incident in which I made a derogatory reference to Representative Barney Frank. I wish to make two points: First, I realize that my remarks were hurtful to Representative Frank and I regret causing this hurt. I respect Barney Frank as a person and as a worthy political adversary. Second, I accept responsibility for what I said. Although I did not knowingly and deliberately intend to use that unfortunate and hurtful expression "fag," the expression was mine. In accepting this responsibility, I commit myself to avoiding such (or similar) expressions in the future, thereby achieving my personal ideals and those of this country."

In another case, driver Bryan Smith of Fryeburg, Maine, temporarily lost control of his vehicle after being distracted by his Rotweiller dog, who was attempting to get into a food cooler on the back seat. Smith hit author Stephen King who was walking along the road. The impact threw King 14 feet into a ditch, and he subsequently had to undergo six surgeries and long-term rehabilitation. In an interview, Smith said, "It was *one time and one time only*. I'm very, very sorry."[37] (Italics added.) Smith's explanation might have been more believable had he not accumulated several driving convictions during the preceding ten-year period. However, given his driving record, the claim that "it was one time and one time only" undermined his credibility.

In yet another apology, the *Bangor Daily News* reported, "The husband of Princess Caroline of Monaco apologized Friday to the Turkish public for urinating on the side of Turkey's pavilion at the Expo 2000 World's Fair in Germany. Prince Ernst August took out a full-page advertisement in the European edition of the *Turkish Hurriyet* newspaper that said:

'It is my duty to express to the Turkish public that relieving myself during my visit to the Expo 2000 was *definitely not a conscious act.* I and my family would like to express with our whole hearts that we are fans of Turkish culture and friends of the Turkish people.'"[38] (Italics added.) This explanation is obviously inaccurate and even ludicrous. Everyone knows that urinating while awake is a conscious act. To claim, therefore, he was not conscious of his act strains the credulity of most. Prince August's apology might have been more believable if, by way of explanation, he had said the men's room was far away and he was physically incapable of controlling himself (assuming that this explanation was true). Perhaps an even better alternative in such circumstances, where no explanation would suffice, would be to say, "there is no excuse for such behavior," and offer some meaningful reparations to the Turks. Most people could appreciate such a dilemma. It is also difficult to understand why he urinated on a pavilion instead of finding some more isolated spot.

In an attack of rage, professional basketball player Latrell Sprewell attempted to choke his coach during practice. He was suspended and later traded to the New York Knickerbockers. In making his apology, Sprewell said, "I think it's fair to say *I had a bad day.* . . . That's not me. I don't have a problem. I don't walk around angry."[39] He eventually told Commissioner David Stern "how wrong he was for his attack on the coach," and reassured him that he would be a positive influence in the NBA.[40] Here is another explanation that compounds the original offense. Suggesting that having a "bad day" is sufficient justification for choking someone trivializes the gravity of the offense. We all have bad days, but we do not go around choking people as a result. Furthermore, saying, "That's not me," undermines the explanation, since it was clearly Sprewell and no one else who attacked the coach.

Another example of a deficient explanation is a comment by Senator Conrad Burns of Billings, Montana, who referred to Arabs as "rag heads"[41] during a speech to the Montana Equipment Dealers Association. He later apologized to the group by saying that *"he speaks faster than he thinks."*[42] (Italics added.) Once again we have an explanation that compounds the original offense. To suggest that rapid speech can somehow justify demeaning an entire culture insults the intelligence of the party to whom this "explanation" is offered. Rather than helping the offended party understand why the offense occurred, this rationale only deepens the wound.

There are many explanations that offenders commonly use in everyday life, in hopes of diminishing their responsibility, but which diminish the apology and even insult the offended parties. I offer the following list of such explanations to alert the reader: "I just could not help myself." "I was not myself." "I was careless." "I was not thinking straight." "I was overtired." "I was preoccupied." "I was sick." "I do not have a good memory." "I was being selfish." "I was angry at someone else." "I was under stress." "I did not really mean it." "I was only joking." "I must have been out of my mind." "I had a bad hair day." "I am only human." "I was drinking." "I let my emotions get the best of my judgment." "I gave in to an irresistible impulse." "I just snapped." "I was in love." "I was hormonal." "The devil made me do it."

I believe that offenders are best served when they offer no explanations at all, rather than explanations that are dishonest, manipulative, or insulting. The simple message, "I was responsible. I deeply regret it. I have no excuse," can restore the victim's dignity and repair damaged pride. In such situations, the offended party realizes that the offender did not shirk responsibility or hide behind a shallow attempt to manipulate the victim. The following apologies are example of this honest humility.

A U.S. sailor apologized at his court martial for brutally beating a homosexual shipmate to death. "I can't apologize enough for my actions," he said. "I am not trying to make any excuses for what happened that night. It was horrible, but I am not a horrible person."[43] This apology would have been even better had the sailor not tried to separate himself from the crime he had committed ("I am not a horrible person").

In the following story, my wife and I were the ones who received an honest apology. My daughter Jackie's oncologist had just arranged for her hospital admission for intractable pain resulting from breast cancer that had metastasized to the bones. The prescribed doses of pain medicine taken at home had been inadequate to relieve Jackie's pain, and increased calcium in the blood was causing mental changes. After she was admitted to the hospital, she lay in the hospital bed in obvious distress for six hours waiting for the physician to arrive. My wife and I had been at her side throughout this agonizing wait for relief. The nurses were obviously upset that the resident physician had not appeared despite having been paged numerous times. When she finally arrived, the nurses told her that the family was irate. The physician, appearing distressed and exhausted, offered what we experienced as a simple but heartfelt apology. "I feel terrible that it took so long," she said. *"There is no excuse."*[44] Moved by the sincerity of her apology, as well as by her apparent suffering, I replied, "I was once a resident. It must have been quite a day." The physician, with some supportive prodding on my part, then told us that she had been awake all night tending to patients suffering from cardiac arrests and gastrointestinal bleeding. As I think about her apology years later, I wonder whether by offering "no excuses," she meant that there is no excuse for hospitals (a famous and distinguished one in this case) to mercilessly overwork their residents, or whether there was an unfortunately heavy workload that day.

Had the resident begun her apology with a series of explanations or excuses for the delay in treatment, my wife and I might not have felt so empathic toward her. But her statement, "There is no excuse," carried a certain dignity: She recognized the distress her delay had caused, and she accepted responsibility for it, without trying to blame others or justify her lateness. In addition, we shared a common experience of helplessness, the feeling of being unable to change our current, painful circumstances. Perhaps the physician's suffering mirrored our own and helped us forgive.

REPARATIONS

In chapter 3, I showed how, for some apologies, reparations can be the dominant feature of the apology, because they completely restore the loss. Examples include replacing or cleaning a garment accidentally stained by a spilled beverage at a party, returning a stolen automobile, or replacing a lost camera. Offering reparations shows the victim and/or society that the offender takes the grievance seriously and is willing to "repair" the harm done.

On the other hand, when such reparations are available but not acted upon, the apology fails. Consider this personal story. I allowed a photographer who was an acquaintance to use my office for a photography session. He dropped a piece of his equipment on my antique lampshade, shattering a glass panel. He proceeded to apologize profusely with apparent compassion and remorse. I asked what he intended to do about the lamp. "Nothing," he answered.[45] I experienced his apology as just cheap words and was angry that he was not prepared to repair the damage. He eventually pasted the broken pieces together and acted as if he had done me a favor. No apology would have satisfied me without some kind of tangible reparation: paying for, replacing, or repairing the lamp. The fact that I had to "coerce" the pasting of the broken pieces detracted from the genuineness of the reparative action.

A similar situation occurred in Stockholm, Sweden, when a car thief stole a car containing expensive fishing gear, a snowboard, some home video tapes, and an unemployment claim form. The thief wrote a letter of apology saying that he had to "borrow" the car but added, "I hope you can forgive me."[46] The thief explained that he was in great need of the car. He sent the unemployment claim form back with his letter, but he did not return the car. In this case, the only acceptable reparation would be to return, pay for, or replace the car. Failing that, the apology is only a sham, evidenced by the fact that the thief apparently believed returning an easy-to-replace application form is a good exchange for a car.

Steven Glass, former reporter for the *New Republic*, fabricated at least 27 articles, and then subsequently wrote a book about the experience. Glass also lectured to students and journalists at George Washington University, which provoked Marc Fisher, a columnist for *The Washington Post,* to write, [Glass] "has done nothing to show remorse or make amends, other than to say how sorry he is. Is he lending his considerable talents to worthy causes? Did he donate his winnings from his nasty book to those in need? No and no."[47] Fisher quoted Andrew Sullivan, the editor who hired Glass for the *New Republic,* as saying, "How can you convince me or anybody else that this isn't bull—from beginning to end?"[48]

When the offense is intangible, such as insults or humiliations, reparations may be symbolic in nature, such as buying a drink, treating for dinner, arranging a party in honor of the person, giving tickets to a show or athletic contest, offering an award, or making a donation to the offended party's favorite charity. If an offender cannot think of an appropriate reparation, he or she can ask, "Is there anything I can do to make it up to you?"

In an unusual but effective symbolic reparation, Victor Crawford, a former lobbyist for the tobacco industry and former senator of Maryland, after being stricken with cancer of the throat, apologized to the public for his lobbying activities. "I lied and I am sorry," he said.[49] His reparation came in the form of public statements against the tobacco industry.

Despite generous reparations, an apology may fail because other aspects of the apology are not handled well. Such is the case in Homer's *Iliad,* when Agamemnon's apology to Achilles inflames rather than heals. In this classic tale (as translated by Robert Fitzgerald), the gods determine that the Greek general, Agamemnon, must give up the concubine he won as spoils in the conquest of Troy.[50] Agamemnon replaces his loss by taking the concubine of Achilles, the greatest warrior in the Greek army. In doing so, he publicly humiliates Achilles, causing him great dishonor. Achilles, in his rage, refuses to fight in battle, with the result that the Greeks suffer great losses on the battlefield. On reflection, Agamemnon admits to his comrades that he had committed "blind errors."[51] His mitigating explanation is that he yielded to "black anger."[52] His idea of reparation is to return Achilles' concubine without having ever slept with her. In addition, Agamemnon promises his comrades that he will give Achilles seven additional concubines as well as enormous wealth. But he demands that Achilles must "bow to me, considering that I [Agamemnon] hold higher rank and claim the precedence of age."[53]

When these comrades take the news to Achilles, they fail to communicate the apology that Agamemnon had admitted to committing "blind errors" that were influenced, in part, by "black anger." Instead, they offer a deal (an attempt at reparation) in which Achilles should "abandon heart-wounding anger"[54] in return for gifts. Achilles refuses the offer and through the emissaries, accuses Agamemnon of shamelessly tricking him, defrauding him, breaking faith, playing him for a fool, and robbing him blind. He further accuses Agamemnon of not looking him in the eye [apologizing face to face]. Achilles says Agamemnon will not appease him, "not till he pays me back full measure, pain for pain, dishonor for dishonor."[55]

Although Achilles is usually portrayed as hardheaded and rigid, I would argue that in this situation, it is Agamemnon who is at fault. The apology he offered was inadequate in at least three ways. First, he failed to make the apology face to face. Second, his emissaries failed to communicate how much he had suffered and the remorse he felt. Third, he demands that Achilles, already humiliated, bow to him. In this case, although the tangible reparations Agamemnon offered were more than generous, the apology failed because one of Achilles' essential needs—the restoration of honor or dignity—was left unsatisfied.

In contrast to Agamemnon's failed apology, the next apology is an unqualified success, due in large part to a successful reparation. A lesbian couple was ejected from Dodger Stadium during a baseball game because the two women shared a kiss. Some people complained and said that their children should not be exposed to such behavior. The couple threatened to file a civil rights lawsuit if the team ownership failed to apologize. Team president Bob Graziano responded by telling the couple, "I was troubled . . . because of what it implied about the Dodger organization. . . . It means a lot to me that you are Dodger fans. We will continue to do the right thing."[56] In addition to the apology, the Dodgers donated 5,000 tickets to three gay and lesbian organizations, provided sensitivity training for all of its employees, and gave the lesbian couple prime seats to make up for the game they had missed. In this case, all parties were pleased with the apology and its outcome. A member of a gay advocacy group commented, "This result is a 'home run' for all concerned."[57] Graziano, in contrast to Agamemnon, spoke directly to the offended couple, and his apology both restored their dignity and demonstrated his respect for them. In this case, the offered reparations served to confirm his good will.

Although offering financial reparation commonly reinforces the offender's shame and remorse, at times it can have a decidedly negative effect on the victim. For example, when a Japanese American received $20,000 for being interned in a camp from ages five to nine during World War II, he commented, "the American government stole 4 years of my childhood and has now put a price of $5,000 for each stolen year." He added, "It would have been better to receive no financial settlement."[58] It is clear from his comment that this man considered the reparation to be an inadequate statement of his personal worth, as if each year of his stolen childhood was worth only $5,000. Perhaps no amount of money would have satisfied his feeling of profound loss. Such reparations may have been well intentioned, symbolic acknowledgments of the victim's loss, but were understandably received as inappropriate and insulting.

A variation of the negative impact that can result from attempting to offer financial reparations can be seen in some of the reactions of victims to the clergy abuse settlement. One lawyer involved in the settlement said accepting the settlement mimicked abuse since each time his client had been molested, he had been given money by the priest who abused him. Another victim, in a similar vein, said that "plaintiffs feel almost like 'prostitutes' now that they've been compensated financially for having been sexually violated."[59] Given the nature of the abuse, the reparations may be experienced by the victims and others as "hush money."

The most difficult reparations to attempt are for those offenses against large groups where the causes of the offense are complex and longstanding and do not easily lend themselves to financial repair. Examples include U.S. slavery and South African Apartheid. In both situations, historical circumstances produced an environment in which offenses were able to continue for many years, with resulting damage to both the psychology as well as the material living conditions of the victims. These historical wrongs in turn led to institutions that perpetuated the unequal treatment of large numbers of affected parties. Making appropriate reparations raises a number of difficult questions. To whom are reparations owed? How should the suffering and damage be measured? What would count as adequate reparations? How could reparations change the social conditions that perpetuate the offense?

I have heard it said that since Abraham Lincoln already apologized for slavery, there is no need for the United States to continue to debate this question. Lincoln ends his second inaugural address with a call for reparations, which have never been adequately implemented: "with malice toward none and charity for all . . . let us strive on to finish the work we are in; to bind up the nation's wounds . . . to do all which may achieve and cherish a just, and lasting peace, among ourselves, and with all nations."[60] The current debate is about the implementation of such reparations.

PERSONAL REFLECTIONS

Chapter 4 and chapter 5 discuss the apology process: how apologies work to achieve healing goals such as restoring self-respect and dignity, assuring shared values between offender and offended, and demonstrating the suffering of the offender. I am struck by the complexity of the process by which various combinations of acknowledgments, attitudes and behaviors, explanations, and reparations work together to meet the needs of offended parties. The metaphor for communicating apologies that comes to mind is the performance of a small orchestral group. Sometimes composers use only one instrument to provide a satisfying sound. Other times, a combination of instruments is necessary. In any case, a successful performance requires years of training and lots of practice. So it is with apologies. Success or failure depends on how successfully we can train ourselves to "hear" what is needed and to respond with just the right combination of elements, emphases, and empathy.

SIX

Why People Apologize

In chapter 3, we considered why people, groups, or nations want apologies. We asked what apologies mean to the offended parties: How do apologies heal? Now we will reverse the direction of our inquiry and look at the apology process from the viewpoint of the offenders: Why do they apologize? What motivates them to risk humiliation and rejection if their apology fails?

Motives to apologize can be meaningfully divided into two categories. In the first, people apologize in response to strong internal feelings: for example, their empathic concern for others or their inner distress of guilt and shame. By apologizing, they seek to restore and maintain their own dignity and self-esteem. In the second category, offenders apologize in response to strong external pressures: They want to influence how others perceive and behave toward them. The motives for any given apology can be described as either primarily internal, external, or a combination of both.

The stories that follow will illustrate both kinds of motives, as well as the variations that can occur within each category. Although my primary purpose in presenting these stories is to explore the two types of motives for apologizing, I will also discuss the complexity and uniqueness of each apology, pointing out some of the features of apologies we have discussed previously.

"I FEEL SO GUILTY AND ASHAMED FOR WHAT I DID"

Three psychological ideas or concepts help us understand how our emotions can move us to apologize. The first is empathy, a person's ability to be aware of and understand how another person thinks and feels. The second concept is guilt, the capacity to apply standards of right and wrong to our behavior toward others and to punish ourselves emotionally when we hurt others. Some writers view empathy as a necessary part of guilt. Martin L. Hoffman, for example, describes what he calls empathy-based guilt as "an intensely unpleasant feeling of disesteem for oneself that results from empathic feeling for someone in distress combined with an awareness of being the cause of that distress."[1] These guilt experiences can be constructive because they push us to acknowledge culpability and subsequently to attempt to repair the damage we have done, often by means of apologies. Behavioral researchers have shown that this kind of guilt is socially adaptive and does not lead to psychiatric symptoms or mental illness. For this reason, they distinguish between healthy guilt and neurotic or pathologic guilt.[2]

The third concept is shame, an emotional reaction to the experience of failing to live up to one's image of oneself.

Although guilt and shame seem closely allied, one difference between them is that guilt usually attaches to a specific instance of wrongdoing toward another ("I feel guilt because I did not keep my promise to you"), whereas shame appears to be a response to a more general judgment about the self ("I am ashamed that I seem unable to do the things I say I will do"). A common response to guilt is to make amends, whereas the most common response to shame is to hide—to avoid contact or to turn away with body posture. People who are shamed, however, often try to restore themselves to good standing in the eyes of themselves and others.

Although I have described each of these psychological ideas separately, we often experience them simultaneously. For example, a person who accidentally damages a pedestrian with his automobile while driving under the influence of alcohol may feel empathy and guilt for the damage he inflicted on the pedestrian, and shame because of his poor judgment and loss of status in his community.[3]

The capacity of people to experience empathy, guilt, and shame and to aspire to a healthy sense of dignity, pride, and self-esteem constitutes in large part what we regard as character and integrity. We trust and count on people with these qualities. When they violate standards of acceptable behaviors, they usually apologize in an attempt to undo the damage to others or to restore their own sense of dignity, self-respect, or honor.

The next set of stories illustrates how maintaining honor, dignity, and self-esteem and avoiding guilt and shame can serve as motives for both private and public apologies. In all of them, a strong internal feeling motivates the apology, whether it is empathy-based guilt, shame, or a combination of both.

The first story is a personal experience in which guilt and shame were the motivating forces for the apology. In my role as medical school dean, I made a progress report to the hospital trustees on the search for a new department chair. I remarked that the search was going well and that the two leading candidates were women (we were making considerable efforts to recruit women chairs). Twenty minutes later, I realized that the acting chair was in the room (it was unusual for any chair to be present at this meeting). He is a very fine person who was doing an excellent job in the interim position and who was a candidate for the permanent position. I felt mortified that I might have inadvertently humiliated him by discussing the leading candidates in a way that made clear he was not included. After a restless night of imagining his humiliation (empathy and guilt) and then feeling stupid for not realizing he was at the meeting (shame), I went to his office the next morning to apologize. I told him how terrible I felt about the events of the previous day, particularly how insensitive it was of me not to realize he was present. My apology was not for what I had said but for giving my report in a way that may have publicly humiliated him. We spoke for a few minutes and shook hands. He appeared surprised and smiled warmly as I departed.

Two weeks later at a routine meeting between the interim chair and myself, I asked him how he felt about our previous encounter. He said that it had been a very important event for him and that as a result, his respect for me had grown significantly. A month later at another scheduled meeting between the two of us, he told me that he had offended a colleague, and as a result, his relationship with that colleague was strained. He asked me to teach him how to apologize—how to do for others what my apology had done for him.

As I reflected on the apology I had made to him, I realized I had been motivated by a combination of empathy, shame, and guilt. Shame was evident as I berated myself during a restless night ("What kind of a leader do I want to be? How can I teach people the value of apology if I cannot do it myself?") Guilt was clear as I realized how I had hurt his feelings. I was also aware of my resistance to apologizing. I asked myself, "What if he refuses to speak to me? What if he insults me? Am I making a mountain out of a molehill? Why not just forget the whole matter and move on? After all, I am his boss."

The outcome of my apology—increased respect from the offended for the offender and a stronger relationship between the two—is quite common in genuine apologies. This apology succeeded because it met at least some of the offended party's needs: For example, it restored his dignity and respect, affirmed shared values (we both agree about the importance of treating people with dignity), and reestablished his sense of safety in the relationship (I can be counted on not to hurt him).

What is interesting about the chair's request is that he seems to be asking to be taught something that "everyone" already knows—or should know: How to make a good apology. In fact, many people do not know how to apologize. His request was indicative of his openness. His request prompted me to consider the best way to teach people to apologize, and I have concluded that the most effective approach is to model the process for them; that is, by apologizing to them when appropriate. We know that modeling good behavior works with children: Why should it not also work for friends and colleagues?

The next story illustrates the importance of guilt as a motive for apology, even for the most fleeting of relationships. Paul, a neighborhood friend and retired psychologist, told me of an experience that occurred several years ago and that has had, to this day, a significant emotional impact on him.[4] Paul and his wife, Jean, had moved temporarily to a condominium in the next town during the summer while their permanent home was being renovated. The couple continued their habitual early morning walks in their new neighborhood, exploring the ethnically diverse neighborhood with its Chassidic synagogue.

As the couple followed their usual walking route each day, they regularly passed a man in his seventies going to synagogue. He wore a yarmulke and informal summer clothes. "He had a refined, serious and intelligent face and a dignified bearing," Paul told me. Over time, this couple and the Jewish man developed a limited but cordial relationship—"a smile, a wave, a greeting"—and the couple found themselves wondering about the man's profession and life circumstances.

One day, after not having seen the stranger for about three weeks, the couple noticed him walking behind them. He quickened his step in order to give them a warm and enthusiastic greeting, which Paul and Jean returned. However, the couple had already picked up their own pace and now, feeling somewhat awkward with the man so close, they moved ahead even faster, in effect, walking away from him. On their return trip, they passed the man again, but this time he "looked detached and remote," Paul reported. "Averting his gaze, he barely acknowledged us as we passed." It seemed clear to Paul that the man felt snubbed and rejected by their having walked away from him earlier.

Paul told me this story with tears in his eyes. He said that he "felt very badly. It hung over me all day. That night when I went to bed, I stayed awake a long time, thinking and praying.

I wanted to undo the hurt; I craved redemption. I started to rehearse what I would do and say the next time we saw him." After two weeks of not seeing him on their daily walks, the Jewish man reappeared, coming toward them in the customary manner. "As he drew near, I angled toward him with a smile, holding out my hand. He held out his hand and we shook. I apologized immediately for our having kept going without inviting him to walk with us the previous time, explaining that I had been preoccupied, but that we had wanted to meet him. We had a friendly conversation for the next several minutes." Paul told him that he and his wife would be returning to their permanent home in a few days. Paul ended his story by commenting that the apology gave him peace about his rejection of the man.

I was quite touched by Paul's story. It was clear to me that his motivation was internal: He was not trying to cultivate a personal or business relationship, nor was he trying to avoid punishment. The pain he experienced for having caused unnecessary harm to another person was a form of empathy-based guilt, and the resulting apology healed by both making amends (reassuring the stranger that he did not deserve to be ignored) and removing his own shame.

The next story is taken from a narrative written by noted Civil War historian Shelby Foote. Foote describes an apology Confederate General Robert E. Lee gave to his field generals after a crucial battle that was lost. Confederate General George E. Pickett, during his disastrous charge on a Union stronghold at the battle of Gettysburg, had seen two-thirds of his division destroyed. However, upon his return to the main line, Lee commanded this dejected and bewildered man to position his troops to repel the anticipated counterattack of the Union soldiers.[5] Pickett said tearfully, "General Lee, I have no division now."[6] "Come, General Pickett," Lee broke in after realizing what had happened, "This has been my fight, and upon my shoulders rests the blame. The men and officers of your command have written the name of Virginia as high today as it has ever been written before. . . . Your men have done all that men can do. . . . The fault is entirely my own."[7] Lee repeated this statement as he approached each of his field commanders. "It is I who have lost this fight, and you must help me out of it the best way you can." The next day, Lee told General Longstreet, "It's all my fault. I thought my men were invincible."[8]

According to Foote, ". . . his ready acceptance of total blame for the failure of the assault was not merely a temporary burden he assumed for the sake of encouraging his troops to resist the counterattack he believed the Union general Meade was about to launch at them; he continued to say the same things in the future, after the immediate need for them was past and the quite different but altogether human need for self-justification might have been expected to set in."[9] The British officer who was present at Gettysburg, Colonel Fremantle, thought it "impossible to look at [Lee] or listen to him without feeling the strongest admiration."[10] From what we know about General Lee, he enjoyed an empathic bond with his subordinates who, in turn, had a great deal of respect for him. With this apology, he healed his generals' psychological wounds by relieving their guilt and responsibility and by restoring their dignity and self-respect. Lee willingly accepted blame for defeat while extolling their valiant efforts. The courage and generosity that marks some apologies can elevate the stature of the offender, as this story so poignantly demonstrates.

In the next two stories, dignity, pride, and the removal of shame provide the predominant motives for the apologies. The first involves a 75-year-old machinist who came to me after a lecture I had given and volunteered an apology "for your book, Doc."[11] He said, "I worked at my machine for 30 years. One day, something happened between me and the fellow next to me. Some unpleasant words were exchanged. I do not remember what was said or who was at fault, but we stopped talking. We did not speak to each other for the next six years. One day, I turned to him and said, 'I have been a damned fool,' and I stretched out my hand for him to shake. We shook hands. The grudge was over. Several workers nearby came over and asked what was going on. I said: 'I do not have to be a damned fool all of my life.' That was my apology."[12]

This gentleman felt like a fool for holding the grudge for so many years, particularly since it was caused by a trivial event that he could no longer remember. He wanted to be a better person, not a "damned fool." His dignity and pride were at stake: He was ashamed of himself. Apologizing required that he take four risks. First, he risked being viewed as the original instigator of the unpleasantness since we expect apologies from those who "start" a fight. Second, since he was publicly admitting that he had been foolish, he risked being ridiculed by coworkers. Third, he risked being perceived as weak since he was the one who conceded. Fourth, he risked rejection and humiliation if the other person refused to shake his hand or to resume the relationship. Once again we see courage displayed in the act of apologizing.

It is difficult to explain how such an abbreviated apology was able to heal. Perhaps it healed because the man humbled himself by acknowledging that he had been a fool, an admission that returned respect and esteem to the other party. Perhaps the apology opened a dialogue in which both parties were able to clarify whether in fact they held important values in common and wanted to continue the relationship. Perhaps the "offended party" could see that he shared responsibility for letting the grudge continue for so many years. In any case, it is clear that this apology—although delayed and unusually brief—had the power to heal and repair a damaged relationship and dissolve a grudge that had festered for six years.

The second story, involving celebrities, again illustrates how shame can motivate an apology. David Brinkley, a 76-year-old television pioneer, made his final appearance on his Sunday news program, *This Week with David Brinkley*, in early November 1996. His guest on the show was President Bill Clinton. Brinkley began with an apology to his guest for comments he made at the end of election night coverage the previous week. Believing he was off the air at the time, Brinkley had opined that the president would give Americans four more years of "god-damned nonsense" and added that the president "has not a creative bone in his body. Therefore, he is a bore, and will always be a bore."[13] He ended his extemporaneous comments by referring to Clinton's speech as "one of the worst things I've ever heard."[14]

Brinkley began his show by recalling something he wrote many years ago—that even though it may be impossible to be objective, it was important to "always be fair." He acknowledged that after a long day on the set covering election day activities, he was "both impolite and unfair."[15] Brinkley then acknowledged his sorrow and regret. The president responded by graciously accepting his apology and adding that he understood Brinkley had been through a difficult day. He explained that he too had regretted saying things when he was tired. He opined that "you have to judge people on their whole work."[16] Brinkley concurred. Later in the interview, the president joked that Brinkley had made the vice president happy when he referred to the president as "boring. You've made me very popular around the White House."[17] (During the campaign, Vice President Albert Gore had frequently been criticized for being boring.)

It is evident from his remarks that Brinkley believed he had not lived up to his personal goal of fairness, and his apology was a desire to restore his honor and to avoid or diminish shame. He not only acknowledged the offense he had committed but also offered an explanation as to why he did not behave in his usual manner: The remarks came after a "long day" on the set. Such an explanation, implying that his behavior that night was an aberration, might be viewed as an attempt to diminish his culpability. Such explanations are commonly found in apologies. As long as they are reasonable and do not attempt to deny responsibility for the offense, these explanations are not offensive. In this case, by establishing that under normal circumstances he and Clinton share important values (e.g., one does not gratuitously inflict harm on another), Brinkley acknowledged that his behavior was clearly unacceptable.

President Clinton's response to Brinkley's apology is interesting. Rather than playing the role of a wounded victim, he turned the apology to great advantage. First, he showed that he is a forgiving person, not a spiteful or vindictive one. Second, he demonstrated compassion by understanding that David Brinkley had been through a rough day. Third, the president was able to suggest that others judge Brinkley on his whole work, not on a single event, perhaps as a request for compassion and forgiveness for Clinton's own past misdeeds. Finally, the president demonstrated the capacity to make fun of himself, with his comparison to Vice President Gore, who was frequently described as boring. In essence, Clinton portrayed himself as a forgiving, compassionate, humorous person who should also be forgiven whenever he fails to measure up to people's expectations. With his humor and wit, Clinton took total charge of the situation, without damaging Brinkley. Both parties were victorious, and, presumably, the public enjoyed the entire interchange.

"PLEASE DO NOT DISRUPT MY SOCIAL SUPPORTS"

Turning from apologies offered by offenders seeking to relieve internal emotional states, this second group of stories involves offenders who are responding to (and hoping to change) external circumstances. Specifically, they are using the apology to avoid abandonment, stigmatization, damage to reputation, retaliation, or punishment of any kind.

The first story comes from a friend who, in 1940 as a young boy, witnessed a profound apology whose goal was to preserve the cohesiveness of his family.[18]

"I come from a large, extended, close-knit family,"[19] he began. "My father was one of six children, my mother one of four. They spent their adult years living within a few miles of their respective families and visiting each other often. The 1940s were very anti-Semitic years, even in New York City, where we lived. The family members often reminded each other 'in times of trouble, all we have is family.' In retrospect, it is significant that World War II had begun and we had many relatives in Poland, Russia, and other parts of Eastern Europe, a fact which must have been in the forefront of the minds of the adults." He continued, "On this occasion, my father, mother, myself, and my sister were visiting one of my father's sisters (along with all of my father's other brothers and sisters, their spouses, children, and my father's mother). My mother, who had a strong 'sweet tooth,' spotted a dish of candies on a coffee table— the confection now called 'turtles'—rich chocolate candies with caramel, almonds, and cashews. She said, 'Turtles! I love turtles.' (She used the Jewish word for the confection.) These were expensive candies at that time and were considered a very special treat. My mother closed her eyes, took a bite of one of the turtles, smiled ecstatically, and said, 'mmm.' My sister and I watched, awaiting my mother's permission for each of us to help ourselves to a piece.

"My aunt, the hostess, rushed over and said to her sister-in-law, 'Oh Frieda, I didn't mean to leave those candies out. I was saving them as a special treat for my husband.' My mother opened her eyes and then widened them in mock surprise. She was furious. She said, 'Oh, excuse me. I am sorry. I naturally thought that if you left them out, you meant them for your guests. Oh do excuse me, etc., etc.' My mother continued in this way for some moments, her voice dripping with sarcasm and mock apologetic sincerity. She then placed the piece of candy, out of which she had taken a bite, back in the dish and said, 'By all means, give this to your husband.' My aunt withered under the barrage. She then left the room followed by her husband, who gave my mother a long, angry glance. The party continued without the host and hostess, while my grandmother (my father's mother) quietly stepped into the hostess role. The room was silent with none of the customary laughter, loud voices, and good fellowship. After a while my aunt and uncle returned, but the atmosphere was glacial. I remember feeling very frightened. 'In time of trouble, all we have is family.' I had never seen the family like this. Eventually we left, without the usual hugs and kisses all around.

"On the ride home, my mother, seeking reassurance, asked my father, 'Dear, was I right?' My father, a wise man who knew what was best for him replied, 'Yes, dear, you were right.' Aside from that, no one spoke on the long ride home, a very unusual situation.

"That night, my grandmother phoned my mother while I sat in a corner of the room doing my homework. I learned my grandmother's part of the conversation from my parents' discussion of the phone call. My grandmother told my mother that she should apologize to her sister-in-law. My mother protested that she herself was in the right and it was she who deserved the apology. My grandmother said that whoever was in the right didn't matter, it was my mother who humiliated my aunt, and not the reverse, and that, therefore, my mother must apologize. Her unanswerable argument, as far as my mother was concerned, was my grandmother's statement, 'It's important for the family.' Without further discussion, *my mother acceded to my grandmother's request.*

"I was present when my mother called my aunt. The conversation went something like, 'I am very, very sorry I hurt your feelings. I was wrong to embarrass you in front of the family, and especially in your own house where I was invited as a guest. It was very wrong of me. Please forgive me.' There was a long silence from my mother, while my aunt spoke. My mother was crying. She said, 'thank you, thank you so very much for forgiving me.'

"The next time the family got together my mother walked up to my aunt and said, 'There is something I must say to you, in front of the family' and repeated the apology. My aunt, crying, said, 'I forgive you, I forgive you.' The two women hugged and both began to cry, and then all the women and children cried, including me, and there were hugs and kisses all around, and everything was all right again."[19]

In this situation, it did not matter who was right: After all, each woman had been humiliated. What mattered was the peace that was restored to the family. What is interesting is that the third party arbitrator was the grandmother, someone who had the standing and the authority to speak for the family and the influence to win cooperation. She decided who had committed the offense and who would apologize to whom. The primary motive was not a matter involving dignity, pride, guilt, or shame but was aimed at an external goal: to please the grandmother and to support her effort to preserve family cohesiveness. The need of the aunt, the offended party, was the restoration of her dignity and, perhaps, reassurance that she was not at fault. Even though the designated offender (the narrator's mother) may have believed she was treated unjustly, I suspect she ultimately realized that her relationship to her mother-in-law was strengthened.

I recall growing up in this same era among a large extended family. Frequently I was "commanded" by my mother to make peace with my younger sister or cousins regardless of whether I was in the right. I was ordered to apologize because "You must be the bigger one," or "you are wiser," or "you are older." My childhood answer, "but it wasn't my fault," fell on deaf ears.

The next apology was related to me by a 45-year-old woman and describes an event that occurred when she was 16 years old.[20] Although she has a vivid picture of her mother's response, she does not recall any offense. Her mother, nevertheless, was very upset with her. "She froze me out. She was sick and tired of me," she told me. "Her face became a cold mask. She was stern and remote. She did not speak to me. I felt abandoned, homesick, and desperate. I felt blown apart and on the verge of panic. I said, 'I was sorry. I was sorry. I was really sorry, really sorry.' I kept apologizing and apologizing, even though I did not feel I did anything wrong. This happened at about 2 P.M. I went to sleep in my mother's bed. I did not feel OK until I awoke the next morning. By then, my mother seemed to have forgiven me."

The primary motives for the apology in this story were the 16-year-old girl's fear of abandonment and her intense desire for reunion with her mother. (Sleeping in her mother's bed after the incident gives further evidence of her desire for reunion.) The girl could not acknowledge committing an offense because, from her vantage point, there was none. Consequently, she could not express genuine remorse or offer a meaningful explanation. And yet she apologized. Her apology is an echo of young children who apologize and immediately want to know whether they have been restored to good graces. "I am sorry, Mommy, for taking all of the cookies. Do you love me again?"

The next story offers a variation on the theme of apologizing to keep the social order intact. An African American man and a Caucasian woman gave birth to a baby girl in Thomasville, Georgia. The baby's skull was deformed and she died before the end of her first day. She was buried beside her maternal grandfather in a Baptist Church cemetery. Three days after the funeral, when the Board of Deacons of the church learned that the child had an African American father, they voted to remove the coffin from the cemetery so they could keep the graveyard exclusively white.[21]

The child's grandmother said the deacons' response exposed something ugly that went beyond racism. "It was inhuman," she said.[22] The deacons' request shocked the townspeople and outsiders who learned of the situation and an official of the Southern Baptist Convention remarked that it was "an embarrassment to the gospel of Christ."[23]

This explosive town reaction, sympathetic to the bereaved couple, led to a barrage of TV cameras and reporters. The deacons then changed their mind and ultimately apologized, "Our church family humbly asks you to accept our apology."[24] The grandmother said she had to goad them into making the apology. "I wanted them to admit to what they did and say they were sorry for it."[25] The grandmother noted that whenever she went to town, she was offered sympathy from people she met who told her how badly they felt for such happenings. The baby's parents said the hurt would take a long time to heal. The deacons apologized because of external pressure from the community and the governing church, not from an internal feeling of guilt or shame. Sincerity was not necessary.

The next apology is by a religious figure, the Reverend Jerry Falwell, who offended many groups with insensitive comments made two days after the terrorist destruction of the World Trade Center. During a television broadcast, Falwell expressed his belief that "God, angered by the secular groups, had lifted a 'curtain' of protection and allowed the terrorists to strike."[26]

Four days later, following a communication from the White House stating that President Bush considered Falwell's comments to be inappropriate and that the president did not agree with him, Rev. Falwell issued an apology. "I made a statement that I should not have made and which I sincerely regret," he said, "I apologize that . . . I singled out for blame certain groups of Americans. This was insensitive, *uncalled for at the time*, and unnecessary as part of the commentary on this destruction. . . . In conclusion, I blame no one but the hijackers and terrorists for the barbaric happenings of September 11."[27] (Italics added.)

His apology continued, "I do not know if the horrific events of September 11 are the judgment of God . . . ," [28] and he concluded with a quotation from Abraham Lincoln's second inaugural address: "The Almighty has his own purposes. . . . The judgments of the Lord are true and righteous altogether."[29] Falwell also added in his apology that he had stated his theological convictions at a *"bad time."*[30] (Italics added.)

Falwell's apology is clearly an attempt to manipulate the situation to avoid being rebuked and rejected by the president. He retracted what he said to please President Bush, but he framed his apology in such a way that his audience is quite aware that it is only the timing of the apology that he regrets and not its contents (see italics). In other words, he is apologizing for bad taste in making such statements so soon after 9/11, not for making them at all. He does not repudiate his belief that the nation is suffering God's wrath because of its secular diversity. I find it ironic that Falwell cloaked himself in President Lincoln's second inaugural address, since that is the speech in which Lincoln also declared that slavery is the sin that divides us and that we must move on "with malice toward none and charity for all."[31] In her column, "Apology Not Accepted,"

Ellen Goodman makes a similar observation. "The preacher and the terrorist both claim that we must agree with their religious or political views—or be damned. So now we know who the dividers are." Her final line is one of cutting sarcasm, "But of course, I forgot again. Mr. Falwell apologized, didn't he?"[32] In my opinion, Falwell's apology is simply an attempt to manipulate circumstances so that he remains in favor with President Bush, avoids the wrath of most Americans, and remains a credible voice for his own followers.

The next apology was offered by former boxing heavyweight champion Mike Tyson to heavyweight fighter Evander Holyfield after he bit off part of Holyfield's ear during a World Boxing Association bout. Tyson, who previously lost to Holyfield in a major upset, had been regarded as the biggest star in boxing since Muhammad Ali. During the third round of a 15-round fight in Las Vegas, Tyson bit both of Holyfield's ears. The bite to the right ear occurred with 38 seconds left in the round. (Fifteen percent of the ear, skin and cartilage were completely removed: The wound required between 12 and 15 stitches to close.) The fight was stopped for two minutes to treat Holyfield, and then, shortly after action resumed, Tyson bit Holyfield again, this time on the left ear. The referee disqualified Tyson and declared Holyfield the victor. Immediately following the disqualification, Tyson brawled with policemen who tried to maintain order between the two camps. Two million people watched the fight on pay-for-view TV for approximately $50 per person, and 17,000 fans were in attendance.

At the time of the fight, Tyson was on probation following his release from an Indiana prison, where he had served three years of a six-year sentence for raping a contestant in a beauty pageant. The judge in the case, Patricia Gifford, had the power to revoke Tyson's probation because of his behavior at the fight.

Two days after the fight, Tyson called an impromptu news conference to apologize. After keeping 100 people waiting for nearly an hour, he read his apology from a prepared text and left without taking any questions. In his apology, Tyson asked for forgiveness for "snapping in that ring . . . and doing something that I have never done before and will never do again."[33] He addressed his apology to a series of people or groups: his family, the Nevada State Athletic Commission, Judge Patricia Gifford who is responsible for his probation, MGM, Showtime, promoter Don King, his team, and the city of Las Vegas. In attempting to explain his reaction—snapping—he said he feared losing the fight because of a cut above his eye, and so he reacted aggressively, as many other athletes have done. He acknowledged his behavior was wrong and that he expected to pay a price, but he asked that he not be "penalized for life for this mistake."[34] He explained that he grew up in the streets without proper schooling or people to help him in his times of need, and he assured those listening that he is now seeking help: "from God" for help in renewing his faith as a true believer[35] and from medical professionals "to tell me why I did what I did."[36] He asked to be forgiven so that he could later redeem himself.

Tyson included mention of Holyfield only in passing and in a manner that may be described as the "fallacy of the empty disclaimer": He conveyed an attitude of "I am sorry, but you started it by head-butting me and I would have won anyway." What Tyson said was, "I am only saddened that this fight did not go further so that the boxing fans of the world might see for themselves who would come out on top. When you

[Holyfield] butted me in that first round, accidentally or not, I snapped in reaction and the rest is history."[37]

It is apparent to me that the primary motive for this apology was to avoid punishment. Tyson directed his apology to those who had the power to punish him: the Nevada State Athletic Commission, which was considering a $3 million fine (10 percent of the purse and an indefinite suspension from boxing) and Judge Patricia Gifford, whom he acknowledges as having the power to revoke his probation. His apology to the offended party, Evander Holyfield, comes near the end of his prepared statement, almost as an afterthought. Aside from his injury to Holyfield, Tyson also caused his audience to experience distress: His offense is equivalent to a performer who walks off the stage shortly after being introduced. Tyson does not appear to recognize that the major parties owed an apology were Holyfield and the audience who paid to see a fight that ended after less than three rounds. He even presumes to describe the terms of the commission's forgiveness (that he not be banned from boxing for life).

Even if the words and emotions of the apology were changed to address these deficits, I believe this apology would be meaningful only if Tyson offered reparations: a return of most of the $30 million to the paying audience, for example, or a comparable donation to some public charity.

The next story is a humorous one, but as is commonly recognized, humor often masks serious ideas and attitudes. At the end of the 1995 baseball season, three Red Sox fans wrote a letter to the editor of the *Boston Globe* to propose an interesting strategy for the Red Sox organization. Observing that 1995 marked the hundredth anniversary of Babe Ruth's birth, they noted that at the time Ruth was sold to the New York Yankees in 1920, the Red Sox had won one-fourth of all World Series ever played. As everyone who follows Boston baseball knows, the Red Sox have not won a Series title since. The strategy suggested in the letter was for the Red Sox owners to "publicly acknowledge that they, as subsequent owners, regret that such a sale ever took place."[38] The letter continued, "Such an acknowledgment would lift 'the curse of the Babe' from the hearts and minds of Red Sox players and fans and give the team a fair shot at winning the series this year and forever after."[39]

I discussed this proposal with several of my colleagues who are Red Sox fans. They were quite interested in it and enthusiastically described how such an apology could be handled. A special ceremony would be held in center field before Opening Day, at which a copy of Babe Ruth's 1920 contract would be solemnly burned. Beer would flow freely as token reparation to the team's long-suffering fans and as a libation for whatever baseball gods there may be. The curse of the Bambino would be lifted forever.

Although in jest, the fans are asking the current owners of the Red Sox to apologize for selling Babe Ruth. As the latest in an unbroken string of owners, the current owners can "stand in" for the original culprits. The motive of the apology is not to assuage some internal emotional state, but purely and simply to manipulate a negative (and hence unacceptable) set of circumstances.

The next proposed apology makes no pretense at humor despite its similar motive. According to the Associated Press, villagers of Nabutautau in a remote island of Fiji "staged an elaborate ceremony of apology . . . for the relatives of a British missionary killed and eaten here 136 years ago."[40] As the story goes, the community has been cursed for their earlier imprudence by being deprived of modern developments enjoyed by other Fiji villagers and by the persistence of poverty. Although apologies had been made on two previous occasions, this apology was directed to the family of the victim, the Rev. Thomas Baker. The village chief, a great-grandson of the chief responsible for cooking the missionary, apologized to one of Baker's descendants by kissing him and asking for forgiveness. Apology-related rituals continued for over a month, culminating in a series of reparations given to ten Australian descendants of Baker: "cows, specially woven mats, and 30 carved sperm-whale teeth. . . ."[41]

I find this apology remarkably similar to contemporary apologies. For example, the villagers were determined to "make things right," despite the failure of two previous apologies. As we will see in chapter 10, a commitment to negotiate the terms of an apology is an important part of the apology process and increases the likelihood of a successful outcome. In this case, the villagers revised their earlier apologies by reconsidering who should speak for the offenders (the village chief and great-grandson of the original offender), and who should receive the apology (a relative of the victim of the cannibals). Whether or not this apology will prove more successful than previous attempts, the villagers appear to understand the power of the apology process and the role of negotiation and persistence in it.

BOTH CATEGORIES OF MOTIVES FOR APOLOGIES HAVE THEIR PLACE IN THE WORLD OF RECONCILIATION

Having examined two sets of apologies spurred by internal and external motivation, respectively, can we assess the value of these two types of motives for apologies? If we think of times when we have been offended by someone we cared about, we may want to believe that they were motivated by an empathic concern for us, and their feeling of guilt or shame because they offended a good friend. We might even expect them to treat strangers in a similar fashion, because we admire people of character who are committed to fairness and to preserving the dignity of others. We trust them as individuals. We can count on them. They are reliable. They are sincere. These are the kind of people who would return your lost wallet, even if they did not know you, because they know how they would feel if they lost their wallet (empathy) or because it is simply the right thing to do (a healthy sense of guilt). Does our admiration for these people suggest that apologies motivated by a desire to avoid punishment or to restore peace between nations, groups, families, and individuals have less value?

I believe that these "strategic" apologies—motivated by the offenders' attempt to change how others perceive them or keep their relationships intact or enhance their social stature— are valuable even if the offenders do not exhibit or experience shame, guilt, and empathy. How can we argue against social harmony among individuals, families, and nations? How can we argue against the avoidance of war? As we saw in chapter 3, in order to be successful, an apology must meet the needs of the offended party, such as the restoration of dignity, acknowledgment of shared values, reparations, and the like. To believe that a "pragmatic" apology is somehow less truthful or less effective than a more impassioned one is to value style over substance, as if we believe that the manner in which an apology is delivered is more important than the goals it seeks to achieve. I believe such an attitude shortchanges both the personal and social value of the apology process. As long as an apology meets important psychological needs of the offended, or, by being public, it reestablishes harmony and reaffirms important social values, we should not diminish its effectiveness by becoming critics. We can also learn from Japanese and Chinese cultures that reestablishing social harmony is often the major function of apologies.

SEVEN

Why People
Do Not Apologize

The forces enhancing or propelling the apology process are substantial, as we have seen in the previous chapter. From within the person, there is empathy, guilt, and shame, elements we may refer to loosely as "conscience." External forces for apologizing include threats of abandonment and other punishments as well as opportunities for enhanced reputation and social harmony. Despite these forces to apologize, there are many situations in which people fail to apologize or do so with much reluctance, emotional distress, and clumsiness. The stories in the previous chapters illustrate again and again how people avoid or undermine apologizing through all sorts of techniques, such as acting oblivious to the offense, failing to acknowledge the offense, offering trivial and shallow explanations, failing to show remorse, or offering inadequate reparations. In addition, many apologies are delayed by years, decades, and even centuries after the offense. Many of these failed apologies turn out to be insults, which in retrospect would have been better left unsaid.

To understand some of the reasons why people find it difficult to apologize, I asked several groups of high school students, medical students, and colleagues why they find it difficult to apologize. (Several of the following statements are paraphrased and synthesized from several sources.) Their responses fall into two categories: First, they fear the reactions of the people to whom they apologize, and second, they are embarrassed or ashamed of the image they would have of themselves.

The fears of the other party's reactions as a result of the apology are illustrated in the following statements:

- "They might decide to end the relationship right on the spot."
- "They would change their regard for me."
- "They would feel superior to me."
- "The punishment that I would receive could be quite severe."
- "I would just be opening myself up for hurt. Once, when I apologized to my mother, she told me I should be more than sorry for what I did and that I better never do that again."
- "My friend would become smug and self-satisfied that she was right and I was wrong. I do not believe I could bear such a reaction."
- "I might never be forgiven."
- "Apologizing gives someone else the god-like power to forgive you."
- "She might make a scene, especially in public."
- "She might never want to see me again."

- "He might hold a grudge, just waiting for the opportunity to get even."
- "My professor might publicly humiliate me in front of my friends."
- "You never know how the other person will react."

The second group of responses illustrates the feared negative self-image of the person offering the apology, regardless of the reactions of the offended.

- "It makes me feel weak to apologize."
- "Apologizing is an admission of fault, an example of incompetence, an example of below-expected performance, an acknowledgment of a mistake someone else would have to repair, a mistake that could damage a patient. I couldn't stand to think of myself as incompetent."
- "Our general practice as human beings is to define our self or ego in terms of who we are, what we have, etc. We try to protect that mental image because we have no other structure to our mind. Emotions are one of the most powerful forms of this experience. When we are angry, hurt, or sad, we are loath to give up that emotion because it serves to define us in that moment. It is fuel for the fire. I would say this is the crux of the difficulty in apologizing: We feel that by apologizing, we will lose ground, lose our self-image, lose our 'self.'"
- "It is difficult to apologize because it is giving in to the other person and that makes you feel as if you lost."
- "It is difficult to apologize because I might show hidden inner emotions like sadness or anger and start to cry. I might then be perceived as weak."

- "A lot of people like to hide their feelings, and saying 'sorry' shows they do have feelings."
- "In order to apologize you have to show emotion in order for people to believe you."
- "Saying 'I am sorry' is difficult because of the shame it brings. It forces the reality that I am capable of hurting someone and doing something wrong. With that realization comes guilt."
- "When you say you are sorry, you are likely to take a battering to your self-esteem."
- "It is difficult to apologize because it is hard to swallow one's pride. A person wants to feel right, and apologizing is another way of admitting that you are wrong."
- "It is hard to apologize because you know you let the other person down or made them feel sad. You feel so bad about it that it is hard to say."
- "When you apologize, you let your guard down and you are like a soldier going into battle without armor or a gun. I feel that when you say you are sorry, you are opening your inner self up and your guard is let down. You are more likely to take a battering to your self-esteem."

To summarize these sample responses, the first group of offenders fear the recipients of the apologies will lose their regard for them, threaten to or end the relationship, become smug and self-satisfied, feel superior, make a scene, hold a grudge, withhold forgiveness, or dole out punishment, including humiliations. Such offenders convince themselves that if they don't apologize, the offended parties will be unaware of the offenses committed against them. This is often a false assumption. They further assume that the offended's responses to the apologies will be punitive, another question-able assumption.

The second group of offenders are less concerned with how the offended parties will react to their apologies but are more concerned with feeling weak, incompetent, defeated, guilty, ashamed, emotional, like a loser—in essence losing their self-esteem or their very self. What is striking is that it appears the offenders experience these self-perceptions and emotions as a result of acknowledging them in the apology, not as a result of their behavior. In other words, they believe it may be acceptable to behave in a hurtful manner, but to verbally acknowledge that you have behaved in a hurtful manner makes you a hurtful person.

We are left with the paradox that the two major motives for many people to apologize—changing the external world and relieving their inner feelings of guilt and shame—are the same reasons why others avoid apologizing—fearing the reactions of the external world and suffering from the emotions of guilt and shame. It remains to be determined to what degree the difference in these apologizers and non-apologizers is a result of negative experiences and simple learning or a result of more permanent personality features.

These observations about the reasons people resist apologizing certainly apply to person-to-person private apologies. It will be interesting to learn to what degree these principles apply to public apologies.

OTHER REASONS WHY PEOPLE DO NOT APOLOGIZE

A common reason why people fail to apologize is their lack of awareness that their behavior offended the other person. This

may result from several causes. Some offenders may be generally insensitive to the impact of their behaviors. These are bulls
in china shops; they manage to say and do the wrong things
much of the time and offend many people by remaining
blissfully unaware of their actions. The offended people, in
order to get the attention of the offenders, may have to shout
at and confront them about their behaviors.

Some of these offenders may be described as extremely
self-centered. They may ultimately apologize out of regret
that they are no longer liked, in good favor, or admired by
the offended party. Guilt or shame is not a dominant motive
in their lives, and their concern for the suffering of others is
limited. Hence, the apology, after they learn of the offense,
takes the form of "I am sorry that you are upset with me"
rather than "I am sorry that I hurt you." Their "sorry" is a
childlike afterthought. The offended party will not experience such apologies as meaningful. One young man told his
relatives on one hour's notice that he could not be in their
wedding party because he had made other plans. He said he
did not need to apologize because they knew him well
enough to understand. His "apology" consisted of one word,
"sorry."

Sometimes, the so-called failure to apologize is not the
result of the insensitivity of the offender but the oversensitiv-
ity of the offended party who expects an apology. The so-
called offenders may be understandably unaware of what they
have done. This commonly happens at home or at the
workplace in the relationship between those in positions of
authority and those with lesser power. At work, for instance,
the manager's assignment of offices, annual evaluations,
determination of salaries and bonuses, or termination of

someone's employment may be considered work as usual for the manager but a serious offense by the employee.

Among families and friends, someone may be offended by not being invited to a particular event, by having a relative or friend fail to come to certain events (weddings, funerals, confirmations, etc.), by having a guest wear inappropriate dress, or by receiving inappropriate gifts. Someone may feel offended because of a belief that other siblings are not doing their fair share for elderly parents. One sibling may feel offended that another sibling received a disproportionate share of the family estate. In all of these situations, one party may be unaware that another party is offended and therefore does not consider offering an apology.

At first glance, it would seem reasonable in the above situations for the offended parties to inform the other of the offense. There are several reasons why this may not occur. The offended parties run the risk of appearing weak or thin-skinned for feeling so offended. They may feel that if the offenders really cared they would know what they did and the impact it made without having to be told. They may feel justified and morally superior in observing the other's offense, thereby providing justification for maintaining distance in the relationship. Finally, in the work situation, the offended parties are often reluctant to inform the offenders when such people are superiors, since the latter may experience the communication as criticism and hold it against the subordinates.

When the offended party wants the other to know of the offense but is reluctant to communicate the message for fear of appearing weak or risking retribution, the choice of words can reduce these dangers. The offended party, instead of accusing the offender of insensitivity, can say, "I was bothered [troubled] [upset] by something that you did [said]." Instead of acknowledging being embarrassed, one can talk about an embarrassing moment. Instead of acknowledging being insulted or being offended, one can speak of the insulting remark or offensive comments. Another method of facilitating communication is for the offended party to use a third party to deliver the message to the offender about his behavior. The offended party can then appear not to be complaining. Finally, the offended party can communicate through humor.

There are many situations in which a person behaves in an offensive manner for which he has no regrets and for which he may even feel pride. At the same time, people who are the objects of such behaviors feel aggrieved or offended. The offensive person in this matter believes he owes no one an apology because he has no regrets. He may apologize, however, to avoid punishment.

Some people offend others just to feel superior and in control of the situation. They may ask inappropriately intimate questions such as: "How come you do not have children? Do you have a fertility problem?" "How come you never married?" They may attempt to establish their intellectual superiority with questions such as: "Have you read Shakespeare's collected works?" or "Have you seen a particular play on Broadway?" Such behavior is offensive, but the offenders would never apologize because they intended to be offensive.

Finally, there are people who offend in order to create distance from others they perceive as getting too close or making too many demands in the relationship. This may also be an attempt to gain power in the relationship and to keep the other off balance. Sarcastic and insulting behavior, offensive language, and attacking the other's cherished beliefs offends the other, thereby enhancing power and creating distance. These offenders have no regrets.

Most readers suspect or realize they have at times inadvertently offended others. They often consider making apologies but seem incapable of doing so. I believe such people would do well to explore the forces that hold them back. Is it a fear of the responses of the other parties? Is it losing or giving up power to the other parties? Is it the shame of apologizing or the idea that expressing fearful emotions makes us lesser people? Is it the concern of acknowledging to the aggrieved parties more than they already know?

I believe that thoughtfulness about such questions can help people make the decision to apologize, since the fears, on closer examination, turn out to be much exaggerated. Most responses to genuine apologies are expressions of gratitude. The power we give to the offended parties is usually no more than a compensation for the power we took from them in the offense. Finally, although in apologizing we often experience the emotion of shame, such an emotion is a signal to us that we have not lived up to our standards and should try to do better. Shame in this sense is not a moral failure but a sign of integrity. Most of us would rather feel shame than be shameless.

There are many times with family, friends, and coworkers when we offend others without knowing it. We should suspect this has happened when such people unexpectedly offend us with emotional withdrawal, slights, insults, or even humiliations. An effective response to such a situation is asking such people, "Have I offended you in some way?" This is based on the possibility that their hostility toward you is a response to your offense. If they answer in the affirmative, a very common experience, you have several options depending on the circumstance. You can offer the rationale for your behavior without apologizing. For example, "This is something I had to do. It was part of my job. I am sorry it was so upsetting." (The use of "sorry" is not intended to be an apology.) Alternatively, you can clarify any misunderstanding. For example, "I did not show up for your dinner party because you did not confirm the date." Finally, you can apologize. For example, "I am very sorry. I was so distracted that I did not realize my behavior was so hurtful. I was very insensitive."

We can surmise what personality traits in people make it particularly difficult for them to apologize: They need to be in firm control of interpersonal situations. They need to be in control of their emotions. They need to feel right or morally superior most of the time; they believe they rarely make mistakes. They assume the world is hostile and that relationships are inherently dangerous. In contrast, people who find it easy to apologize accept sharing control of interpersonal situations and enjoy relationships with others. They accept, respect, and even enjoy their emotions. They can acknowledge their vulnerabilities, weaknesses, and flaws while constantly trying to improve. They believe they are reasonable and decent people and assume that others share these traits. When they apologize, they are merely admitting they made a mistake. Such an admission is not a threat so long as they feel good about themselves and feel that *they* are not a mistake.

A final reason why offenders do not apologize even though they regret committing an offense and want to heal the relationship is that they do not know how to apologize, or they never thought of an apology as an option for dealing with their hurtful behaviors. In other words, apology has not been a skill set with which the offender is familiar, either in its structure or application. Several years ago, I would have thought this to be an outlandish statement. Everyone knows how to apologize, I assumed.

During the past several years, immersed in my interest in apologies, I freely discussed this subject with friends, my children and their friends, my siblings, and colleagues. These were discussions about why I thought the subject of apology to be so interesting and engaging, not advice or problem-solving sessions—so I thought. Months or years later, several of these people told me about apologies they offered that had profound impacts on their lives. Some of these people had not understood the apology process and literally did not know how to apologize. Others understood the apology process but never thought of applying it. I conclude from these experiences that learning about apologies is wanting and discouraged in our broader culture. I have since held discussion groups on apologies in high schools and religious after-school or Sunday school classes. The interest of these students has been enthusiastic and their insights keen. I recommend formal teaching of this topic in high schools or colleges under the subjects of psychology, ethics, or communications.

EIGHT

The Timing of Apologies

Senator Fred Thompson expressed an important truth about the timing of apologies during his own apology to President William Clinton on October 8, 1997. Referring to his mistaken implication that President Clinton had been involved in some fund-swapping conspiracy between the Teamsters union and the Democratic National Committee, Thompson observed, "If you've got to eat any crow, or maybe even half a crow, it's better to do it warm than when it gets cold."[1] In my opinion, it is only sometimes true that eating warm crow is better than eating cold crow.

I asked a high school class what they thought about the timing of apologies. In response to my question, "When should you make an apology?" most of the students, like the senator, advocated immediate responses. One student, obviously streetwise, disagreed. "When I cheated on my girlfriend and she found out," he said, "right away I told her we would talk about it; but I did not apologize to her at that moment. I needed to give her enough time to get the anger out of her system. Many days later, I apologized and everything came back to normal."[2] I agree with this student, not that it was all right to cheat on his girlfriend but that timing is an important and complex ingredient in delivering effective apologies.

The issue of the timing of apologies raises a number of questions. Can a person apologize before committing the offense? When is it best to apologize: immediately after committing the offense, or at least while the crow is still warm? What about hours, days, or weeks after the offense? Can the offended party influence the timing of the apology? Are there differences in the timing of apologies following private and public offenses? Is it ever too late to apologize?

"I WANT TO APOLOGIZE IN ADVANCE"

Some people attempt to apologize in anticipation of committing an offense. Two examples illustrate this point. Many years ago, my four-year-old son, while recuperating from surgery in a pediatric ward, told me, "If I run over that little girl with my cart, I will say I'm sorry." The second example, a cartoon, shows a husband announcing to his wife, that he wants to pre-apologize before going out for the evening.

Despite the humor involved in the idea of "pre-apologizing," I do not believe that a person can meaningfully apologize before the event. It is part of the very meaning of "apology" that the offending party acknowledge and regret an offense already committed, and then plan not to repeat the offense, even if the opportunity presents itself. My son and the husband in the cartoon cannot successfully apologize in anticipation of committing the offense. The fact that I need to look to amusing childhood anecdotes or cartoons to make my point illustrates that such apologies are childish or laughable.

A common "pre-apology" occurs when people "apologize" in anticipation of leaving a meeting early. As I was working on this book, a newly appointed member of my management team apologized at the beginning of the meeting for having to leave well before the meeting's conclusion. With tongue in cheek, I explained that it was not possible to apologize in advance of the offense. I further suggested that instead of "apology," he should use the word "sorry" or "regret" as in, "I regret I must leave early" or "I am sorry that I must leave early." As the time neared for him to leave, another member of the management team asked him why he had to depart before the meeting would end. He told the group that he was taking his mother-in-law to the airport after her three-week vacation with his family and that completing this task would be a great relief to him. We all laughed together, realizing not only that it was semantically incorrect to use the word "apology" when the event had not yet occurred, but that it was also factually incorrect to say that he regretted leaving the meeting early to send his mother-in-law on her way.

"IT ISN'T PERSONAL"

Senator Thompson's advice about eating crow when it is warm applies to apologies that are not personal or, if personal, are not serious. Nonpersonal offenses are offenses that happen inadvertently or coincidentally. They are not directed at a specific individual or group with the intention of causing harm or lowering that person or group in the estimation of others. For example, accidentally bumping into someone at a cocktail party and spilling a beverage on that person's clothing would not ordinarily be regarded as a personal offense, because the incident could have happened to anyone occupying that space at that time. No planning or deliberate intent was involved; the person was not singled out because of his/her character, relationships, or choices. The offending party in nonpersonal offenses should apologize immediately, clearly communicate that the offense was accidental, and offer meaningful reparation when feasible. A person who fails to apologize immediately for a nonpersonal offense is usually considered impolite, insensitive, socially obtuse, or a boor. If, on the other hand, the offended party perceives such an offense as a deliberate hostile act in the context of an already strained relationship, the offense becomes personal, and offering and accepting a successful apology may take more time and effort on the part of both parties.

In some nonpersonal offenses, however, an apology may be interpreted as an acknowledgment of guilt, and as a result, the offender may withhold the apology for fear of legal repercussions. A driver at fault in an automobile accident and a physician who errs in providing medical treatment are common examples. However, legal scholars are now revisiting the wisdom of this practice in medicine, since studies have shown that the absence of an apology can be taken as an insult or humiliation and may, in fact, spur the victim to file a lawsuit. In studies of the doctor-patient relationship, researchers found that not all adverse outcomes result in litigation, and not all lawsuits are the result of medical malfeasance. One of the factors that appears to influence whether a malpractice suit is filed is the quality of the relationship between the doctor and the patient, and the degree to which the patient feels his or her views, values, and perspectives have been respected.[3]

"IF I APOLOGIZE IMMEDIATELY, I DO NOT HAVE
TO HEAR HOW UPSET YOU ARE"

At times, apologies are offered before the offended parties understand the full meaning of the offense, or before they have had an opportunity to express how they feel about the offense. For example, a child who breaks a vase rushes to his mother with remorse and contrition pleading for forgiveness, "I am so sorry mother. Don't be mad at me." The mother may not even yet know what the child did. The purpose of the timing of this apology is not for the offender (the child) to meet the needs of the offended party but to avoid hearing the distress of the offended party (the mother), which may include sentiments of anger, disappointment, withdrawal of love, and other threats. In other words, the offender wants to get off easy.

I was recently the recipient of such a premature apology in one the most distressing days of my life. The day began with a four-hour wait for a cancer specialist who was to evaluate my wife's sister for lymphoma. (Her husband, my wife, and I were present for the visit.) The physician confirmed that the disease was far advanced. She died several months later.

The distress of that day, for me, began with the impending loss of a cherished sister-in-law; the anguish of my wife and brother-in-law, both of whom are important to me; and my own helplessness and powerlessness as a physician to make a difference in the final outcome. As if these issues were not enough, this experience reawakened for my wife and me earlier experiences of being with our 28-year-old daughter during her medical visits for breast cancer, which eventually led to her death. My daughter and sister-in-law had many natural physical features in common, in addition to those features common to many cancer patients, such as an emaciated body and a baseball cap covering a bald head caused by chemotherapy. The acute crisis of the day had yet to occur.

After the medical visit, my sister-in-law's husband brought her to our home, while I drove to a pharmacy for a few items. As I was leaving the parking lot, I waited a few seconds for a lull in traffic to enter the main street. At that moment, a young man leaped in front of the open window on the driver's side, moved his arms to a position suggesting that he had a weapon, and said "stick um up." I was stunned, frightened, and over-whelmed with fear for what seemed an eternity (actually several seconds) until I realized the young man was my nephew, my sister-in-law's 30-year-old son, who was playing a practical joke. He had just driven 250 miles from his home in Maine to see his mother and, coincidentally, found himself at the same pharmacy I was leaving.

When I arrived at home, emotionally exhausted from the experience in the hospital and shaken by the faked "holdup," my nephew had already arrived. He greeted me with a sheepish grin and said: "I really gotcha Uncle Aaron." I exploded at him with all sorts of profanities and even told him such behavior could have caused a heart attack. I must have gone on with my tirade for a few minutes, but he interrupted after 10 seconds with profuse apologies, which annoyed me and which I pre-tended to ignore.

I must have frightened him because I had never before behaved toward him in that manner. I recall thinking with my rational mind during my irrational attack that his apologies were just a way to quiet me and stop my assault on him, which I wanted to continue. Neither he nor I understood at that moment the context of the offense, which was our mutual stress over his mother's illness, the long wait at the hospital, and my own memories of my daughter's illness and death. I just wanted him to be quiet while I expressed my anger. Then he could apologize.

He left my home minutes after my tirade and returned to his home in Maine. I thought afterward that if he had the forbearance to allow me to vent my anger and then apologize, we could have had a civil conversation and shared the dinner that was about to be placed on the table. I was mortified that I drove him out of my home with my anger at a time when he came to be with his mother. Just as he overwhelmed me with his prank, I overwhelmed him with my irrational anger.

Since neither of us is a grudge-holder, our positive relationship continued as if nothing had happened. In retrospect, it was an embarrassing event for both of us, because neither of us behaved in our usual manner. We have since apologized to the other for our behaviors. After reading a draft of this story, my nephew said he felt proud to have contributed to my education about apologies and to this book.

APOLOGIES FOR SERIOUS PERSONAL OFFENSES TAKE TIME

Senator Thompson's advice about eating crow when it is warm does not usually apply to serious personal offenses such as humiliating someone in public, cheating or lying to a friend, or otherwise betraying a person's trust. It can be a serious mistake to assume that apologizing immediately after such behavior is the best way to restore the relationship. Doing so may communicate to the offended party that the offender does not realize the impact of the behavior, is trying to get off too quickly and too easily, or is fearful of the emotions of the offended party and does not value the relationship. If, for example, a person discovered by a spouse to be unfaithful in marriage acknowledges committing the misdeed, expresses regret, offers an explanation, and promises a gift for reparation, all within minutes of the accusation, the marriage is in serious trouble—if that is the end of the apology. The offended party often needs days, weeks, or longer to understand and psychologically assimilate what happened. If the relationship is to continue, both parties may need to meet on several occasions for varying periods of time and in designated places (e.g., a quiet place away from the children or at a psychotherapist's office) to discuss and understand the meaning of what happened, the explanations of the offending party, the appropriate reparations, and the future of the relationship. In other words, if a meaningful relationship is to have any chance of being restored following a serious personal offense, the apology must be a complex process conducted over time.

These same timing principles apply to large group interactions in the public arena, where both parties may be culpable and have a great deal at stake. In labor-management situations, for example, "cooling off" periods are offered to allow rational ideas to evolve. During wars or warlike conditions, ceasefires and some kind of truce may be necessary to give combatants an opportunity to arrive at rational decisions regarding settlements, blame, and (sometimes) apologies. The apology may even require waiting for the arrival of the next generation of leaders when those immediately responsible for the offense are no longer on the scene and cooler heads, or at least fresh faces untainted by offenses of the past, can prevail.

The reverse is often true for public apologies in which one party is clearly to blame, such as Senator Trent Lott for his segregationist comments, Cardinal Bernard Law for his reassignment of child-abusing clergy, and Commander Scott Waddle for his role in the sinking of a Japanese fishing boat. In such cases, the public will demand an unambiguous apology as soon as the offense becomes known. Any delays or "hedging" will be met with suspicion and increasing pressure to "come clean," unlike the slowly developing process that can unfold with personal apologies or conflict in which blame is yet to be determined. In the private realm, the offender often has the luxury of time and reflection in order to deliver an appropriate apology, but in the public arena, the offender must get it right the first time.

BEING UNAVAILABLE TO ACCEPT AN APOLOGY

Another way in which timing affects the apology process occurs when the offended party refuses to or is unavailable to accept the apology at the time it is first offered. This practice enables that party to inflict suffering on the offender by denying him or her the desired outcome (such as relief of guilt or restoration of the relationship). It further transfers power to the party who felt powerless. In private apologies, the offended party refuses to meet with and talk to the offender until they are "good and ready." China's response to the U.S. bombing of the Chinese embassy in Belgrade in May 1999 is an example in the public arena. The Chinese waited one week before it would accept President Clinton's phone call of condolences, regrets, and apology. During that interval, China took the opportunity to castigate the United States.[4]

THE FAILURE TO APOLOGIZE IN GOOD TIME
IS UNFORTUNATE, BUT NOT ALL IS LOST

When important grievances, both in private and public apologies, are not settled within days, weeks, or months, the relationship can be at risk for permanent damage or even rupture. In addition, grudges and vengeance-seeking may develop in the aggrieved. Such grudges may persist without resolution for years, decades, and even centuries. When the unresolved grievance involves relatives or close friends, the death of one party before there is time for reconciliation, can lead to permanent psychological damage to the survivor.

When apologies are not forthcoming, both parties may create their own stories that justify their behaviors. The aggrieved parties may say that the offending parties are insensitive, uncaring, and even cruel, that they are not the people they thought they knew. The offenders may say that the aggrieved parties are too sensitive, too demanding, too rigid, too unreasonable, and too unforgiving, that they are not the people they thought they knew. Both parties seek out others to justify their positions. Both parties may say that it is just as well the relationship ended, despite their nagging sense that the conflict resulting in the ruptured relationship could have been avoided or resolved. Nevertheless, as we shall see in the next chapter on delayed apologies, it is never too late to apologize.

NINE

Delayed Apologies

Some apologies are offered or requested years, decades, and even centuries after the offense has been committed. It seems to me that these delayed apologies have become increasingly common since the early 1990s. What are we to make of such phenomena? Why the delay and why the apology now? Can individuals, groups, or nations meaningfully and successfully apologize for offenses they committed decades ago? Can people or groups successfully apologize for offenses committed by their predecessors? Should we take such apologies seriously?

In this chapter, we will explore these questions by examining a number of apologies, both private and public, that were offered years and even decades after the offending event. The apologies fall into four major groups. The first group includes apologies to relieve an unbearable sense of guilt or shame. The second group includes apologies arising out of an awareness of growing old and even facing death. In the third group, the offender is attempting to manipulate his or her external environment in hopes of influencing public reaction or of repairing a damaged relationship that has recently assumed value. The last group of apologies includes those motivated by a new understanding or a new application of an ethical ideal, who perhaps see for the first time that their actions violate an important moral value.

ATTEMPTS TO RELIEVE AN
UNBEARABLE SENSE OF GUILT AND SHAME

A common cause for delayed apologies is the unbearable sense of guilt that accompanies the realization that we have caused harm. Consider the case of John Plummer, a 24-year-old helicopter pilot and operations officer whose job during the Vietnam War was to assist in the coordination of Allied bombing strikes. On June 8, 1972, heavy explosives and napalm were dropped on the village of Trang Bang.[1] The next morning, the U.S. military newspaper *Stars and Stripes* carried a story about the bombing raid, accompanied by the now-famous photograph of 9-year-old Kim Phuc fleeing her burning village. Years later, Plummer ". . . looked at the picture and saw the jellied gasoline had burned off her clothes. Her eyes are screwed shut, her mouth spread wide in terror, and uncomprehending pain. Her arms flap awkwardly, as though she does not recognize them as her own. . . . 'It just knocked me to my knees.'"[2]

For decades after the war, John Plummer suffered from excessive drinking and two failed marriages. He eventually left his job as a defense contractor to become a minister of the United Methodist Church. Despite this career change, he continued to struggle with the photograph which was imprinted on his brain. It hurt every time he thought of it.[3] He dreamed of the photograph, accompanied by screams of the victims. "If she could look into my eyes, Plummer thought, she would see my pain and remorse for what I did to her."[4]

Twenty-four years after the event, John Plummer and Kim Phuc met at the Vietnam War Memorial in Washington, D.C. Plummer described their encounter. "She opened her arms to me. . . . All I could say is, 'I'm so sorry. I'm just so sorry.'" She responded by patting Plummer on the back and saying: "It's all right. I forgive, I forgive."[5] They spent two hours together that day. "Since meeting Kim, I don't hear anything in that dream. I don't hear any more screams. It's all quiet."[6]

This story presents a situation in which guilt provided the motive for an apology that came 24 years after the event that caused harm. Plummer was not under prosecution: The victim did not even know his identity. He was not trying to manipulate the situation or escape punishment for his actions. The pain he felt was internal—he simply lacked inner peace. On his own account, apologizing face-to-face and receiving forgiveness seems to have silenced the screams and given him peace. Nothing else—not even a career change and a dramatic reorientation of his life—had been able to relieve his guilt.

Another story of delayed apology motivated by guilt and shame and the desire to make amends involves a Japanese intelligence officer, Nagase Takashi, who tortured British P.O.W. soldiers sentenced to work on the River Kwai during World War II. Takashi tried to relieve his inner torment by writing about his activities and creating religious temples at the site of the torture. However, like Plummer, Takashi was unable to relieve his psychological pain by these "good works." A fortuitous meeting with one of his victims 60 years after the torture gave him an opportunity to apologize directly for his crime. In response, perhaps to relieve his own passion for revenge, the British soldier, Eric Lomax, gave the officer a written letter of forgiveness. Lomax tells this story in his own book, *Railway Man*,[7] which we will discuss in greater detail in chapter 11.

Guilt is clearly the motive for the next apology, involving an incident that occurred in 1976 during a violent anti-busing protest. Several teenagers and young men pummeled Theodore Landsmark, an African American lawyer, on the steps of Boston City Hall. In addition, one young man, using an American flag for a weapon, aimed the pole of the flag at Landsmark with the stars and stripes vertically furled. Stanley Forman's Pulitzer Prize–winning photograph of the incident, along with the occasion (the nation's bicentennial), the site of the event, the prominence of the American flag as a weapon, the race of the victim, and the color of his attackers, presented a powerful message of bigotry and hatred. Mr. Landsmark never got a look at his attackers and no arrests were made.

Eighteen years later, one of the assailants, Bobby Powers, sought out Mr. Landsmark to apologize and to confess "with great humility"[8] that he was responsible for the attack and that he now wanted to make amends. "I'm not a hateful person," he explained. "I always blamed busing for a lot of my problems . . . but a lot of my problems were with myself."[9] Powers said that he was the one who had tripped Landsmark, and then he had stepped aside so that the "jackals" could attack. Powers, who was 17 years old when the incident occurred, said he was not a racist. "I was just an angry young man, a boy really."[10] At the time of the incident, Powers's father was dying and his grandmother was sick. He had been in trouble periodically. Powers felt he could not get on with his life until he made amends for what he had done. He said he felt he was wearing a "burlap T-shirt" for almost 20 years. Powers said, "I know Ted has forgiven me. But I'm having a hard time forgiving myself."[11]

Powers appears to be genuine in his acknowledgment (confession) of the offense as well as in his acceptance of his responsibility ("I always blamed busing for a lot of my problems . . . but a lot of my problems were with myself"). His remorse and suffering are significant, and his explanation is credible (not a racist "just an angry young man" whose grandmother was sick and whose father was dying).

The next story presents an offender whose delayed apology for his guilty feelings was set in motion by his membership in Alcoholics Anonymous (AA). Membership in this organization, other "12-step" organizations, and some religious groups encourage apologies for offenses that occurred years and decades earlier. Steps 8 and 9 of the AA 12-step program for recovery are specifically related to apology. Step 8 states, "Made a list of all persons we had harmed, and became willing to make amends to them all."[12] AA requires that members make an attempt to "repair the damage we have done"[13] and clean away the "debris of the past."[14] In a similar manner, Step 9 says, "Made direct amends to such people wherever possible, except when to do so would injure them or others."[15] AA warns about the appropriate timing of such apologies to avoid harming others. The following story illustrates a successful apology motivated by membership in AA.

A research assistant working for psychologist George F. Mahl had developed a pilot study whose positive results Dr.

Mahl found very exciting. Before submitting the results to a scientific journal for publication, Mahl asked two other assistants to repeat the measurements, but they were unable to do so, and in fact, their measurements contradicted the earlier work. About a year later, Dr. Mahl happened to meet his former assistant and casually began discussing possible reasons for the discrepancy. Mahl noticed that his former assistant seemed uncomfortable. "[He] cringed and his facial expression changed in a manner that I have always described to myself as 'turning green,'" Dr. Mahl wrote in an article describing the event. "This change in expression was unique, and produced a lasting impression in me."[16]

As Dr. Mahl relates the story, he received a letter from his former assistant some 25 years later. The letter read:

> I am writing to let you know that I consciously altered the results . . . to try and make the study support the hypothesis. I was very concerned at the time with the approval of others and I felt that if the results supported your hypothesis, I would be more acceptable to you.
>
> I apologize for doing this and for jeopardizing your reputation and professional standing which might have occurred had the study been published or presented by you. . . . Again, I apologize for my dishonesty while I was working for you.[17]

Dr. Mahl responded a week later with this reply:

> I accept your apology. And I'm very touched by your courage in telling me about it. Your doing so confirms my faith in mankind, and in my sense about you 25 years ago—

that you were a good person. I wished I could have sensed your deep need for approval and responded in some way that would have relieved you of the sense of guilt and shame you have borne all these years. At any rate, let me assure you that you have now won it forever.

I notice that you wrote your letter September 7 and posted it on September 30. This suggests that the letter caused you considerable conflict and turmoil. I appreciate and acknowledge the struggle you have endured. . . .

I'm keeping your letter in my files, but have cut off your signature at the end of it. Sincerely yours. . . .[18]

The former assistant's next letter expressed his gratitude: "Thank you for your beautiful response to my letter of amends. I appreciate it very much. It's real important for me to feel clean inside."[19]

Seven years later, Dr. Mahl asked his former student why he waited for 25 years before telling him of the falsification. "He answered that he had been a sober member of AA for over 11 years and explained that the recovery program encourages participants 'to make amends for past harms we have done to others,'"[20] Mahl wrote.

These apologies described above illustrate the common reactions of the people receiving the apologies, which is to be generous and forgiving and, sometimes, to accept some of the blame. Dr. Mahl, in his first written communication to his former research assistant, acknowledges not being sensitive enough to be aware of his assistant's deep need for approval. People's generosity comes from feeling that they were treated respectfully and given a gift, the validation and clarification that the thing that went wrong was not of their doing.

AN AWARENESS OF
GROWING OLD AND EVEN FACING DEATH

Another common cause of delayed apologies is our desire to make amends as we mature, age, or experience serious illness and loss. We seek to reestablish personal ties with friends and family members in part because we want to "put our own house in order," and in part to ameliorate our sense of loneliness and isolation. Perhaps we come to see the trivial nature of the offense in the context of the complex nature of human existence. Or we decide to relinquish our false pride about "never being wrong" and take on a new willingness to acknowledge our mistakes. Whatever the precise reason may be, it seems clear that these "life milestones" provide occasion for apologies that have been long delayed, as the next several stories will illustrate.

New York Yankees owner George Steinbrenner fired former player and manager Yogi Berra through a third party by telephone just 16 games into the 1985 season. At the time, Berra vowed never to set foot in Yankee Stadium as long as Steinbrenner was the owner. Fourteen years later, when Steinbrenner was 68 and Berra was 74, Steinbrenner came to Berra's home, took him by the hand, looked him in the eye, and said, "I know I made a mistake by not letting you go personally. It's the worst mistake I ever made in baseball."[21] Berra responded by admitting that he, too, had made mistakes during his baseball career. Steinbrenner said that if Berra would come to Yankee Stadium for a future celebration, he (Steinbrenner) would bring him across the George Washington Bridge in a rickshaw. According to *New York Times* sportswriter Harvey Araton, Steinbrenner acknowledged that his desire to make amends was directly related to the death of Mickey Mantle and the serious illness of Joe DiMaggio only one month earlier.[22] Araton commented that Berra reminded him of the "wandering son returning to a paternal embrace, when the two men hugged at the door, and said goodbye."[23] Berra's wife Carmen attributed the apology to the millennium, a time when people want peace and to make things right.[24]

Another apology energized by maturing perspectives on life involved former heavyweight boxing champions Muhammad Ali and Joe Frazier. Before their first of three fights, Ali had called Frazier an "Uncle Tom" and "too ugly to be the champ."[25] Before the third fight, Ali compared Frazier to a gorilla. On the thirtieth anniversary of Frazier's victory over Ali in their first fight, Frazier, who was said to be embittered over Ali's comments, said, "Hey man, just come on and give me a hug and let's get on with our lives."[26] In a subsequent media interview, Ali responded, "In a way, Joe's right. I said a lot of things in the heat of the moment that I shouldn't have said. Called him names I shouldn't have called him. I apologize for that. I'm sorry. It was all meant to promote the fight."[27] He added, "I like Joe Frazier. Me and him was a good show. It was a good traveling show."[28] In a telephone interview, Frazier said he would accept the apology. "I'll accept it, shake his hand and hug him when I see him. We're grown guys. This has been going on too long. It's like we've been fighting the Vietnam War. We're two athletes of the world. Why we been biting off bullets? We have to embrace each other. It's time to talk and get together. Life's too short."[29]

This brief exchange is very moving for me. It was Frazier who initiated the apology with a simple request: a hug would suffice (a nonverbal apology). His rationale was clear, "We're grown guys. . . . Life's too short." Ali gave more than a promised hug. He acknowledged the offense (calling Frazier names), concurred that it was wrong, expressed regret, and explained that the attack was not personal: It occurred in the "heat of the moment" and was meant to promote the fight. Frazier's use of the Vietnam metaphor suggests that, at least for him, their dispute was an ongoing battle with much suffering, done for no good cause, and apparently without end. He beautifully reframes the situation by reminding Ali and himself that both are "two athletes of the world." An apology called a halt to the needless suffering of two aging and maturing men. I was particularly moved by Frazier's comment to Ali: ". . . let's get on with our lives." This comment suggests that, at least for Frazier, some part of his life had been stalled for 30 years.

The last story is about a former Royal Air Force pilot who stole a 6-ft by 4-ft flag from a flagpole outside of a pub near Exeter, Devon, during a party to celebrate Victory in Europe day in 1945. Almost 50 years later, the former pilot, now in his seventies, returned the flag by mail without divulging his name. In a note accompanying the flag, the airman explained that the theft was "an unforgivable act of vandalism for which I have never stopped being ashamed."[30] He described himself, further, as "a remorseful, penitent, mature delinquent."[31] Upon receiving the flag the current landlord of the pub remarked, "I think all is forgiven now and I would like to meet this man and invite him down to the hotel to stay."[32]

ATTEMPTS TO MANIPULATE THE SITUATION FOR PERSONAL GAIN

Another common reason for delayed apologies is the offender's attempt to manipulate his/her environment for personal gain or to mitigate the negative consequences of the offense. Especially if the offense is only recently discovered, the offender might attempt to disavow the offense by saying, in effect, "That was then, this is now: I would never do such a thing at this point in my life." The first example of such an apology involves President Richard Nixon and the Reverend Billy Graham. Secret tapes made by President Nixon revealed that Nixon and Graham had exchanged anti-Semitic comments following a prayer breakfast in 1972. Nixon had initiated the conversation by ranting about how Jews dominate the media and how he could not express this view publicly without being pilloried by the press. Graham's response indicated his agreement with Nixon. "This stranglehold has got to be broken or the country's going down the drain," he said, adding, ". . . if you get elected a second time, then we might be able to do something."[33]

Thirty-one years later, after the tapes had been made public, Graham, now 83, apologized. "I don't ever recall having those feelings about any group, especially the Jews, and I certainly do not have them now. My remarks did not reflect my love for the Jewish people. I humbly ask the Jewish community to reflect on my actions on behalf of Jews over the years that contradict my words in the Oval Office that day."[34]

The passage of time gave Graham an opportunity to recant the view without ever having to admit that it was his ("I don't ever recall. . . ."), while denying that he would say such a thing now (". . . I certainly do not have them now"). Even the verbs used in his apology give evidence of the paradoxical nature of Graham's predicament: How could remarks made 31 years ago reflect his current love for the Jewish people? In any case, Graham urges the Jews to balance his "actions on behalf of Jews over the years" against "my words in the Oval Office that day"—an implicit assurance to the Jews that whatever was the case then, his present beliefs and values would not permit such behavior.

The next illustration involves romance novelist Janet Dailey, who was discovered to have plagiarized the work of novelist Nora Roberts. Dailey admitted that two of her books, *Aspen Gold* and *Notorious,* written in the early 1990s, contained material taken from several of Ms. Roberts's novels. "I can only apologize to Nora whom I've considered a friend, and to my readers for any pain or embarrassment my conduct has caused. . . . I recently learned that my essentially random and non-pervasive acts of copying are attributable to a psychological problem that I never even suspected I had. . . . I have already begun treatment for the disorder and have been assured that, with treatment, this behavior can be prevented in the future."[35] In this apology, it is the explanation that attempts to mitigate the consequences. By claiming that she suffered from "a psychological problem that I never even suspected I had," Dailey is suggesting that perhaps, because of her illness, she should not be held fully responsible for the plagiarism at all. In this case, her apology was offered only after her offense had been discovered by others, and it included an explanation that dodged responsibility while appealing for pity. One wonders if her reparations—payment to the Literacy Volunteers of America and discontinuing sales of *Notorious* (*Aspen Gold* being already out of print)—was similarly only a bid to escape a civil lawsuit.

The third illustration involves the Swiss government as offender. From the end of World War II until 1996, the Swiss maintained a low profile regarding their relationship with the Nazis during the war and the fate of the Swiss bank accounts of Jews who were killed in the Holocaust. The status quo of minimal discussion was disrupted by the declassification of U.S. documents 50 years after World War II and the availability of documents following the collapse of the Soviet Union.

Beginning in 1996, accusations were leveled against the Swiss that they turned away Jewish refugees during the war, traded with and provided hard currency for Germany, profited significantly from such trade, and rejected requests to return money in bank accounts to victims of the war or their relatives. The accusations were devastating to the image of the Swiss as a humanitarian and fair-minded people.[36]

The Swiss have responded to the accusations with public apologies and reparations. These apologies can be understood both as attempts to assuage feelings of national guilt by making amends as well as change the world's negative perception of their past behavior. In addition, the Swiss continue to review their history to understand how such actions could be undertaken by fair-minded and humane people. None of these efforts would be forthcoming had not new information appeared that exposed and documented their offenses.

In these three examples, it is unlikely that apologies would have been offered without an exposure of the offenses. Should we consider these apologies to be without value? I think not. Billy Graham has long been regarded as a friend to people of the Jewish religion. He was able to make the point in his apology that his actions toward the Jewish people since making the alleged anti-Semitic remark should be regarded as a form of reparation. Although Janet Dailey's apology leaves much to be desired in terms of forthrightness and a convincing explanation, she, too, offered reparations (perhaps under threat of legal action). The apology of the Swiss government also acknowl-

edged a truth that needed to be known and provided reparations that needed to be made. Regardless of the lateness of these
apologies, and despite the questionable "purity" of their motivation, all three cases achieved something of value.

A subset of this group of apologies we could describe as
"strategic" are those in which the offender is attempting to
achieve personal gain. An example is Governor George Wallace's apology to African Americans. Wallace, a staunch segregationist once described by journalist Theodore White as "a
Southern populist of the meanest streak" and a "narrow-
minded grotesquely provincial man,"[37] ran for president of the
United States several times as a third-party candidate. During
the presidential campaign of 1972, as he discussed the "big
nigger vote," Wallace was quoted by a *New York Times* reporter
as saying he "didn't give them much nigger talk today. . . .
Shoot, people are going to start saying that I've gone soft."[38]
Later in this campaign, a would-be assassin shot Wallace,
paralyzing him from the waist down.

By the late 1970s, Wallace began to apologize to the
African Americans he had wronged. He met, for example, with
John Lewis, a black civil rights leader and then city councilman
of Atlanta, to list the things he regretted he had done and to
"ask for forgiveness for anything I've done to wrong you."[39]
Wallace appeared at Martin Luther King, Jr.'s old church in
Montgomery, Alabama, where he related his own suffering "to
the suffering of black people and asked for their forgiveness."[40]
He repeatedly defended his past behaviors as merely support-
ing states' rights.

Confronted with this total reversal of position, we have a
choice: either to believe that Governor Wallace, following his
paralysis, genuinely apologized (repented) for his racist views;

or to believe that as he saw the changing political tide and his diminishing voter base, he apologized to bolster his future political career.

Another apology that appears to be motivated primarily by career enhancement was offered by conservative author David Brock to Anita Hill, a former employee of current Supreme Court Justice Clarence Thomas and a major critic during Thomas's confirmation hearings. In writing a book highly critical of Anita Hill (*The Real Anita Hill*), Brock now admits that he fabricated material evidence, intimidated supporters of Anita Hill, suppressed evidence, and falsified the record.[41] As quoted by Howard Kurtz in a *Washington Post* article, Brock said, "I not only wrote a book I now believe was wrong, I consciously lied in print in a book review on the subject. I think I owe a debt to the historical record to correct it. If I made a mistake here, the mistake would be that I knew these facts five years ago and didn't disclose them."[42]

Brock now believes that writing a truthful book will redeem him. According to a National Public Radio interview, he says he sent Anita Hill an apology. He added, "My intention there was to reach a private reconciliation. It was a first step, essentially. I thought maybe it would be enough then—ease my conscience."[43] After Brock wrote another article, Hill phoned and left a voice mail message, but Brock said he "didn't have the guts to call her back at that point because I felt I could not handle . . . telling the truth totally because I would be admitting that the two things that I was most known for were both wrong, and I just didn't have the courage to do it."[44]

We can speculate as to why Brock confessed at this time. First, he knew that the statute of limitations protects him from slander claims that could have been brought against him based on his writings of 1994. Second, he recently announced the publication of a new book, *Blinded by the Right: The Conscience of an Ex-Conservative.* His confession, some believe, might increase the sale of the new book. Should we consider his various "confessions" a form of apology? Examining those remarks carefully, we find several indications that if he meant to offer a valid apology, he fell considerably short of the goal. For example, in the *Washington Post* article, he uses the conditional expression, ". . . if I made a mistake . . . ," suggesting that he is uncertain that he made a mistake. And the fact that he never spoke directly to Anita Hill suggests that he neither wanted to acknowledge fully the wrong he had done nor pay for his wrongdoing in the form of shame or suffering. Given these facts, the apology seems to be a bid for publicity rather than a sincere attempt to make amends.

A NEW UNDERSTANDING OR APPLICATION OF AN ETHICAL IDEAL

One set of examples of apologies motivated by newly recognized ethical ideals involves the behavior of children and adolescents as they transition to adulthood. A colleague shared with me a personal story of such an apology. She told me that she entered medical school when her son began kindergarten. Throughout childhood and adolescence, he continually berated her for not being a good mother. But recently, he began his first year of medical school, and now he is apologizing profusely and repeatedly to his mother for his childhood criticisms of her.[45] He is probably not the only adult child who would like to apologize to parents for all they put their parents through during adolescence.

The next apology that I believe fits the criteria of emerging out of a growing understanding of ethical ideals was offered by author Richard Reeves to President Gerald Ford in 1996 for writing a book highly critical of the president. Titled *A Ford, Not a Lincoln,* the 1975 book argued convincingly, with documentation, that Ford's pardon of President Nixon was part of a deal brokered by Alexander Haig, Nixon's chief of staff. A *New York Magazine* article that excerpted the book displayed a faked photo of Bozo the Clown in the Oval Office, with the headline "Ladies and Gentlemen, the President of the United States."[46]

Reeves's apology appeared in a 1996 *American Heritage* article entitled "I'm Sorry, Mr. President." He wrote of his book, "But it was . . . cruel, unnecessarily so. As a national leader President Ford was a man with many flaws and more inadequacies. But he had become President by accident, done the best he knew how, and, we now know, muddled through a very dangerous time."[47] Reeves explained that he now believes that Ford pardoned Nixon so that he could govern the nation, even though his move probably cost him the election. He also believes his book contributed to poisoning "the wells of democratic faith and our political dialogue"[48] by using a style of reporting that trashes politicians and that continues to this day. The article ended with Reeves's *mea culpa:* "I wish I had not been part of the problem, and perhaps I will find a way to be part of the solution. I'll begin by saying to Gerald Ford that I know he did his best and did what he thought he had to do: You have my respect and thanks, Mr. President."[49] Reeves's apology, appearing some 20 years after the publication of his book, suggests that in the interim, he had engaged in serious reflection about Ford and the context of his pardon of Nixon, as well as his own practice of journalism. Out of such reconsideration often comes wisdom and new apologies for old offenses, as it happened in this case.

The next illustration was an apology offered by Pope John Paul II in an apostolic letter urging, "the Roman Catholic Church to confess the sins its members may have committed over the last 2000 years. . . ."[50] The pope commented that the Roman Catholic Church "cannot cross the threshold of the new millennium without encouraging her children to purify themselves through repentance of past errors and instances of infidelity, inconsistency, and slowness to act."[51] He urged that the Church recall "all those times in history" when its members "indulged in ways of thinking and acting which were truly forms of counter witness and scandal."[52] The apology is only one in a long line of apologies from this pope, as documented in a book titled *When a Pope Asks Forgiveness: The Mea Culpas of John Paul II*. The 21 pronouncements and requests for forgiveness (for behaviors involving the Crusades, women, Jews, Galileo, the Inquisition, Islam, Martin Luther, the Mafia, racism, the history of the papacy, and blacks) indicate that John Paul II is a thoughtful student of history as well as a pope who is committed to discovering, acknowledging, and repenting, on behalf of the church's members, for past deviations from ethical ideals.[53]

The final illustration of an apology made possible by reflecting on past practice is the presidential response to the infamous "Tuskegee Experiments," during which the U.S. Public Health Service withheld treatment from 399 African American men between 1932 and 1972 in order to study the natural history of syphilis—how it spreads and kills. The men, who were recruited at churches with the promise of free medical care, were never told whether they had syphilis and received no treatment if they had the disease. Twenty-eight men died of syphilis and an additional 100 died of syphilis-related complications. Transmission of the disease to children and spouses also occurred.[54] A class-action lawsuit on behalf of the victims was settled in 1973 for $10 million.

In January 1996, a committee met at Tuskegee to consider a request for a formal apology and to assess whether human subjects of research currently received sufficient protection from risk of harm (that is, whether the research being done could be justified and whether the subjects who participate are giving truly informed, voluntary consent).[55] The committee consisted of Tuskegee University scholars, officials from the Centers for Disease Control, historians, and Macon County public health administrators. The next year, following pressure from the Black Congressional Caucus, together with considerable media attention, President Clinton offered an apology 25 years after the study had been declared inappropriate and terminated.[56] The apology, eloquently and passionately delivered, was a moral statement on behalf of the United States. Although it meant a great deal to the victims, this apology was diminished, at least in my eyes, on several counts. First, we need to ask, why did it take so long? Previous presidents had apologized to Japanese Americans for being interned during World War II. Secondly, what motivated the apology? Many people remained cynical, believing that the Tuskegee apology was politically motivated, perhaps offered as Clinton's bid for African American votes during the next campaign. And finally, President Clinton was apologizing for someone else's misdeeds, not his own, at a time when the nation wanted him to apologize for his own inappropriate actions. However, giving Clinton the full benefit of the doubt, this apology might have been offered because Clinton—or others in his administration—believed that the experiments were wrong, even though they had been accepted practice at an earlier time.

Some world grievances that occurred decades and centuries ago call for apologies that so far have not been forthcoming. In chapter 3, for example, I described the importance of acknowledging the genocide of Armenians by the Turks. Over two million Armenians from eastern Anatolia were forcibly deported by the Ottoman Empire. It is believed that one-third were massacred, one-third died after deportation, and one-third survived, totaling perhaps 1.5 million Armenians killed in what has been called the first modern genocide. (Adolf Hitler used this example as a precedent for his subsequent genocidal behaviors. "Who, after all," he declared, "speaks today of the annihilation of the Armenians?"[57]) I have met many American-born Armenians who now, more than eight decades after the event, continue to be pained by this massive human tragedy. Their desire is for validation by the Turkish government of what happened: Denial of the event is a denial of their history and their identity.[58] Perhaps someday their pleas will be answered and at least an acknowledgment of what occurred will be made by the Turkish government.

Japan, unlike Germany, has been reluctant to express apologies for various war atrocities its armies committed before and during World War II. These include the Nanking massacre, the surprise attack on Pearl Harbor, unnecessary cruelty to prisoners of war of Western nations, and the use of sex slaves from Asian nations. The growth of the Pacific Rim nations and Japan's economic need for positive trade relations with these countries are some of the forces exerting increasing pressure on Japan to apologize to these victims.

The Australian Aborigines, with a population of 400,000 are arguing for an official apology for "injustices suffered by aborigines over past generations."[59] The Aborigines are the most disadvantaged group in Australia in terms of life expectancy, infant mortality, and health and financial status. One of the most publicized offenses committed against the Aborigines was the forcible adoption of Aboriginal children by Caucasian Australians over a period of many decades. The nation is currently divided over its willingness to apologize.[60]

Closer to home, a growing consensus has been emerging since the end of the Vietnam War that the U.S. government's rationale for fighting was dubious and that the war seriously and unnecessarily damaged our nation and the Vietnamese people. In fact, many of our citizens now believe that our leaders deceived us, and that the 58,000 U.S. soldiers and 3 million Vietnamese were killed in vain. Many of the U.S. Vietnam veterans who were never welcomed home after the war are particularly bitter. I believe that it is likely, in the years to come, that the U.S. government will be called upon to apologize for our prolonged involvement in this war.

Although a significant reconciliation between the Roman Catholic Church and Jewish people has occurred, a complete apology for centuries of violence against the Jews has not yet been offered. Beginning with the Second Vatican Council in 1965, the church formally repudiated the idea of collective Jewish guilt for the crucifixion of Jesus and condemned anti-Semitism. The *Nostra Aetate* read, "The Church . . . decries the hatred, persecutions, and displays of anti-Semitism directed against the Jews at any time and by anyone."[61] From 1987 until the present, Pope John Paul II has been a firm advocate for such reconciliation.[62]

In 1998, the Vatican issued a long-awaited document on the Holocaust, titled *"We Remember: A Reflection on the Shoah."*[63] Many Roman Catholics and Jews hoped for an apology from the Church for its centuries-old behavior against the Jews, but it was not forthcoming. Jewish organizations want acknowledgment that it was not simply a group of deviant Christians but rather the Church itself, along with some of its popes, who were responsible for crimes against Jews.[64] Jewish organizations await a statement similar to the one made by the Evangelical Church of the Rhineland in 1980: "We confess that we as German Christians are also responsible and at fault for the Holocaust."[65]

Another example of an apology that might yet be forth-coming is an American apology for slavery. Demands for an apology for the slavery of African Americans gained significant momentum during the middle 1990s. Making this apology is problematic for a variety of reasons, and much discussion is still needed on issues such as defining who the victims are, and who has standing to make the apology, and agreeing about the nature and extent of reparations.[66] Yet without question, slavery was a blot on our nation's history and a challenge to our national pride. It remains, in my opinion, our most significant "unfinished business."

PERSONAL REFLECTIONS

Apologies that have been delayed for years, decades, and centuries have become more frequent and significant since the end of World War II. I believe that being aware of and receptive to delayed apologies can have great significance to those who have committed grievances but have not apologized, as well as to those who have been aggrieved and continue to nurse their grudges. Those who have committed grievances in the past, particularly those who suffer from guilt and shame and who want to restore damaged relationships, should consider making amends, regardless of how much time has passed. Those who have been wounded in the past and feel hemmed in by long-standing grudges may consider doing as Joe Frazier did: asking for an apology and offering forgiveness. For those of us who witness conflicts among our friends and relatives, perhaps our wise counsel can facilitate the apology process. I believe that the examples in this chapter illustrate how such apologies may be a significant source of emotional satisfaction to both parties. As we have seen, most of the recipients of such apologies are welcoming and grateful, not hostile and rejecting. Some of these apologies, of course, will fail; but these apologies, I believe, tend to be self-serving or fail to meet the standards for successful apologies described in earlier chapters.

Apologies by nations for old grievances inflicted upon ethnic groups, religious groups, and nations present challenges considerably more complex than apologies between two individuals. Part of the reason for this complexity is that many people who are called to apologize were not even born at the time of the grievance, or their ancestors were not in the country at the time the grievance occurred. They may say, "I am not guilty." "It was not my fault." "Why should I apologize and make reparations? I didn't harm those people." Many other questions arise. Who speaks for the nation? How do we decide who has the credentials to speak for the offending party and for the offended party? Who determines the membership of the offended party? How do we assess appropriate reparations? Despite these difficulties, however, I believe the apology process holds out a promise to us that is well worth the effort it requires: the prospect of restored respect, of healed relationships, of civility, and of a clearer sense of morality among individuals and nations who inhabit an ever-shrinking world.

TEN

Negotiating Apologies

For many years, I have been interested in studying and understanding the role of negotiation in human interactions. In the 1970s, I wrote that many physician-patient interactions are best understood as negotiated exchanges. For example, the doctor and patient commonly negotiate over what is wrong, the causes of the problem, the goals of treatment, the methods of treatment, and even the nature of their relationship. This analysis contradicted, or at least supplanted, the common belief at the time that the physician should always control the agenda while the patient should passively follow the physician's orders.[1] Today, experts who study the medical interview generally agree that a negotiated approach best describes what actually happens between physician and patient and is more likely to produce satisfaction for both parties and greater patient adherence to the treatment plan. In my view, the apology process shares several important characteristics with the medical encounter. Like the doctor-patient interaction, an apology is best understood not as what one party (the offender) does or offers to another party (the offended) but as a process in which both parties reach agreement through a "give and take" as a way to deal with the initial problem.

Much of the content of an apology is negotiable, such as: 1) who should apologize to whom; 2) how much responsibility the offender and offended each accepts for causing the grievance; 3) the specificity with which the offender acknowledges the offense; 4) whether mitigating explanations are acceptable; 5) how much remorse, shame, humility, and sincerity the offender must communicate; 6) the amount of suffering the offender must bear; 7) the acceptability of reparations to the offended parties; 8) the timing of the apology (when, how often, and how long the two parties must meet); 9) the opportunity of the offended parties to verbalize their suffering; and 10) the degree to which the offended parties are willing to accept that their needs have been adequately met so that they can offer forgiveness. The best negotiated apologies result in "win-win" situations for both parties, in contrast to a "zero-sum game" in which one party wins at the expense of the other.[2] Many times, the only way a relationship can continue after a serious offense has occurred is through an apology that results in both parties feeling they have gained something, or at least "enough," in the end.

The multitude of issues involved in such negotiations makes each apology a complex and unique event with an outcome not entirely anticipated at the start. I will illustrate many aspects of negotiated apologies, both public and private, in the stories that follow. I intend to show that understanding apology as a negotiation can be helpful to both the offender and the offended in effecting successful apologies. The stories will be presented in three groups: 1) negotiations between individuals, 2) negotiations between nations, and 3) negotiations between public figures and their constituencies.

NEGOTIATIONS BETWEEN INDIVIDUALS

The first example of a negotiated apology between individuals involves my administrator and administrative assistant as the offended parties, and myself as the offending party. Although both the administrator and administrative assistant report directly to me, the three of us work together in a collegial manner to accomplish the tasks of the office of chancellor/dean of a medical school.

As I was leaving work at the end of the day, my assistant told me that we were far behind in routine activities such as deciding between conflicting appointments and responding to various requests. My administrator, my assistant, and I all agreed to come to work early the next day so we could "catch up" before the official workday began. I forgot about our early morning meeting and arrived at work 40 minutes past the time we had agreed to meet. I cheerfully greeted my administrator and my assistant but noticed that they kept their backs to me while they muttered a cold "good morning." They soon reminded me of our appointment. Mortified by my lapse, I apologized profusely. (Days later, my assistant told me that she had never seen me look so ashamed. With scarcely concealed amusement, she informed me that I had been unable to look her in the eye.) I hoped my verbal apology, together with my nonverbal communication of shame and remorse, would be enough to earn forgiveness, but this outcome proved elusive. (At this point, although my initial apology was clearly unsuccessful, negotiations had begun.) Realizing that I needed to understand their view of the situation, I settled down to listen as they described the impact of my offense on them. They began by telling me what they sacrificed to come in early. My administrator, for example, told me that she had given up her early morning yoga session to keep our appointment. Despite my best efforts to respond empathetically to their accounts, tension persisted. (My enhanced apology was not sufficient and thus our negotiations were still incomplete.) My administrator wanted assurance that I had not knowingly ignored the meeting. I, in turn, felt wounded that she would even consider such a possibility and wondered if she wanted to hurt me. (Her request for clarification about my explanation for being late was another step in the negotiation. Still, no success.) I then offered to take both parties for lunch to make up for my oversight. (My attempt to offer reparations was another step in the negotiation.) They refused, saying that such an activity would only worsen the administrative backlog our morning meeting was supposed to have resolved. (So far, all of my efforts at negotiation had failed—verbal apology, expression of shame, listening to the impact of the offense, offer of reparation, reassurance of no disrespect intended.) Finally, as I passed their desks a few hours later, the administrator, smiling, said to the assistant, "I think he has suffered enough." (Our negotiations were now complete. They needed to know how distressed I was.) We joked about the episode for the rest of the day.

Several weeks later, I asked each of the offended parties to describe how they perceived our interactions. One of the offended parties said, "Since you are the boss, you could have said 'enough is enough' or 'let's just drop it,' but you would not let it go until we all felt better." The other party said, "The most important part of the interchange to me was your acknowledging that our personal time was as valuable as yours and that your missing the appointment was not intentional. Had it been intentional, our relationship of mutual respect would have been harmed."[3]

I view this apology as a successful negotiation in which mutual "give and take" occurred. I felt that a heartfelt verbal apology would suffice. They demanded much more, including confirmation that we shared common values about keeping appointments, assurance that they were not at fault, assurance that I respected their time, an opportunity to express what they had lost as a result of my offense, confirmation that I cared enough about them to offer tangible reparations, and proof that my oversight caused me distress. I could do no more. Had I offered less, our relationship would have lost something that makes our working relationship so effective and enjoyable.

The second illustration of a negotiated apology occurred between Judge Lance Ito and Assistant District Attorney Christopher A. Darden during the highly publicized murder trial of O. J. Simpson. Ito cited Darden for contempt of court because Darden had argued with the defense attorney at the judge's bench, out of hearing range of the jury. With the jury out of the room, Ito issued the contempt citation and then strongly suggested that Darden apologize. After initial reluctance, Darden agreed that his response may have been "somewhat inappropriate. . . . I apologize to the Court. I meant no disrespect."[4] The judge accepted Darden's apologies and added, "I apologize to you for my reaction as well. You and I have known each other for a number of years, and I know your response was out of character, and I'll note it as such."[5]

Judge Ito commanded District Attorney Darden to apologize, probably in an attempt to show he was "in charge" and to address what he perceived as disrespect. Darden offered a weak or failed apology, stating that it "appears" the court is correct and that his comments "may have been or are somewhat inappropriate." Even with such a flimsy apology, Ito was more than satisfied that Darden had demonstrated his respect for the court. The judge then declared that he had overreacted and had demanded too much from Darden. Ito concluded the negotiation by apologizing to Darden and offering reparation in the form of a comment that Darden's behavior was out of character. (Usually, it is the offending parties, in their own defense, who declare that a behavior is "out of character.") Ito's remarks suggest that he believed he had asked too much from Darden, thus unnecessarily or unfairly humiliating him.

In these two stories, the parties involved had good working relationships. All wanted and accepted a timely restoration of goodwill and respect. All participants came out of the negotiation with something they valued. I believe this kind of negotiated apology occurs frequently in everyday life. Often, the result is that the offended party echoes Judge Ito's sentiment, saying, in effect, "I appreciate your apology, but part of the fault is mine."

NEGOTIATIONS BETWEEN NATIONS

Negotiations between nations are similar to those between individuals in the sense that both parties want a "win-win" resolution within a reasonable amount of time. Nation-to-nation apologies are complicated, however, by differences in protocol, legal concerns, cultural and language differences, and the involvement of several parties on either side. The next four stories highlight the confounding effect of these added elements.

In the first story, during a routine training mission, the submarine USS *Greeneville* crashed into the Japanese fishing boat (used for training) *Ehime Maru,* which sank, resulting in the death of four teenage high school students and five crew members. The maneuver that caused the accident, an emergency surfacing procedure, was apparently performed as a demonstration for civilian guests onboard. At the conclusion of an administrative hearing (an "Admiral's mast"), Commander Scott Waddle received a "punitive letter of reprimand" from Admiral Thomas Fargo for "dereliction of duty" and "subjecting a vessel to hazard." Waddle was removed from command of his submarine and given a desk job. He resigned from the Navy with an honorable discharge and was allowed to keep his pension and other privileges.[6]

What did the aggrieved party, the Japanese, want from Waddle and the U.S. Navy? According to numerous reports from Japan, Hawaii, and the United States mainland, the Japanese, particularly the 26 survivors and the family members of the nine fatalities of the collision, wanted four things. First, they wanted a condolence visit from Waddle within a short period of time after the accident, during which he would go to the homes of the families of the deceased and personally apologize. Japanese custom demanded that the apology be sincere and that Waddle be in full dress uniform. Second, they wanted an explanation of what led to the accident. Third, they wanted the sunken fishing vessel raised and the remains of the deceased recovered. Finally, they wanted Waddle to receive appropriate punishment.[7]

Following the incident, a court of inquiry was conducted. Family members and a Japanese submarine admiral who witnessed the administrative hearings were not satisfied with the explanation of what happened and were disappointed with what they perceived as insufficient punishment.[8] As a negotiated apology, the U.S. response fell short on every count. Although apologies for the accident were offered by leaders of the U.S. government and the Navy, either in person or by message, the needs of the Japanese officials and the victims' families were not met. They wanted apologies from the person responsible, not from third parties.

Several weeks after the accident, Waddle released a quasi-apology through his lawyer's office. "It is with heavy heart that I express my most sincere regret to the Japanese people and most importantly, to the families of those lost and injured in the collision between the USS *Greeneville* and the *Ehime Maru*," Waddle's statement read. "No words can adequately express my condolences and concern for those who have lost their loved ones. I too grieve for the families and the catastrophic losses that the families have endured." He added that he hoped that the subsequent inquiry would "resolve the questions and uncertainties surrounding this tragedy. . . . It is my most sincere desire to determine the truth about what happened."[9] The Japanese were unconvinced. The brother of one of the victims commented, "Frankly speaking, at this stage, we don't know even if he wrote it [the quasi-apology described above]. We can't see him and we don't hear him. . . . It's so late, it does not convey his sincerity."[10] Others remarked that Waddle's statement failed to acknowledge responsibility for the accident and were angry that a court martial did not take place. In addition, the Japanese said the punishment is "absolutely not one that the families can accept."[11]

At the end of the hearing, Waddle said through his lawyer, "To those families, I again offer my most sincere apology and my hope that our government will promptly and fairly settle all claims made by the families against the United States."[12] Almost a month after the accident, Waddle, at last, met privately with families of the victims who came to Honolulu. He bowed deeply and apologized tearfully to them, and accepted responsibility for the accident. He also went to the Japanese consulate in Honolulu with 13 letters to the families, bowed deeply, and presented them to the Japanese vice minister. The vice minister said, "When Waddle handed the letters to me, tears fell from his eyes . . . Commander Waddle 'had used the word apology so I accepted it as an apology.'"[13]

After the legal proceedings began, Waddle promised he would visit the families in Japan to make formal apologies, saying he said he would come even if he had to row the boat. On December 15, 2002, 22 months after the fatal accident, Waddle, dressed in civilian clothes and accompanied by his lawyer, visited Japan. He visited a monument at the high school where four of the victims had been students, apologized to the four students who survived the crash, laid a wreath of white lilies on the high school grounds, and bowed in front of the nine pillars in memory of each of the victims. He read a message from a small piece of paper, said each dead person's name, heard the demands for an explanation from survivors, and offered a letter of apology to them. Later, the U.S. Navy compensated the survivors and families of the dead with $14 million.[14] The Japanese ultimately felt that what the United States and Waddle brought to the table was inadequate. They received the apology in person but not until 22 months after the offense, and even then, he was not in uniform.

The negotiations did not succeed because Commander Waddle initially refused to admit blame and responsibility for the death of nine Japanese citizens and also failed to meet with the family members of the deceased in Japan until 22 months later. Waddle holds the Navy responsible for restraining him from such travel.[15] The U.S. government failed in the eyes of many Japanese because they believed the facts of the case were seemingly withheld and because the U.S. government's punishment of Waddle was too lenient. I believe the United States could have done better. Not only is visiting the families of the deceased and apologizing to them in person in good time important in Japanese culture, it is also important in American culture.

Another international negotiation involved the U.S. government and North Korea. Chief Warrant Officer Bobby Hall, a U.S. helicopter pilot, crashed over North Korean air space on December 17, 1994. His copilot was killed in the accident. The North Korean government wanted the pilot and the U.S. government to admit that the helicopter was on a spying mission. According to an Associated Press story, U.S. officials did not want to antagonize the North Koreans or concede too much. They negotiated a lesser offense by expressing "sincere regret for the incident" and committing to work to prevent similar events.[16]

The Korean Central News Agency released a statement allegedly handwritten and signed by Hall. "I admit that this criminal action is inexcusable and unpardonable. However, at home my parents, wife and kids are anxiously waiting for my return to them. I only hope, and it is my desire, that the Korean People's Army will leniently forgive me for my illegal intrusion so that I may return to my home and be with my family again. . . . Our intrusion deep into the territorial air space of the Democratic People's Republic of Korea is a grave infringement upon the sovereignty of the D.P.R.K. and a flagrant violation of international law."[17]

Even in this statement, whether written under duress by the pilot or by the North Korean government, we see a negotiation. The action of the pilot is called a "criminal action" that is "inexcusable and unpardonable." The statement does not acknowledge that Hall was on a spying mission. In this apology, then, the United States admitted to more than it wanted and North Korea accepted less than it wanted. The negotiation was satisfactory enough to recover the missing pilot. Thirteen days after the accident, Bobby Hall walked to freedom.

The third negotiated apology between nations involved the U.S. government and the People's Republic of China. A U.S. reconnaissance spy plane collided with a Chinese F-8 jet in disputed air space off the coast of China. The Chinese jet apparently made several provocative approaches to the American plane, eventually clipping the American plane, and then broke apart and crashed. The 33-year-old Chinese pilot, Wang Wei, was killed. The American plane, damaged in the process, was forced to make an emergency landing at a Chinese military airfield on the island of Hainan. All 24 members of the American crew, unharmed, were detained by the Chinese government.[18]

In the ensuing negotiation, the U.S. government wanted to achieve several important goals: to recover both the hostages and the reconnaissance plane as soon as possible, to assign blame to China for allowing its jet plane to fly aggressively in neutral air space, and to maintain national dignity on the world stage. In opposition to this agenda, the goals of the Chinese government were to keep the U.S. spy plane for extended study, to extract an apology from the U.S. government, to embarrass the United States, and to ensure that in the future, the United States would keep a reasonable distance from China's mainland. Central to the negotiation were the diametrically opposed goals of China's desire for an apology and the U.S. desire to assign blame to China.

The Chinese government had as leverage their possession of the U.S. hostages and the spy plane. The American leverage included rebukes by U.S. allies (Britain, France, Brazil, and Canada); the threat of economic sanctions; possible disapproval of China's 2008 Olympic bid; a U.S. weapons deal with Taiwan; and the possibility of moving the aircraft carrier *Kitty Hawk* close to Hainan.

In the end, the United States followed the negotiating strategy devised by Secretary of State Colin Powell of dividing the goals into two parts. The first was the return of all 24 U.S. crewmembers, a goal that was particularly important to U.S. citizens. The second was the return of the plane and continuing U.S. surveillance of the Chinese. It was the first part of the goals that resulted in the negotiated apology. After several exchanges between the two governments, U.S. ambassador Joseph Prueher sent the following letter to the Chinese Minister of Foreign Affairs Tang. China responded by returning the 24 hostages to the United States.

On behalf of the United States government, I now outline steps to resolve this issue.

Both President Bush and Secretary of State Powell have expressed their *sincere regret* over your missing pilot and aircraft. Please convey to the Chinese people and the family of pilot Wang Wei that we are *very sorry* for their loss.

Although the full picture of what transpired is still unclear, according to our information, our severely crippled aircraft made an emergency landing after following international emergency procedures. We are *very sorry* the entering of China's air space and the landing did not have verbal clearance, but very pleased the crew landed safely. We appreciate China's efforts to see to the well being of our crew.

In view of the tragic incident and based on my discussions with your representative, we have agreed to the following actions: Both sides agree to hold a meeting to discuss the incident. My government understands and expects that our aircrew will be permitted to depart China as soon as possible. The meeting would start April 18, 2001. The meeting agenda would include discussion of the causes of the incident, possible recommendations whereby such collisions could be avoided in the future, development of a plan for prompt return of the EP-3 aircraft, and other related issues. We acknowledge your government's intention to raise U.S. reconnaissance missions near China in the meeting." [19] (Italics added.)

The ultimate resolution of the conflict between the two nations involved a series of negotiations that went beyond the scope of the letter to Tang. On the U.S. side, the ambassador, not the president or other high officials, offered the written statement. (China undoubtedly would have preferred to receive the "apology" from an official with higher status.) Furthermore, the United States acknowledged both the loss of the Chinese aircraft and its pilot, and entry into Chinese air space and landing without permission. However, the letter stopped short of accepting blame, offering instead empathic expressions such as "very sorry" and "sincere regret."

On the other hand, the Chinese detained the crew for 11 days, making the United States appear helpless. During that time, they were able to study the U.S. spy plane in considerable detail, thus gaining access to U.S. intelligence information. They portrayed the United States' empathic "very sorry" as an acknowledgment of blame, with the state run news agency Xinhua reporting that this admission of blame, together with Chinese generosity, was the reason for the release of the American hostages. "As the U.S. government has said, 'very sorry' to the Chinese people," the agency stated, "the Chinese government has, out of humanitarian considerations, decided to allow the crew members to leave China."[20] The state-run *People's Daily* similarly reported, "the firm struggle by the Chinese government and people against U.S. hegemony has forced the U.S. government to change from its initial rude and unreasonable attitude to saying 'very sorry' to the Chinese people."[21]

The United States received less than it wanted, which was the immediate return of the plane and its crew. The Chinese received less than they wanted, which was presumably an apology from a higher official than the ambassador, the U.S. acceptance of blame, and a U.S. commitment to discontinue reconnaissance flights near the Chinese coast. The language of the letter to Tang was interpreted very differently by the two governments: The United States declared that it did not apologize, while the Chinese declared that the United States did apologize.

The final illustration of a negotiation involving an apology between nations is the Trent Affair, a diplomatic crisis between the United States and Great Britain that occurred during the first year of the American Civil War. I include this example because it provides some historical perspective on negotiated apologies between nations.

Captain Charles D. Wilkes, commanding the U.S. gunboat *San Jacinto*, stopped a British mail steamer 300 miles east of

Havana. His men boarded the ship and took as hostage two Confederate diplomats and their secretaries, whose mission was to enlist Great Britain in the war against the North. Wilkes, who had "a well-deserved reputation for insubordination and ill temper,"[22] had no authorization from the U.S. government for his actions. Furthermore, the act of removing the passengers and the circumstances surrounding the event were eventually regarded by both parties, as well as other countries, as a violation of international law.

Because the North had been losing ground in the war, the seizure of the prisoners and their transfer to Fort Warren in Massachusetts received great acclaim: Wilkes was even honored by the Massachusetts House of Representatives. At the same time, the British government perceived the event as an "outrage on the British flag," an intolerable insult.[23] According to historian Gordon H. Warren, London "crackled with anger"[24] and the citizens were frantic with rage. The official British government dispatch requested that the United States free the four Confederates and apologize for the U.S. insult to Great Britain.[25] At the same time, Great Britain embarked its troops to Canada in preparation for war with the United States should negotiations prove unsuccessful.

As with most international negotiations, the leader or spokesperson for each nation has the benefit of hearing multiple voices within the government as well as informal communications from the other side. With the help of such input, the decision to avoid war prevailed on all sides. The United States agreed to return the hostages while acknowledging that Capt. Wilkes acted without authorization. In addition, the United States suggested that the maritime law they were acknowledging owed its source to a position previously espoused by President

James Madison. No formal apology was offered, but U.S. concessions appear to have met the spirit of an apology.[26] In effect, the United States saved face by dissociating itself from the offense while making reparations without a formal apology. The British refrained from mobilizing troops and accepted the U.S. gestures as adequate concessions in order to preserve their honor.

NEGOTIATED APOLOGIES FROM PUBLIC FIGURES TO THEIR CONSTITUENCIES

In this third group of negotiated apologies, the offenders are public figures whose behaviors threaten to compromise their stature with their constituency.

The first example of such a negotiated apology involved Joseph J. Ellis, a Pulitzer Prize-winning author and professor of history at Mt. Holyoke College. His offense was fabricating Vietnam War experiences and exaggerating his participation in anti-war activities. His initial apology (see chapter 5), issued by his attorney, was: "Even in the best of lives, mistakes are made. I deeply regret having let stand and later confirming the assumption that I went to Vietnam. For this and any other distortions about my personal life, I want to apologize to my family, friends, colleagues and students. . . ."[27] This apology had three major flaws: It may not have recognized the full list of offended parties, it suggested that there were "other distortions" that he did not specify, and it lacked humility. His first offering must have been perceived by his constituency as inadequate since his attorney offered a second apology two months later. In this negotiated apology, Professor Ellis adds to his list of offended parties Vietnam veterans "who have expressed their understandable anger," and he explicitly characterized the offense as a "lie" and a violation of "the implicit covenant of trust that must exist in the classroom."[28] He further characterized his behavior as "both stupid and wrong," and removed the less-than-humble sentence, "Even in the best of lives, mistakes are made" as well as the provocative comment that he is apologizing "for this and any other distortions about my personal life." There are two other items in the second apology that might have offended some people: The first is that by announcing that he would take a sabbatical and write another book, he made it seem that he was being rewarded for his behaviors; and the second is that he delivered the apology in a written statement through his lawyer, rather than in person. All things considered, however, I suspect most people would regard the second apology as the outcome of a successful negotiation.

The next story begins with Senator Trent Lott announcing at a birthday party for 100-year-old Senator Strom Thurmond, "I want to say this about my state: When Strom Thurmond ran for president, we voted for him. . . . If the rest of the country had followed our lead, we wouldn't have had all these problems."[29] The media did not comment on Lott's remark for several days. Then the story exploded: Newspapers, magazines, and TV shows seized on its racist overtones, since Thurmond had previously campaigned for the presidency with a segregationist platform. The inference drawn was that Lott wished to return to the days of segregation and that Thurmond's election to the presidency would have prevented the racial problems that the nation had subsequently experienced.

Lott eventually apologized, saying, "A poor choice of words conveyed to some the impression that I embraced the discarded policies of the past. Nothing could be further from the truth, and I apologize to anyone who was offended by my statement."[30]

I believe that this apology fails on several counts. First, Lott tells us that the offense was his choice of words, not the meaning of his words, a claim many people doubted. Second, his apology is directed at "anyone who was offended," leaving open the possibility that only a few people had actually been offended by his remarks. Finally, the apology shows very little explanation, remorse, or reparation, suggesting that Lott did not take the alleged offense seriously. However, the public furor over his comments did not end. Two days later he made a second apology in a written statement and on a radio interview.

In this apology, Lott said repeatedly that the comments were "a mistake of the head—and not the heart . . . poorly chosen and insensitive . . . I regret the way it has been interpreted."[31]

Soon afterward, during a speech to a multiracial audience, President Bush rebuked Senator Lott for his statements, in effect, apologizing to the nation for Lott's comments. Bush declared that Lott's statements, "do not reflect the spirit of our country. . . . Any suggestions that the segregated past was acceptable or positive is offensive, and it is wrong. . . . Every day our nation was segregated was a day that America was unfaithful to our founding ideals."[32]

Taken as an apology, the president's words were very powerful. Addressing the entire nation as the offended party, Bush clearly stated the nature of the offense—"the segregated past"—and called it a moral violation of the "founding ideals of the nation." By offering a better apology, Bush humiliated the man who had stumbled so badly with his own words of regret. Not only was the president attempting to salvage the dignity of his party with the prestige of the presidency, but he was also publicly showing the nation that he had lost confidence in Lott's judgment and commitment to American ideals.

Senator Lott apologized yet again several days later during a televised news conference in Pascagoula, Mississippi. He read a prepared statement and took questions. The heart of his apology is contained in the first few paragraphs: "Segregation is a stain on our nation's soul. . . . I grew up in an environment that condoned policies and views that we now know were wrong and immoral. . . . I will dedicate myself to undo the hurt I have caused."[33]

Viewed from the perspective of a negotiation, it is clear that Lott repeatedly increased his offering to the public under the watchful eye of President Bush and the Republican Party. The negotiation ultimately failed, in part because Lott lost all credibility in the early stages (first by denying he had even committed an offense and then by arguing he had been misunderstood), and in part because the president withdrew his support. Lott's final offering might have succeeded as an apology had he not shown his "true colors" first. His statement acknowledges "the hurt I have caused" and pledges to work for "a society where every American has an opportunity to succeed." However, the gap between this statement of contrition and his initial arrogance was too large and took too long and too many attempts to bridge. Viewing the apology process as a negotiation might prevent offenders from opening with a position that dooms the process before it ever begins.

In the negotiated apologies described previously in this chapter, the challenge of the offender and the offended was to propose an apology that would meet the needs of both parties. The next story illustrates how the apology itself, as opposed to other outcomes, became the instrument of the successful negotiation.

General George S. Patton, Jr., widely regarded as the most successful field commander in the European Theater during World War II, slapped two soldiers who were patients in evacuation hospitals in Sicily during August 1943.[34] This was a court martial offense that almost resulted in his removal from command by his superior, General Dwight D. Eisenhower.

General Patton was described as flamboyant, profanely outspoken, of a volatile temperament, and prone to posturing and exhibitionism. To many generals (not under his command), congressmen, and members of the press, he was a highly controversial figure.

After a successful but exhausting campaign, Patton visited the field hospitals to greet his wounded soldiers. At one hospital, he came across a private who had no visible wounds, in contrast to other soldiers around him who were bloodied and crippled. The soldier acknowledged to Patton that he was not wounded but that he just couldn't take it.

An enraged Patton called the soldier a coward, ordered him out of the tent, and slapped him in the face. The soldier later developed a temperature of 102.2 degrees and a case of dysentery and malaria.[35]

A second soldier suffered Patton's wrath during a visit to another field hospital. Patton found the soldier shivering on his cot. He responded to Patton's query about his condition with "It's my nerves." Patton, shaking with anger, called him a coward and told him he should be shot. He then slapped the soldier numerous times and with such force that his helmet lines were knocked loose. Later in the day, following the second slapping event, Patton bragged to his immediate subordinate about what he had done and justified his behavior by his belief that the slap would make the soldier mad in order to cause him to fight back.

These events soon came to the attention of Eisenhower, a man who, besides being an excellent military strategist, was widely known for his interpersonal skills of humility, amiable personality, and ability to compromise and develop a consensus between strong personalities in conflict. With respect to these traits, Eisenhower was the antithesis of Patton.

Patton received a letter from Eisenhower in which Eisenhower demanded that Patton make an apology to the soldiers he had slapped, and to all divisions of the Seventh Army, and promise not to repeat such behavior. At the same time that Eisenhower received the report about Patton's slapping the soldiers, several reporters heard and confirmed the story through informal sources and asked to meet with Eisenhower. At their meeting, Eisenhower shared with them his unofficial reprimand to Patton together with his order for him to apologize and asked the correspondents to refrain from publishing the story in order to keep Patton on the battlefield.

Eisenhower's stroke of genius was to ask Patton to apologize. It was a punishment that would teach Patton a lesson; quiet the reporters; and give the soldiers, medical corps, and reporters the satisfaction of seeing Patton humiliated. It would also provide "cover" for Eisenhower, showing his superiors, particularly Army Chief of Staff George C. Marshall, that he was conscientiously performing his duties. In effect, Patton's apology eliminated the pressure to relieve him of his duties, thereby preserving him for future combat.

Patton had no regret or remorse for slapping the soldiers. He was remorseful only for alienating Eisenhower. He was regretful only that he was in trouble. His singular desire was to return to combat and assume his role in history as a great leader. "I regret the incident as I hate to make Ike mad when it is my earnest study to please him."[36]

His letter to Eisenhower, personally delivered on August 29, was more a justification or an *apologia* than an apology for the behaviors in question. He began by thanking Eisenhower for his fairness and expressing his chagrin for causing him displeasure. Patton explained that his only desire was to restore in the soldiers "a just appreciation of their obligation as men and soldiers."[37]

From the letter, we see again that Patton saw his offense not as slapping the soldiers but as upsetting Eisenhower. He not only offered an explanation for the slap—an attempt to mitigate the slapping offense—but he also explained it away. The slap, according to Patton, had only a positive intent, to save the characters of these soldiers. Patton fulfilled his obligation to Eisenhower by making a series of pseudo-apologies.

In sum, we have an apology delivered without remorse and full of self-righteous justification, behaviors on the part of Patton that were offensive to some parties. This put Eisenhower in the difficult position of having to dismiss or court martial his most effective general when the nation's highest priority was winning the war. His alternative to dismissing Patton was to humiliate him by demanding an apology. Eisenhower, however, could say to all those concerned that he adequately punished his general.

Apologies, genuine or not, can be effective (or regarded as successful) when the offender is humiliated and the offended has their dignity restored. This was the case with the Patton apology. Respect for medical patients and medical facilities was restored by Patton's apologies. Even more important, the other offended parties—reporters, legislators, and the American public—took satisfaction in seeing Patton punished. In their minds, justice was served. We have, therefore, a fraudulent apology, that was the culmination of a successful apology. The apology became the negotiated punishment.

THE VALUE OF UNDERSTANDING APOLOGIES AS NEGOTIATIONS

During the question-and-answer period following a lecture I gave on the subject of apology, one of the participants asked: "I made a good apology to an acquaintance who responded that my apology was unsatisfactory. Well, that ended our relationship. What do you suggest?" Having learned from this chapter, I told the participant that apologies are negotiations and that he is just beginning this one. If I had more time during the question-and-answer period, I would have suggested that he should try to explore what the offended party wants and needs. "Find out whether you fully understand the meaning of the offense. Has the offended party had an opportunity to tell you how upset the offense made her or him feel? Does the offended party need more time to assimilate what happened? Are reparations required? Were yours appropriate? Do you feel humbled and remorseful? Was your apology offensive in any way?" All of these questions suggest possible areas for negotiation between both parties. Only when the offender is unwilling to offer what the offended believes are minimal conditions for acceptance can we say the apology failed.

Elazar Barkan comments in the *Guilt of Nations: Restitution and Negotiating Historical Injustices*, "An apology doesn't mean the dispute is resolved, but it is in most cases a first step, part of the process of negotiation but not the satisfactory end result. Often, lack of apologies, demands for apologies, and the refusal of them all are pre-steps in negotiations, a diplomatic dance that may last for a while, a testimony to the wish and the need of both sides to reach the negotiations stage."[38]

ELEVEN

Apology and Forgiveness

I find it interesting that so many books and newspaper stories have been written in recent years on the subject of forgiveness, while comparatively few have been written about apology. It suggests that people in general would rather forgive or be forgiven than apologize or receive apologies. But this preference is based on a misperception and idealized view of the forgiveness process. According to this view, when we are forgiven by another, we often understand this experience as a consequence of the generosity and grace of another party (whether God or man). We experience forgiveness as a gift that releases us from the twin burdens of guilt and shame. In addition, if we are the ones doing the forgiving, we are proud of our generous behavior in forgiving the offending party. We had the power to forgive and we used that power benevolently. As if these gifts of forgiving were not enough, behavioral psychologists now tell us that forgiving contributes to a person's mental and physical health.[1] In contrast to this idealized view, forgiveness, as serious books on the subject tell us, is an extremely difficult task. As I will illustrate in this chapter, there are many people who cannot forgive under any circumstances or who forgive only following a meaningful and demanding apology.

By contrast, the apology process is accurately perceived as hard work. Two parties must participate in an interaction at high risk of producing discomfort: the offender, in the position of a supplicant who exposes weaknesses and risks rejection or retaliation; and the offended party, who may be uncomfortable with the other person's embarrassment or may be reluctant to relinquish a treasured grudge or even admit being hurt. Thus, the entire process of offering, negotiating, or accepting an apology can be emotionally demanding for both parties. Given a choice between the seemingly positive experience of forgiveness and the arduous and often uncomfortable process of apology, who wouldn't prefer forgiveness? In this chapter, I will argue that we cannot choose between apology and forgiveness because they are inextricably bound together.

APOLOGY, REPENTANCE, AND FORGIVENESS

Although this book deals primarily with secular relationships, in this chapter, I will frequently turn to various religious traditions, the source of a wealth of psychological wisdom on apology as well as forgiveness. The discussions in religion that refer to apology are most often found under the topic of "repentance," a subject closely related to and often used synonymously with apology. Apology, as I have explained throughout the book, is the acknowledgment of an offense followed by an expression of remorse and, commonly, expressions of shame and acts of reparations. "Repentance," in Judaism, Christianity,

and Islam, refers to a turning away from evil and sin and a
returning to righteousness or to God, not because of a single sin
but because of a sinful way of life.[2] This turning away can be
abrupt, as in conversion experiences, or it can consist of a series
of smaller movements in the correct direction.[3] Sincere apologies can be viewed as manifestations, mechanisms, or steps to
repentance. Religious authorities commonly describe the process of repentance in language similar or even identical to the
descriptions of apology in chapters 4 and 5. For example,
Maimonides, a twelfth-century Jewish scholar, carefully details
the steps of repentance as including confession, humility,
remorse, forbearance, and reparation, behaviors that also apply
to apology.[4] A contemporary Christian scholar, Harvey Cox,
professor at the Harvard Divinity School, suggests four essential
components of repentance: remorse (an acknowledgment of
the harm done together with being genuinely sorry for such
deeds), resolution (determination not to repeat the offending
behaviors), restitution (taking modest steps toward restoring
what has been damaged), and restoration ("full integration into
the human community").[5] Having established the close relationship of sincere apology to manifestations of repentance in
the writings of Maimonides and Cox, I will use these terms
interchangeably in the remainder of this chapter, bearing in
mind that "repentance" is generally used in religious contexts
while "apology" is generally used in secular contexts.

Forgiveness can refer to three different kinds of relationships: the interpersonal or social forgiveness between two
parties, a person's forgiveness of him or herself, and God's
forgiveness. This chapter will consider primarily forgiveness
between two parties. The customary meaning of forgiveness between two parties is a process by which the offended

party or victim relinquishes grudges, feelings of hatred, bitterness, animosity, or resentment toward the offender. In addition, the person who forgives forgoes wishes and plans for retaliation, revenge, and claims for restitution. Some writers include in the definition of forgiveness attitudes of compassion, generosity, and even love toward the offender.[6] Forgiveness is, therefore, both a cognitive and an emotional process, a change of mind and heart on the part of the victim toward the wrongdoer. It is, in addition, a voluntary act that cannot be forced on the victim. Forgiveness is not the same as forgetting, because one must remember the offense in order to forgive. Forgiveness also differs from "pardon," which is a legal or administrative act that may reduce the formal punishment of the offender. When Pope John Paul II forgave the man who attempted to assassinate him, he did not recommend pardoning him from his jail sentence. That judgment was left to the authorities.

There can be varying degrees of forgiveness, so that even a forgiving person who feels renewed positive feelings of empathy, caring, and generosity toward another may also harbor remnants of anger and bitterness. The degree of forgiveness may be related to the seriousness of the offense, the quality of the apology, and the forgiving nature of the victim.

RELATIONSHIPS BETWEEN
APOLOGY (REPENTANCE) AND FORGIVENESS

In order to provide some clarity to the complex relationship between apology and forgiveness, I organize these interactions into four distinct but familiar categories: 1) forgiveness without apology; 2) no forgiveness regardless of the apology; 3)forgiveness that precedes apology; and 4) apology that precedes forgiveness. I believe these categories encompass the way people think about apology and forgiveness. Some people behave predominantly according to one of these categories (e.g., "I never forgive" or "I always forgive," or "I only forgive after I receive an apology"), while others behave according to any one of these categories at different times depending on the nature of the offense and the offender. Each category has its relevance to secular as well as religious teaching and practice.

FORGIVENESS WITHOUT APOLOGY

We all know of situations in which offended parties forgive without receiving an apology. If such interactions have not occurred in our own lives or those of friends, we may have read about them in newspaper articles that feature the uniqueness or nobility of such actions. The circumstances of these interactions vary. Sometimes the offenders are unwilling to acknowledge obvious offenses. Other times, they may believe they had a right to act as they did and that the alleged victims deserved the alleged offenses. In other situations, the offenders may no longer be alive, or their whereabouts may be unknown. Common examples of such interactions in everyday life are adults whose abusive parents died before they were reconciled. In both these situations, the offended parties forgive in order to be freed from anger, resentment, and grudges. In still other situations, the offended parties "forgive" to avoid hearing apologies that may be too painful to bear or that threaten to strengthen or restore the relationships that they wish to avoid.

In such circumstances where there are no apologies, reconciliation is unlikely. The offended party is saying, in effect, "I no longer hate you. Sometimes I even wish you well. But I do not want you in my life or my thoughts because I cannot trust you not to hurt me again." We refer to this interaction as forgiveness without reconciliation. Or they may be saying, "You made me miserable while you were alive. I am not going to let you torment me from your grave. I will try to remember the good part of our relationship. Rest in peace."

This notion of forgiving without an apology is more complex than it first appears. Consider the following. First, a moral critic may argue that forgiving an offense without an apology is tantamount to reinforcing immoral behavior, since the offender experiences no sanction for bad behavior. Second, forgiving without an apology may be a way for the victim to avoid a sometimes unpleasant confrontation with the offender over asking for and receiving an apology that may be necessary for restoring the relationship. Third, forgiving others without letting them know they have been forgiven may be regarded as self-centered behavior. The forgiving person is only taking care of him or herself, an act involving only one person. In sum, forgiving without an apology, except when the offender is deceased, may be an easy way out of a difficult situation in which so much more could have been accomplished.

NO FORGIVENESS WITH OR WITHOUT AN APOLOGY

How are we to understand people who will not forgive regardless of the presence of an apology? To those of us offering a good-faith apology, we may feel bewildered, thwarted, frustrated, rejected, and even humiliated when forgiveness is not forthcoming. In such cases, we should first consider whether our apology was inadequate or even insulting. We have seen how easy it is to offer an apology that is unsuccessful. When an apology fails, we should ask ourselves if it in fact has met the important needs of the offended party. If this approach does not explain why our apology failed, we can tactfully ask the offended party why he or she is still angry or hurt and respond accordingly, when we believe such comments are valid.

The problem of not forgiving may have nothing to do with the apology itself but with the meaning of forgiveness to the offended party. For instance, forgiving may cause multiple fears in the offended party: fear of appearing weak, giving in, being an easy mark, being prone to being taken advantage of, or letting the offender off too easily. The offended party may not want to acknowledge that the offender had the power to hurt, and forgiving is an acknowledgment of that power. The offended party can avoid having to forgive by denying that an offense even occurred. The offended party says, in effect, "There is no need for you to apologize. It was nothing. There is nothing to forgive."

Just as forgiving makes some people feel weak, harboring or nursing a grudge makes some people feel strong. Until some resolution is reached, the offended party continues to have power over the offended. Perhaps it is somehow pleasurable to be able to remind the offender of his failings. Or else, the offended party feels that the offending party has not yet suffered enough, and so withholds forgiveness until the score is evened. It may also be that giving up the grudge and forgiving means that now the relationship is restored, with all its earlier problems and demands.

Another reason for refusing to forgive, regardless of the apology, may be the offended party's belief that the offense is too great to forgive and that reparations can never replace what was lost, such as damage to a person's reputation, irreversible physical damage to the victim, or loss of life of a loved one. In situations in which a third party has been damaged, the person from whom forgiveness is required may feel he or she does not have the standing or moral right to forgive. For example, consider slavery, genocide, or other third-party injuries. In these cases, the loss is so great that we believe only the victim or God has the right to forgive.

To summarize the reasons why people fail to forgive despite antecedent apologies are, 1) the apology fails to meet the needs of the offended party; 2) forgiveness makes the offended party feel weak, whereas harboring the grudge provides the offended party with the sense of strength; and 3) the offense is regarded as too great to forgive or the forgiveness belongs to the victims or to God.

FORGIVENESS FOLLOWED BY APOLOGY

In the third kind of relationship between forgiveness and apology, the offended party initially forgives, or partially forgives, with the hope and expectation that repentance will follow. Christian theologian L. Gregory Jones describes this position in a religious context: ". . . we are forgiven of our sin so that we can learn to become holy through lifelong repentance and forgiveness."[7] In other words, forgiveness of a person who sins will lead to repentance. Jones adds a cautionary note: ". . . what seems to be virtually unthinkable—namely, to find unrepentant Christians, who assume that God's forgiveness can be received without any cost—has happened and continues to happen all too frequently."[8] Christian theologian Donald W. Shriver, Jr., past president of the Union Theological Seminary, shares this view of the relationship of forgiveness and apology. He comments that the act of forgiveness and reconciliation "is paved simultaneously with corresponding steps of repentance, all of which intertwine like eight matching strands of cable. A party offered forgiveness matches the offer with repentance, with gratitude that revenge is not in the offing, with counter-empathy for victims' suffering, and with hope that reconciliation is now possible."[9] Shriver warns us that forgiveness, like other changes in human affairs, takes time.

If we extrapolate this theological position to common behaviors of secular life, a person who is offended has the opportunity to bypass grudges and vengeance and preserve the relationship in some positive ways, while still expressing criticism of the offender. It is also possible to acknowledge hurt feelings and not feign compassion and love. This partial or tentative forgiveness allows the offended party to maintain a position of holding the offender accountable while giving the latter the opportunity to apologize. I call this forgiveness "partial" because, unlike full forgiveness, the negative impact of the offense is not automatically transformed into positive feelings toward the offender.

We see such partial forgiveness followed by apologies in relationships between nations and between groups within nations. Germany, after a devastating defeat in World War II, was treated by the Allies with generosity and respect. Such partial forgiveness was rewarded in subsequent decades by profound statements of repentance and substantial reparations. In the Truth and Reconciliation Commission of South Africa, political criminals were pardoned for their offenses, including mass murder, in return for telling the truth about their criminal activities. Some of these political criminals subsequently apologized and some were spontaneously forgiven by their victims in return for the gift of learning what happened to the victims' loved ones (see chapter 3).

The most common example of such forgiveness in family life is the relationship between parents and adolescents who experience prolonged and difficult rebellious states. I have seen several such situations in which these parents feel humiliated, enraged, helpless, defeated, and even hateful. Through all of this, they communicate some degree of tolerance, love, and forgiveness as they wait hopefully for months and years for signs of maturity. In all the situations with which I am familiar (including a situation in our own family), apologies and reconciliation eventually occurred. Friends in Northern Maine consoled us by saying, "Some day she'll get over fool's hill." Often the apology comes when the teenagers have children of their own (hopefully several years later) who inflict the same suffering on them that they inflicted on their parents. They finally appreciate what they put their parents through and offer meaningful apologies. Their parents receive some satisfaction (retributive justice) in seeing their children undergo the same suffering they endured, a phenomenon referred to as "grandparent's revenge."

I offer three illustrations of forgiveness that precedes apology, two from real life and one from literature. In all three, I believe there is a suggestion of a causal relationship between forgiveness and apology. In the first illustration, Steven Cook accused Cardinal Joseph Bernadin in 1993 of sexually abusing him sometime between 1975 and 1977, while Cook was a teenage seminary student and the cardinal was the archbishop of Cincinnati.[10] Cook simultaneously filed a lawsuit for $10 million against the cardinal and other members of the archdiocese. The cardinal denied the charges while making it clear how humiliated, hurt, and deeply wounded he felt. After a federal judge subsequently dismissed the lawsuit and Mr. Cook dropped the charges, the cardinal arranged a meeting with Cook. The Cardinal began by telling Cook that he requested the meeting to bring "closure to the traumatic events of last winter by personally letting him know that I harbored no ill feelings toward him," [11] and added that he would pray for Cook's physical and spiritual well-being. Cook then apologized for the embarrassment and hurt he had caused. The cardinal found the apology "simple, direct, and deeply moving."[12] He gave a Bible and a chalice to Cook, who received these objects with tears in his eyes. The cardinal later commented, "Never in my 43 years as a priest have I witnessed a more profound reconciliation."[13] He later told Cook, ". . . in every family there are times when there is hurt, anger, alienation. But we cannot run away from our family. We have only one family so we must make every effort to be reconciled."[14] Cook told the cardinal before they parted ways, "a big burden had been lifted from him. He felt healed and was at peace."[15]

In the next illustration, the mother of a murder victim offered forgiveness to one of the murderers, conditional on his repentance. In 1922, three right-wing German terrorists assassinated Walter Rathenau, a Jewish Reich Minister of Foreign Affairs for Germany. It was widely believed that anti-Semitism was a motive for the murder. Two of the terrorists were captured and committed suicide before they could go to trial. The remaining terrorist was Ernst Werner Techow, a 21-year-old man from a distinguished family. After being turned over to the authorities by his relatives, he stood trial and was sentenced to 15 years in prison.[16] Within days after the murder, Rathenau's mother wrote the following letter to Techow's mother: ". . . Say to your son that in the name and spirit of him he has murdered, I forgive, even as God may forgive, if before an earthly judge he make a full and frank confession of his guilt and before a heavenly one repent. . . . May these words give peace to your soul."[17] These words were read in court.

When Techow was released five years later for good behavior, he immediately enlisted in the Foreign Legion, became a naturalized French citizen in 1934, and was decorated for his military activities which included capturing 24 Nazis. While still in the Foreign Legion, he met a nephew of Rathenau and told him that the letter from Rathenau's mother was his most valued possession. As a result of this letter, according to Techow, he read the writings of Rathenau while in prison, and after his release, studied Hebrew and became a scholar of Jewish culture. He subsequently learned that the Nazis excused their barbaric behaviors toward Jews through lies and acknowledged that he was obsessed by the same. He spoke of his internal struggles over the evil in his soul during the 18 years following the assassination. He then told Rathenau's nephew how much he admired Frau Rathenau for conquering herself in writing the letter to Techow's mother and expressed the hope that he could make up, in some way, for his past behavior. After the Armistice between France and Germany in 1940, Techow resigned from the Foreign Legion and found his way to Marseilles where he helped over 700 Jews escape to Spain.[18] Thus, Frau Rathenau's forgiveness had at last borne its fruits.

The final illustration comes from an early episode in Victor Hugo's *Les Misérables*, the French classic novel in which Jean Valjean, the hero of the story, is released from a 19-year sentence in prison for stealing a loaf of bread and repeated escape attempts.[19] After falling on hard times shortly after his discharge, he spends a night's lodging at a bishop's home and departs before dawn, taking the bishop's silver with him. Shortly after breakfast at the bishop's home, three gendarmes appear at the door with Valjean. He apparently had told the authorities that the bishop had given him the silver. The bishop confirms Valjean's alibi and then tells Valjean that, in addition to the silver the gendarmes discovered, he also had intended for him to have the silver candlesticks that he forgot to take. The bishop then hands Valjean the candlesticks and sends him on his way, but not before saying, "Forget not, never forget that you have promised me to use this silver to become an honest man. . . . Jean Valjean, my brother: you belong no longer to evil, but to good. It is your soul that I am buying for you. I withdraw it from dark thoughts and from the spirit of perdition, and I give it to God!"[20] The rest of the book is the unfolding of Valjean's repentance. He becomes the owner of a factory, the mayor of a town, the adoptive father of a young orphaned girl born out of wedlock, and a person dedicated to helping those in need, prepared to sacrifice himself for moral causes.

In all three examples, forgiveness precedes and presumably causes apology: Steven Cook, a former seminary student apologizes to Cardinal Bernadin after the latter forgives him for falsely accusing him of sexual abuse. Ernst Werner Techow, an assassin of Walter Rathenau, offers as reparation saving 700 Jews from Nazi extermination following conditional forgiveness from Rathenau's mother. Valjean spends a life of reparation in response to the bishop's forgiveness for stealing his silver.

APOLOGY IS NECESSARY FOR FORGIVENESS

In the fourth type of relationship between apology and forgiveness, apology (repentance) is an absolute prerequisite for forgiveness. This principle is fundamental to Jewish thought, which adds the corollary that the offended party must inform the offender of the offense so that the latter has an opportunity to respond, and that once the offender has repented, forgiveness is required. Many Christian thinkers hold a similar view, that repentance is a prerequisite for forgiveness. For example, Dietrich Bonhoeffer, a Lutheran minister who was killed by the Nazis in a concentration camp in 1945, argued against the "preaching of forgiveness without requiring repentance."[21] He referred to such forgiveness as "cheap grace . . . which amounts to the justification of sin without the justification of the repentant sinner."[22]

In the secular world, the requirement of an apology before offering forgiveness is a common experience. How can we forgive people who have betrayed our trust without their apologizing? How can we ever trust them again when they have not acknowledged their offense, shown remorse, and made some kind of reparations? Is not our forgiving them under such conditions our abdication of any moral authority? Does not our forgiveness without apology communicate justification of their behaviors toward us?

Some people will not forgive and even appear to be psychologically unable to forgive without a prior apology, despite their knowledge that some degree of forgiveness could relieve them of their lifelong grudges and despite the advice of their clergy that their religion preaches the importance of forgiveness. I would venture an estimate that a significant portion of the population of the United States and even the world carry grudges over offenses they will not forgive without a prior apology. I regard this phenomenon as a fact of human nature.

Why do we demand an apology or repentance before we offer forgiveness? The fundamental reason for this demand is that the apology meets the psychological needs of the offended party. It restores the damage that was done. It heals a wound that will not heal spontaneously. As we saw in chapter 3, the apology restores the dignity of the offended party, assures that both parties share the same value system, assures the safety of the offended party, assures the offended party that the offender has suffered, as well as meets several other needs. When these needs are met, the offended party does not have to will him or herself to forgive. The forgiveness comes spontaneously and effortlessly. There is a sudden letting go of the anger, the grudge, and the vengeance. There is often an instant rush of sympathetic and positive feelings toward the offender in response to what is commonly regarded as the gift of the apology.

Eric Lomax's *The Railway Man*[23] illustrates this kind of spontaneous healing following an apology. The book describes his own experiences while a prisoner of war on the River Kwai during World War II and his subsequent attempts to cope with life following the war. The story shows how, despite his efforts to live a normal life following his discharge, Lomax was consumed by hatred and vengeance until he received an apology from the Japanese interpreter whom he believed was responsible for his suffering. At the time of their meeting, nearly 50 years after Lomax was released from prison, both men were in their seventies.

Lomax, a Scotsman, joined the British Army at the age of 20. He was captured by the Japanese army in Singapore and remained a prisoner of war for three years. In the camps, he was assigned to the construction of a railway near the River Kwai Bridge. At one time, Lomax and other officers secretly built a radio to keep abreast of some of the affairs in the world. The radio was discovered and as punishment, Lomax and the others were severely beaten and tortured.

Lomax was subsequently caged like an animal in a cell five feet long, five feet high, and two and one-half feet wide. He was beaten, tortured, and emotionally abused for days. He began to hate his captors, with the focus of his hatred on the interpreter, a man who announced from the beginning of the interrogation that Lomax would soon be killed. Lomax survived the torture, however, and was sent to prison.

Following the war, Lomax returned to his home in Scotland to find that his mother died while he was in prison and his father remarried. Lomax himself married, but soon learned that he was a different person and that his life had been dramatically changed by his torture and imprisonment. He shut down his emotions, pulled back into cold anger at the first sign of confrontation, and developed traits of "deviousness, prevarication and impassivity"[24] that had been adaptive during captivity. He experienced icy rages, silent hostility, withdrawals of affection and contact, and was unable to be lovingly teased. He had recurrent nightmares of being back in prison, starving and suffocating. His behavior puzzled and frightened others, and undoubtedly contributed to his divorce in 1981.

Throughout the years, Lomax frequently fantasized about the revenge he would exact from the Japanese who tortured him. He focused particularly on the interpreter, whom he wanted to cage, beat, and drown. He then became aware that he wanted to know exactly what had happened to him during his captivity, to "establish an indelible historical record of what happened."[25]

After his retirement in 1982, Lomax's need to know what happened intensified. He wanted to learn the sequence of events leading up to the search. He writes, "It was like trying to reconstruct a coherent story from evidence reduced to tattered rags, faded documents, bones and rusty nails."[26] Perhaps he thought learning these details might help him recover something of his past self before the imprisonment. Perhaps he could seek revenge, particularly toward the translator, who became his "private obsession."[27] He felt some kind of closure was necessary for his emotional survival. He observes, "It is impossible for others to help you come to terms with the past, if for you the past is a pile of wounded memories and angry humiliations, and the future is just a nursery of revenge."[28]

In 1989, Lomax read an article in the *Japan Times* about Nagase Takashi, the interpreter about whom he was obsessed. Lomax immediately recognized the photograph of Takashi in the paper. The article described Takashi's repentance, how he attempted to make up for the Japanese maltreatment of prisoners. Takashi had set up a charitable foundation for survivors of the Asian laborers and laid wreaths at the Allied cemetery. Still, Lomax wanted to damage him for ruining his life. "I wanted to see Nagase's sorrow so that I could live better with my own,"[29] he explains.

Lomax was excited that he had the power to take Takashi by surprise, since he was unaware of Lomax's existence. By knowing who and where Takashi was, "I was in such a strong position: I could if I wished reach out and touch him, to do him real harm. The years of feeling powerless whenever I thought of him and his colleagues were erased."[30] He obtained a book written by Takashi (and translated into English) that described the beatings that followed the confiscation of the radio. In the book Takashi described his own shame while watching Lomax being beaten. He also described his feeling of being forgiven after praying at a cemetery for 7,000 Allied soldiers. Takashi, now a Buddhist, also returned to Thailand over 60 times since 1963 where he built a temple at the bridge. As he read his own story told through the eyes of the interpreter, Lomax wondered whether Takashi's remorse was genuine.

Lomax thought about Takashi's feeling forgiven. "God may have forgiven him, but I had not; mere human forgiveness is another matter,"[31] With her husband's permission, Lomax's wife wrote to Takashi in October 1991. She suggested a meeting of the two, since her husband had so many questions he wanted answered. "How can you feel 'forgiven' Mr. Nagase, if this particular former Far Eastern prisoner-of-war has not yet forgiven you?"[32] she wrote. Takashi responded that her letter about her husband's right to forgive "has beaten me down wholely, reminding me of my dirty old days . . . The dagger of your letter thrusted me into my heart to the bottom."[33] Takashi agreed to a meeting.

As they arrived at the agreed upon meeting place, Lomax thought how important it was to see Takashi before being seen by him. To him, this was a source of power. Minutes later, they exchanged words. Lomax took command and comforted Takashi, protecting him from the force of "the emotions shaking his frail-seeming body."[34] Takashi then spoke. He told Lomax that the 50 years since the end of the war had been a long time filled with his own suffering, but that he never forgot Lomax's face. He held Lomax's arm and stroked it. Lomax noted that Takashi's grief was "far more acute than mine." Takashi continued: "I was a member of Imperial Japanese Army; we treated your countrymen very, very badly. . . ."[35] He told of how he became a student of history after the war and opposed militarism. They reminisced for several hours about their experiences in the prison camp, including the behaviors of the Japanese and the prisoners, hidden objects, reactions to torture, and life after the war. "He was kind enough to say that compared to my suffering his was nothing; and yet it was so obvious that he had suffered too."[36] Lomax commented that "my strange companion was a person who I would have been able to get on with long ago had we met under other circumstances."[37] While visiting the Takashis' home, Lomax felt like "an honoured guest of two good people."[38]

"In all the time I spent in Japan," Lomax recalled, "I never felt a flash of the anger I had harbored against Nagase all those years, no backwash of that surge of murderous intent I had felt on finding out that one of them was still alive."[39] Finally, Lomax asked to meet Takashi alone in his hotel room in Tokyo prior to his return to Britain. Takashi seemed afraid and so did his wife. (As a reader, I found myself wondering when and how Lomax would finally murder Takashi, even though I realized the warmth of their encounter made such an act implausible.) In the hotel room, Lomax gave Takashi a letter of forgiveness. "In the letter I said that the war had been over for almost fifty years; that I had suffered much; and that I knew that although he too had suffered throughout this time, he had been most courageous and brave in arguing against militarism and working for reconciliation. I told him that while I could not forget what happened in Kanburi in 1943, I assured him of my total forgiveness."[40]

At the end of the book, Lomax said: "Meeting Nagase has turned him from a hated enemy, with whom friendship would have been unthinkable, into a blood-brother. If I'd never been able to put a name to the face of one of the men who had harmed me, and never discovered that behind that face there was also a damaged life, the nightmares would always have come from a past without meaning. And I had proved for myself that remembering is not enough, if it simply hardens hate."[41]

I chose this story because it illustrates so clearly the causal relationship between apology and forgiveness. Lomax repeatedly states in his narrative what he wanted from Takashi even before they met. His encounter with Takashi eventually satisfied many of those needs. First, he needed to feel power over Takashi to undo his powerlessness as a prisoner, to undo the humiliation he felt for years. Lomax had the power to see Takashi first and to notice his fragility. He even had the power to kill Takashi. Instead, he chose to use the power to forgive him. Second, Lomax needed to learn that he and Takashi shared basic values, particularly about the war. Learning of Takashi's history of opposing militarism, his commitment to the survivors who built the railroad, and his memorialization of the victims of confinement and forced labor gave Lomax assurance that he and Takashi shared a common view of the world. These actions became expressions of remorse as well as acts of reparation. Third, Lomax needed to have a dialogue with Takashi to secure "an indelible historical record of what happened," which enabled him to master the details of the past so that he could find himself, understand his subsequent suffering, validate what had happened to him, and grieve what he had lost. Fourth, Lomax needed to know that Takashi had suffered adequately for his behavior. Learning that Takashi's was a "damaged life," and that his suffering may have been at least as great as his own, gave Lomax that knowledge.

Before they met, Lomax had been unable to forgive or to be freed from the forces that controlled him: humiliation, grudges, and vengeance. When his needs were met by the apology and the "apologetic interactions," Lomax spontaneously forgave. He not only gave up hateful sentiments, but he also developed feelings of compassion and even a brotherly affection for Takashi.

CONCLUDING COMMENTS ON THE COMPLEXITY
AND SIMPLICITY OF APOLOGIES

As I pondered the complexity of the apology process beginning with the definition of apology and ending with the relationship of apology to forgiveness, I worried that the reader might conclude that apologizing is an overwhelming task. Although the analysis of any given apology involves many variables, the act of apologizing is often a simple task, an intuitive and spontaneous act which is usually gratifying to both parties. While this book was in production, I had the opportunity (and need) to offer such an apology.

I was invited to deliver a lecture on apology as part of a four-day scientific convention on cancer diagnosis and prevention in Nice, France. Mine was the only "humanities" lecture at this scientific meeting. I was the keynote speaker for the second day of the convention with an allotted time of 30 minutes, from 4:30–5:00 P.M. Addressing 350 cancer researchers, I began and finished on time. At the conclusion of my talk, many people in the audience raised their hands to ask questions. I turned to the moderator for permission to take the questions. He responded with an affirmative nod.

After 15 to 20 minutes of an animated question and answer period, I noticed the next speaker standing up in the first row. I realized at that moment that I was inadvertently encroaching on his speaking time which was scheduled from 5:00 to 5:30 P.M. I called the question period to a close and immediately left the auditorium.

I was upset with my insensitivity over my management of time (shame) and the probable negative impact on the next speaker's presentation (guilt). As a result, I felt uncomfortable during the next few days when I passed the speaker, a cancer scientist, and his wife on the streets near the hotel. Neither of us acknowledged each other. He seemed unhappy with me— or so I imagined. On our last evening in Nice, my wife and I entered a restaurant and immediately noticed that the scientist and his wife were already seated. As fate would have it, the waiter seated us next to them. To diminish my discomfort, I turned my chair away from them. We finished dinner and left, while they remained. As we reached the door of the restaurant, on an impulse, I told my wife to wait for me. "There is something I have to do," I said. I walked to the table where the couple was seated. Approaching the scientist who immediately recognized me, I told him that it was insensitive of me to go on with the extended question and answer period while failing to realize I was taking his time. I went on to say that I hoped I had not seriously compromised his presentation. He smiled, stood up, put his hand on my shoulder in a warm brotherly manner and told me how much he enjoyed my talk. (He did mention that his colleague was concerned about missing his flight to Paris.) He went on to say that he regretted that his wife did not attend my presentation. She would have enjoyed it, he said, since she is a retired psychiatric nurse. I experienced his behavior as an expression of genuine forgiveness. I then told him that I understood that he is a very distinguished scientist. He asked how I knew, and I replied that his wife had told me when we recently met during a museum tour. Now they were both smiling. The three of us parted in a friendly manner as I returned to my wife who now had a big smile on her face. I asked her what she was smiling about since she could see but not hear the interaction. Reading the body language of the three of us, she said, it looked like a sit-com with a happy ending. (She subsequently described the interaction as resembling an encounter of three close friends who had unexpectedly met after a long period of separation.) There were now four happy people resulting from a spontaneous 30-second apology and a two-minute conversation. Before leaving for the airport the next morning my wife and I were seated next to the scientist and his wife at breakfast. The four of us engaged in a friendly conversation about their European travel plans for the week.

Understanding the apology process may be complex, but the act of apologizing is often quite simple and immensely fulfilling.

TWELVE

Afterword:
The Future of Apologies

As the previous chapters attest, apologies have the capacity to positively transform relationships between individuals, groups, and nations. They provide processes by which parties in conflict can settle their differences in peaceful and constructive manners, while also preserving or restoring the dignity of both parties. The rapid growth of apologies since the early 1990s suggests that people are more aware of these benefits than ever before. But it also raises additional questions: First, what do we know about apologies (particularly public ones) from past centuries? Second, how did people heal and restore relationships before the apology process emerged as such an accessible and effective mode of reconciliation? And third, will this upsurge in apologies continue throughout the twenty-first century? If so, what can we hope for?

The first signs of change in public attitudes about apology began to appear soon after World War II. Michael Henderson, in the *The Forgiveness Factor: Stories of Hope in a World of Conflict*,[1] illustrates the temporal relationship between war's end and war-related apologies and attempts at reconciliation between former World War II enemies. Perhaps the most important of these stories involves the reconciliation between France and Germany, bitter enemies during and between their previous three wars. Elazar Barkan in *The Guilt of Nations: Restitution and Negotiating Historical Injustices*,[2] further chronicles and analyzes several instances of restitution following World War II, beginning with German reparations to its former enemies.

Three implicit or explicit apologies, occurring between the end of World War II and 1990, are particularly noteworthy because of their breadth and precedent-setting impact. All three apologies are in some way the result of World War II. The first of these apologies was Pope John XXIII's decision to eliminate all negative comments about Jews from the Roman Catholic liturgy.[3] In a continuation of this apology, Pope John XXIII initiated the Declaration on the Relation of the Church to Non-Christian Religions, referred to as *Nostra Aetate*, a part of Vatican II. This document was completed and proclaimed in 1965 by his successor, Pope Paul VI.[4] It states that "the Jews should not be presented as rejected or accursed by God, as if this followed from the Holy Scriptures. . . ." And that the church "decries hatred, persecutions, displays of anti-Semitism, directed against the Jews at any time and by anyone."[5] Michael Phayer, in *The Catholic Church and the Holocaust, 1930-1965*, comments: "Led by a new pope, John

XXIII, and compelled by the memory of the Holocaust, the Catholic church reversed its 2,000-year tradition of anti-Semitism."[6] With regard to the world of Islam, the document states: "The Church regards with esteem also the Moslems. . . . Since in the course of centuries not a few quarrels and hostilities have arisen between Christians and Moslems, this sacred synod urges all to . . . work sincerely for mutual understanding and to preserve as well as to promote together for the benefit of all mankind social justice and moral welfare, as well as peace and freedom."[7] *Nostra Aetate* goes on to address the relationship of the Catholic church to all of civilization, "No foundation therefore remains for any theory or practice that leads to discrimination between man and man or people and people, so far as their human dignity and the right flowing from it are concerned. . . . The Church reproves . . . any discrimination against men or harassment of them because of their race, color, condition of life, or religion."[8] It is widely believed that the Church in *Nostra Aetate* implicitly acknowledged, with this apology, its role as offender while explicitly offering reparations through its profound commitments to future relations to other religions.[9]

A second apology is illustrated by a speech, regarded by many as world famous, delivered by the president of the Federal Republic of Germany, Richard von Weizsacker to the Bundestag in 1985, addressing Germany's war-time offenses.[10] This speech is remarkable for its comprehensive acknowledgment of the offenses of the German nation during World War II, together with an admonition to "look truth straight in the eye"[11] and to regard remembering as a moral obligation. Von Weizsacker's speech had further significance because it followed by three days the controversial Bitburg ceremonies in which President Ronald Reagan honored the memory of the SS who died in the war. Anthony Lewis of the *New York Times* called this address "one of the great speeches of our time."[12] Jeffrey Herf, author of *Divided Memory: The Nazi Past in the Two Germanys,* commented this was "the most important speech about the crimes of the Nazi era delivered in the national political arena"[13] since 1952.

Finally the U.S. government in 1988, after years of debate and negotiations, apologized (including financial reparations) to Japanese American citizens who were interned during World War II.[14] Barkan regarded this resolution as a "model for restitution cases and for redressing historical injustices"[15] partly because the U.S. Congress "underscored the moral obligations of the country even when these come into conflict with political considerations."[16] It further showed that even the victors of the war have responsibilities to apologize for their offenses. This U.S. response to race-based civil liberties offenses has further served as a model for subsequent offenses of this type.

In my judgment, no twentieth-century apology prior to the end of World War II approaches the moral and social significance of these three post-war apologies. Only one U.S. president, Abraham Lincoln, is remembered for an apology, his second inaugural address.[17] This 703-word apology for slavery, engraved on the north wall of the Lincoln Memorial in Washington, D.C., will, I believe, grow in importance as one of the most profound and courageous statements in U.S. and world history. Ulysses S. Grant's last message to Congress, said by some to be an apology, is actually an *apologia,* a justification and explanation.[18]

To my knowledge, no systematic studies of apologies exist in the literature or the history of any nation. (Academic disciplines of sociology, social psychology, and psycholinguistics became interested in research on apologies beginning in the 1970s,[19] and the few books on contemporary apologies and "how to apologize" did not appear until the 1990s.)[20] Students of European history of the Middle Ages may be familiar with two famous apologies. In 1077, Holy Roman Emperor Henry IV traveled to Canossa, a castle in Italy, where he waited barefoot in the snow for three days to apologize to Pope Gregory VII with hopes of having his excommunication rescinded. The second famous apology of the Middle Ages was offered by Henry II for inciting the murder of Thomas à Becket, the Archbishop of Canterbury in 1170. He performed penance four years later by wearing sackcloth and ashes and walking barefoot to a place where 80 monks beat him with twigs of a birch tree. Many historians regard both of these apologies as political maneuvers by the alleged offenders, both of whom were kings in conflict with the clergy. Also of historical interest in the management of humiliations and apologies was the practice of dueling, the beginnings of which can be traced to the Middle Ages. A duel was one method of resolving a conflict following an insult where one party was humiliated or lost honor. The duel would be terminated if the offending party apologized, thus restoring the honor of the offended party.

Quotations of famous apologies that I was able to compile, mostly from the nineteenth and twentieth centuries, all speak negatively about apologies:

> "It is a good rule in life never to apologize. The right sort of people does not want apologies, and the wrong sort takes a mean advantage off them."
>
> (P. G. Wodehouse, 1881–1975, writer)

"Apologies only account for that which they do not alter."
(Benjamin Disraeli, 1804–1881, British Prime Minister)

"No sensible person ever made an apology."
(Ralph W. Emerson, 1803–1882, poet)

"I do not trouble my spirit to vindicate itself . . . I see that the elementary laws never apologize."
(Walt Whitman, 1819–1892, poet)

"Never regret, never explain, never apologize."
(Benjamin Jowett, 1817–1893, Oxford University)

"Never contradict. Never explain. Never apologize."
(Lord Fisher, 1841–1920, British admiral)

"Nine times out of ten the first thing a man's companion knows of his shortcomings is from his apology."
(Oliver Wendell Holmes, 1841–1935,
U.S. supreme court justice)

A noteworthy aspect of this list of British and American dignitaries are the missing voices: There are no women, no minorities, and no members of the so-called "underclass." Perhaps their absences can be explained by the oft-quoted remark that "history is written by the winners" and thus reflects the historically devalued position these groups occupied in society. (Only anecdotes and documents that were considered "valuable" were preserved.) Perhaps those not represented had neither means nor opportunity to express an opinion about the value (or lack thereof) of apologies. Whatever the reason, it is clear that people who did have power and influence did not view the practice of apologizing kindly and—presumably—were quite loath to engage in it themselves.

THE RELATIONSHIP OF APOLOGY TO RELIGION AND THE LAW

If we assume that apologies currently play a greater role in personal and public discourse than at any time before World War II, the question arises how the needs of offended parties in those times were met. I believe that a plausible answer can be found in the function of two timeless institutions, religion and the law.

Limiting ourselves, for the sake of this discussion, to the monotheistic religions of Judaism, Christianity, and Islam, we see the importance of repentance as a cornerstone of faith. Although all three religions speak of repentance in general terms as a turning away from sin and a returning to God, they also describe it as a means of healing relationships that have been damaged because one person committed an offense against another. Religious scholars analyze and describe the steps to repentance in virtually the same manner that social scientists describe the apology process.

An important statement about the importance of repentance as a manner of correcting or undoing offenses against God as well as against other people comes from the Talmud (a document dating from the early third century C.E. to the sixth century C.E.), which declares that God created repentance even before he created humankind.[21] I take this statement to mean that the sages who authored this sentiment were acutely aware of the fallibility of humankind and the need for religion's prescriptions to heal offenses. Repentance (or its secular approximation of apology), therefore, would be so important for sustaining a just and livable society that an infinite and all-powerful God would put it in place before creating humankind.

Another institution that served to manage conflict in its evolution over many centuries is the law. Taking the U.S. judicial system as a body of legal practice and precedent, it is easy to see some of the ways that law shares the structure and function of apology. For instance, in both cases, the offended party ("the people"— i.e., the state or federal government in the case of a criminal trial) seeks to remedy an offense. The difference is that law coerces the offender, if guilty, into attending to the victim's needs while apologies are voluntary, unless they are ordered by the court. The significance of this difference is that only one party is apt to be satisfied by the legal process, whereas the apology process may potentially satisfy both parties.

In fact, I believe that many legal proceedings can be understood as formalized and ritualized substitutes for the apology process, complete with offense, explanation, remorse, reparation, and negotiation. For example, in criminal proceedings, acknowledging and negotiating the offense in the form of plea bargaining can precede or replace a trial. Similarly, in civil suits, pre-trial negotiations can resolve the entire suit. The nature of the crime (the offense) can be mitigated if the accused cooperates by providing new information ("acknowledging the offense") that may benefit victims as well as the authorities. For example, the families of murdered victims might want to know how their loved ones died and the location of the bodies. Explanations can affect the degree of culpability (responsibility) involved, as judge and jury determine whether the offense was premeditated or was a negligent but unfortunate outcome of a quarrel. "Victim impact statements" give the victim an opportunity to explain how the offense has affected his or her life, both at the time of the offense as well as in the indefinite future (explaining what the offense meant to the victim). Even the sentencing phase of a criminal justice process hinges on some of the same variables that determine the effectiveness of an apology: the expression of remorse, the presence of continued danger to the victims and society if the guilty party is placed on parole, and the importance of retributive justice on behalf of the victims.

PERSONAL OBSERVATIONS ON THE CURRENT INTEREST IN APOLOGY

Moving from the past use of apologies to the present, we have seen in chapter 1 how the frequency of apology stories in newspapers has nearly doubled over the past decade. As my own interest in apologies has deepened during this time, I have been able to assess the importance of apology through the nature and responses of audiences I have addressed. I have been struck by the diversity of people interested in learning about apology and also by the extent and intensity of interest. These audiences included lawyers and law students, whose professional journals during the past decade have been publishing an increasing number of articles on apologies. Students of police academies were sent by superiors who wanted them to master the social skills of apologizing so they will become more effective law enforcement agents. Many religious audiences, mostly Roman Catholic, wanted to learn about apology as complementary to their interest in repentance and forgiveness. Groups of high school and Sunday school students attended my

lectures with their teachers who hoped, perhaps, that understanding apologies might encourage their civility in relationships. Groups of retirees may have attended because of an
interest, as they matured and aged, in resolving old grudges and
making peace with friends and relatives. Physicians were struggling over whether and how to apologize to patients who were
victims of their medical mistakes. Finally, I spoke before an
international audience of 500 people from 60 nations who met
at Caux, Switzerland, to search for means of resolving civil and
international wars within and between nations.[22] This group
exhibited both a sense of near desperation and unswerving
determination as they struggled to find ways to heal their war-
torn countries. The net result of addressing these varied audiences was to strengthen my conviction that the growing
interest in the apology process transcends arbitrary boundaries
—of nationality, profession, age, gender, and religion.

SPECULATIONS ON THE FUTURE OF APOLOGIES

In order to speculate on the future direction of apologies, I will
review the social and technological factors that have led to their
recent growth. We have already discussed the world's reaction
to the frightening loss of life as a result of World War II and the
use of weapons of mass destruction. As a result, a cloud of fear
hangs over all of us, whether signaled by orange or yellow
alerts, or not signaled at all. War is no longer the great
adventure it was portrayed to be for many people prior to
World War I. Another important social development is a new
interdependence between nations, companies, and individuals.
We need each other for our mutual economic well-being and
to jointly protect the earth from a rapidly rising population,

global warming, and pollution. We observe yet another emerging interdependence required for success in national governance, business, the university, the church, and the physician's office. Such interdependence requires a departure from a rigid "top down" authoritative organizational structure in which no one apologizes to anyone for anything, rules are immutable, and the leader demands to be treated as infallible. In our new kind of interdependence, it matters more than ever what the voter wants, what the customer wants, what the worker wants, what the student wants, what the parishioner wants, and what the patient wants. It also matters to the economy and to our sense of moral justice what minorities want and what women want. The Internet, the cell phone, and the mass media keep populations on this planet interconnected, thus enabling offenses to be instantly visible on a global level. Finally, as women achieve more power and influence in society, their greater skill with and use of apologies (compared to men) can be expected to alter general discourse in most aspects of life.

All of these developments — the dangers of international war, our fragile planet, the global village in which we live, the growing number of the earth's citizens demanding equality, the interconnectedness of all of us—have led to more human interactions than at any time in history. This volatile climate demands that we renew and focus our energies on the resolution of conflicts, and that we do so in a way that does not simply submerge the resentments that inevitably accompany such conflicts but acknowledges and responds to them. As this book suggests, I believe that the apology process can be a powerful tool in that effort. This is the good news.

But this cautiously optimistic view comes with a major caveat: Nations or groups in states of humiliation cannot participate in relationships of equality and interconnectedness. It is difficult for these parties to humbly acknowledge blame, empathically understand the plight of the other party, and behave in generous and forgiving ways. They are too consumed with fighting for and protecting their dignity, their psychological identity and sense of self, and their physical well-being. In their state of humiliated rage, they are vengeful and unable to see the world as they might see it if their adversaries halted attempts to dehumanize them and their dignity was restored. The world currently offers multitudes of examples of these humiliated groups: terrorists who offer their lives to restore the honor of their group or nation, the Iraqis, the Chechens, the Palestinians and Israelis, the Catholics and Protestants of Northern Ireland, and those living in emotional and physical deprivation in all countries. All of these groups or nations have long histories of subjugation and humiliation. The interconnectedness of our global village has only intensified their humiliation, because now mass media shows exactly what others have and what they are missing. Psychiatrist Robert Jay Lifton makes the point that the United States is currently a humiliated nation as a result of its exposed vulnerability following the 9/11 attacks on the World Trade Center and the Pentagon.[23] Such a state of mind can cause a person or a nation to interpret the external world through the lens of fear and rage and can compromise that person's or nation's judgment and ability to acknowledge and rectify mistakes.

I believe that humiliation is one of the most important emotions we must understand and manage, both in ourselves and in others, and on an individual and national level. This belief, particularly as it relates to international affairs, is supported by the writings of Robert Jay Lifton, Jessica Stern, Thomas Friedman, and even the fifth-century B.C. historian Thucydides.[24] The failure to deal constructively with humiliation has led to grudges and killings in families (e.g., Cain and Abel) and in nations (e.g., France and Germany).[25] The significance of humiliation between nations or major national groups is magnified when either party is capable of inflicting mass destruction. The role of vibrant, prosperous democratic nations should be to humbly and without arrogance assist in restoring the dignity of other nations and groups in need. Only then can they partake in the dialogue of apology and reconciliation.

CONCLUDING THOUGHTS

Apology is more than an acknowledgment of an offense together with an expression of remorse. It is an ongoing commitment by the offending party to change his or her behavior. It is a particular way of resolving conflicts other than by arguing over who is bigger and better. It is a powerful and constructive form of conflict resolution, embedded, in modified form, in religion and the judicial system. It is a method of social healing that has grown in importance as our way of living together on our planet undergoes radical change. It is a social act in which the person, group, or nation apologizing has historically been viewed as weak, but more than ever is now being regarded as strong. It is a behavior that requires of both parties attitudes of honesty, generosity, humility, commitment, and courage.

Notes

ONE: THE GROWING IMPORTANCE OF APOLOGIES

1. Personal correspondence to the author from Manuel Zax, a resident of Worcester, Massachusetts. He introduced himself to me many months after hearing my lecture. After telling me his story, he consented to include the letter he sent to his boyhood friend together with his written comments about their meeting. He wrote me a second time describing his reactions to learning of his friend's death, which occurred 18 months after their meeting. He generously gave me permission to use all of the material as described in chapter one.

2. Linda Greenhouse, "Texas Sodomy Law Held Unconstitutional—Scathing Dissent," *New York Times*, June 27, 2003.

3. Nicholas Tavuchis, *Mea Culpa: A Sociology of Apology and Reconciliation* (Stanford: Stanford University Press, 1991).

4. Ibid., 4.

5. Ibid., 5.

6. "Who's Sorry Now? Last Month Everybody Apologized for Past Horrors," *Time Magazine* (September 13, 1993).

7. The criteria I used to count an article as being an "apology story" was having the word "apology" or "apologize" in the headline, lead paragraph or search terms. I chose the *New York Times* and the *Washington Post* because of their national and international standing and the likelihood, in my opinion, that they would carry major national and international stories. There is, nevertheless, considerable variation among other newspapers that service major cities in the United States in the frequency with which they publish stories on apologies.

8. *Seinfeld*, episode 909, "The Apology." The relevant part of the plot involves George's attempt to get an apology from a former friend named Jason, who is making amends as part of his Alcoholics Anonymous (AA) program. Recalling an occasion during which Jason insulted him, George becomes convinced that Jason should apologize. However, although Jason appears to apologize to everyone else

(including Jerry), he doesn't apologize to George. In fact, Jason's sarcastic refusal to apologize only makes George look foolish, which George in turn takes as another insult. Sure that he now should receive two apologies, George goes to Jason's AA sponsor to complain. The sponsor listens carefully, and then refers George to a recovery group for those with uncontrollable rage. Later, when Jason's offer to apologize still does not satisfy him, George's continued complaints cost Jason both his sanity and his new job. Transcript available at: http://www.sonypictures.com/tv/shows/seinfeld (last accessed 9 March 2004). Executive producers Larry David, George Shapiro, and Howard West.

9. Beverly Engel, *The Power of Apology: Healing Steps to Transform All Your Relationships* (New York: John Wiley, 2001).

10. Ken Blanchard and Margaret McBride, *The One Minute Apology: A Powerful Way to Make Things Better* (New York: William Morrow, 2003).

11. See Jonathan R. Cohen, "Advising Clients to Apologize," *Southern California Law Review* 72, no. 4 (1999): 1009; and Peter H. Rehm and Denise R. Beatty, "Legal Consequences of Apologizing," *Journal of Dispute Resolution*, no. 1 (1996): 115.

12. Andis Robeznieks, "The power of an apology: Patients appreciate open communication," *American Medical News* (July 28, 2003).

13. Elizabeth Rosenthal, "Tianjin Journal; For a Fee, this Chinese Firm Will Beg Pardon for Anyone," *New York Times*, January 3, 2001.

14. "Japanese, South Korean leaders sign 'new partnership' accord," *Patriot Ledger* (Quincy, MA), October 8, 1998.

15. Karl E. Meyer, "Just How Sorry Can You Get? Pretty Sorry," *New York Times*, November 29, 1997.

16. Michael Henderson, "A Year of Reconciliation," *Christian Science Monitor*, December 22, 1998.

17. Lance Morrow, "Is It Enough to Be Sorry? The meaning of the Pope's cosmic apology is deeper than the caviling," *Time Magazine* (March 27, 2000).

18. Pope John Paul II, *Tertio Millennio Adveniente*, November 10, 1994.

19. Harvey Araton, "Yogi and the Boss Complete Makeup Game," *New York Times*, January 6, 1999.

20. Marshall McLuhan and Quentin Fiore, *The Medium Is the Massage*, coordinated by Jerome Agel (New York: Bantam Books, 1967), 61.

21. Robert Wright, *Nonzero: The Logic of Human Destiny* (New York: Vintage Books, 2000).

22. Robert Wright, "Two Years Later, a Thousand Years Ago," *New York Times*, September 11, 2003.

23. Craig S. Smith, "China Backs Away from Initial Denial in School Explosion," *New York Times*, March 16, 2001.

24. Peter Hessler, "China Leader Hints of Errors," *Boston Globe*, March 16, 2001.

25. "Lawmaker forwards supremacist e-mail," *Milwaukee Journal Sentinel*, August 23, 2001.

26. Ibid.

27. "Legislator Apologizes for Controversial E-mail," *Shelby Star* (Shelby, NC), August 23, 2001.

28. Elazar Barkan, *The Guilt of Nations: Restitution and Negotiating Historical Injustices*, (New York: W. W. Norton, 2000), xvi.

29. Ibid., xxix.

30. Aaron Lazare, "A Families Adoption of Eight Children of Three Races," unpublished manuscript. Also, the family story was told on *Good Morning America*, ABC, September 27, 2000.

31. Aaron Lazare, "Shame and Humiliation in the Medical Encounter," *Archives of Internal Medicine* 147 (1987): 1653–58.

32. A summary of this talk, "What makes for a good apology," was published in *For A Change* 16, no. 1 (February/March 2003).

TWO: THE PARADOX OF APOLOGIES

1. Personal correspondence on November 9, 2003, to the author from Manuel Zax.

2. Tavuchis, *Mea Culpa*, 3.

3. Ibid., 4.

4. See Erving Goffman, *Relations in Public: Microstudies of the Public Order*, (New York: Basic Books, 1971), 113; and Elite Olshtain, "Apologies across Languages," in *Cross-Cultural Pragmatics: Requests and Apologies*, ed. Shoshana Blum-Kulka, Juliane House, and Gabriele Kasper (Norwood, N.J.: Ablex, 1989), 157.

5. *Oxford English Dictionary*, 2nd Edition, s.v. "apology."

6. Sharon D. Downey, "The Evolution of the Rhetorical Genre of Apolgia," *Western Journal of Communication* 57 (winter 1993): 42–64.

7. Peter Gomes, *The Good Book: Reading the Bible with Mind and Heart* (New York: William Morrow, 1996), x.

8. Ibid.

9. Editorial, Patrick J. Purcell, "An Apology to Readers," *Boston Herald*, December 8, 1998.

10. Deborah Tannen, "Contrite Makes Right," *Civilization* (April/May 1999): 69.

11. Deborah Tannen, *Talking from 9–5: How Women's and Men's Conversational Styles Affect Who Gets Heard, Who Gets Credit, and What Gets Done at Work* (New York: William Morrow, 1994), 47.

12. Janet Holmes, "Sex Differences and Apologies: One Aspect of Communicative Competence," *Applied Linguistics* 10, no. 2 (1989): 194.

13. Jane Bybee, "The Emergence of Gender Differences in Guilt during Adolescence," in *Guilt and Children*, ed. Jane Bybee (San Diego, CA: Academic Press, 1998), 113–22.

14. Carol Gilligan, *In a Different Voice: Psychological Theory and Women's Development* (Cambridge: Harvard University Press, 1982), 173.

15. Elaine Showalter, "Literary Brutes," *Civilization* (April/May, 1999): 71.

16. Ibid., 72.

17. Hiroshi Wagatsuma and Arthur Rosett, "The Implications of Apology: Law and Culture in Japan and the United States," *Law & Society Review* 20, no. 4 (1986): 465.

18. Naomi Sugimoto, ed., *Japanese Apology across Disciplines* (Commack, NY: Nova Science, 1999).

19. Nicholas D. Kristof, "Why a Nation of Apologizers Makes One Large Exception," *New York Times*, June 12, 1995.

20. David McCullough, *Truman* (New York: Simon & Schuster, 1992), 543.

21. Ibid.

22. James Carroll, *Constantine's Sword: the Church and the Jews* (Boston, MA: Houghton Mifflin, 2001), 600.

23. Tavuchis, *Mea Culpa*, 48. For a comprehensive discussion of public apologies and their distinctiveness from private, interpersonal apologies, I recommend Tavuchis, 45–117.

THREE: HOW APOLOGIES HEAL

1. Donald C. Klein, "The Humiliation Dynamic: Viewing the Task of Prevention from a New Perspective. Part I," *The Journal of Primary Prevention*, 12, no. 2 (winter 1991): 87–123.

2. D. J. Goodspeed, *The German Wars: 1914–1915* (Boston: Houghton Mifflin, 1977), 116.

3. Thomas J. Scheff, *Bloody Revenge: Emotions, Nationalism, and War* (Boulder, CO.: Westview Press, 1994), 108.

4. Donald Kagan, *On the Origins of War and the Preservation of Peace* (New York: Doubleday, 1995), 8.

5. Editorial, Thomas L. Friedman, "The Humiliation Factor," *New York Times*, November 9, 2003.

6. Roy L. Brooks, "The Age of Apology," in *When Sorry Isn't Enough*, ed. Roy L. Brooks (New York: New York University Press, 1999), 7.

7. "Pilot Sues U.S. Over 9/11 Arrest," *BBC News*, September 16, 2003.

8. Alison Mitchell, "Clinton Regrets 'Clearly Racist' U.S. Study," *New York Times*, May 17, 1997.

9. Kevin Johnson, "McVeigh's Only Regret Is That Building Wasn't Leveled," *USA Today*, March 29, 2001.

10. "Japan Balks at MP's Virile Rapists' Remark," *The Statesman* (India), June 29, 2003.

11. "LDP Reprimands Ota for Calling Gang Rapists 'Virile'," *Japan Economic Newswire*, June 27, 2003.

12. "Senior Japanese Lawmaker Apologizes for Remark Tolerating Gang Rape," *Agence France Presse*, June 27, 2003.

13. "LDP Politician Lauds Gang Rapists," *United Press International*, June 27, 2003.

14. "Japan: Outrage Over Rape Remark," *New York Times*, June 28, 2003.

15. "LDP Politician Lauds Gang Rapists," *United Press International*, June 27, 2003.

16. "Japan Balks at MP'S 'Virile Rapists' Remark," *The Statesman* (India), June 29, 2003.

17. "Japanese Editorial Excerpts," *Japan Economic Newswire*, June 29, 2003.

18. "Ota's Praise for Gang Rape Condemned," *Japan Times*, June 28, 2003.

19. "Globe Suspends Columnist for Comment on Kidd's Wife," *Boston Globe*, May 7, 2003.

20. Ibid.

21. Jim Baker, "No Kidding; Globe Slaps Writer Over Comments on Nets Star's Wife," *Boston Herald*, May 7, 2003.

22. Louisa Nesbitt, PA News, "Church Sex Abuse Victim Wins High Court Apology," *United Press Association*, April 9, 2003.

23. Yvonne Daley, "Vermont to Pay Two Sisters $1M for Its Failure to Halt Rapes," *Boston Globe*, May 8, 1997.

24. Ibid.

25. Mark Singelais, "UMASS Accepts Chaney Discipline," *Boston Globe*, February 18, 1994.

26. Steven A. Holmes, "White Supremacist Agrees to Make a Public Apology," *The New York Times*, May 12, 2000.

27. Ibid.

28. Carlo D'Este, *Patton: A Genius for War* (New York: HarperCollins, 1995), 521–526.

29. John S. D. Eisenhower, *General Ike: A Personal Reminiscence* (New York: Free Press, 2003), 56.

30. Brooks, "The Age of Apology," in *When Sorry Isn't Enough*, 8–9.

31. Michael Specter, "In Latvia, the First Token of Swiss Remorse: $400," *New York Times*, November 19, 1997.

32. Martha Minow, "Truth Commissions," in *Between Vengeance and Forgiveness* (Boston: Beacon Press, 1998), 68. See also Buergenthal, "United Nations Truth Commission for El Salavador," 292, 321.

33. Pumla Gobodo-Madikizela, *A Human Being Died That Night: A South African Story of Forgiveness* (Boston: Houghton Mifflin, 2003), 130.

34. Paid Advertisement, "To Honor the 50th Anniversary of the U.N. Genocide Convention," which appeared in the March 24, 1998 edition of the *New York Times* on page A16.

35. Alan Riding, "Rail Ride to Death: Jew Seeks One Euro, Wants French Firm to Express Remorse," *The Gazette* (Montreal, Quebec), March 21, 2003.

36. Alan Riding, "Nazis' Human Cargo Now Haunts French Railway," *New York Times*, March 20, 2003.

37. Daniel Wakin, "Confronting His Abuser, on Tape: Voice of Anguish Demands Remorse of Priest and Bishop," *New York Report*, *New York Times*, February 23, 2003.

38. Ibid.

39. Ibid.

40. Ibid.

FOUR: ACKNOWLEDGING THE OFFENSE

1. Garry Wills, *Lincoln at Gettysburg: The Words that Remade America* (New York: Simon and Schuster, 1992), 177.

2. Brooks, "The Age of Apology," 7.

3. Lincoln's second inaugural speech, delivered on March 4, 1865.

4. Ibid.

5. Ibid.

6. Ibid.

7. Ibid.

8. Richard von Weizsacker, president of the Federal Republic of Germany, in the Bundestag during the ceremony commemorating

the fortieth anniversary of the end of the war in Europe and of national socialist tyranny, May 8, 1985.

9. Ibid.

10. Ibid.

11. Ibid.

12. Ibid.

13. Kevin Gover, assistant secretary of Indian Affairs for the U.S. Department of the Interior in remarks made at a ceremony celebrating the one hundred seventy-fifth anniversary of the establishment of the Bureau of Indian Affairs, September 8, 2000.

14. Ibid.

15. Ibid.

16. Ibid.

17. Ibid.

18. Ibid.

19. Ibid.

20. Ibid.

21. Ibid.

22. Ibid.

23. Allen Thorndike Rice, "Frederick Douglass," in *Reminiscences of Abraham Lincoln* (New York: The North American Review, 1888), 192–3.

24. Ronald C. White, Jr., *Lincoln's Greatest Speech: The Second Inaugural* (New York: Simon and Schuster, 2002), 197.

25. Lincoln's second inaugural speech, delivered on March 4, 1865.

26. Peter Nicholas, Carla Hall, and Michael Finnegan, "'The Recall Campaign: Schwarzenegger Tells Backers He 'Behaved Badly'," *Los Angeles Times*, October 3, 2003.

27. Carol Costello, "Schwarzenegger Speaks Out on 'Times' Article," Cable News Network, CNN Live, October 2, 2003.

28. Rene Sanchez and William Booth, "From Schwarzenegger, an Apology; Candidate Says He Is 'Deeply Sorry' for his Behavior toward Women," *Washington Post*, October 3, 2003.

29. Richard Huff and Bill Hutchinson, "Janet's Sorry for Super Trip, FCC Kicks Off Probe into Halftime Stunt," *Daily News*, February 3, 2004.

30. Julie Chen, "Janet Jackson Issues Another Apology for Halftime Flap," *The Early Show—CBS*, February 4, 2004.

31. Drew Mackenzie, "Pull the Other one Mate; Janet Boob: I was Duped Says Justin," *Daily Star* (Great Britain), February 5, 2004.

32. Shelby Foote, *The Civil War, A Narrative: Fredericksburg to Meridian* (New York: Random House, 1986), 568.

33. President Ulysses S. Grant, *Eighth Annual Message to Congress*, December 5, 1876.

34. Ibid.

35. Ibid.

36. Michael Powell, "Crisis in the Church: Egan Supported Priest Accused of Sexual Abuse, Said Cleric Was not his Responsibility," *Boston Globe*, May 11, 2002.

37. Clyde Haberman, "When Silence Can Seem Like Consent," *New York Times*, April 23, 2002.

38. Richard M. Nixon, President of the United States, in his resignation speech, August 8, 1974.

39. Tavuchis, *Mea Culpa*, 54–58.

40. Ibid. Tavuchis points out on page 57 that Nixon, in his comment to interviewer Frank Gannon, remarked, "There is no way you could apologize or to say that you are sorry which could exceed resigning the presidency of the United States. That said it all. And I don't intend to say any more."

41. Grayden Jones, "One Letter Was Worth 1,000 Words," *Spokesman Review*, March 13, 1999.

42. Ibid.

43. Ibid.

44. David E. Sanger, "Swiss Envoy to U.S. Resigns after His Report on Holocaust Dispute Is Disclosed," *New York Times*, January 28, 1997.

45. Paul Newberry, Associated Press, "Zoeller Apologizes for his Tiger 'Joke'," in *Boston Herald*, April 22, 1997, reprinted with permission of the Associated Press.

46. Ibid.

47. Associated Press, "Woods Accepts Zoeller's Apology," in *Boston Globe*, April 25, 1997, reprinted with permission of the Associated Press.

48. Ibid.

49. Associated Press, "Air Canada Cuts more Flights Due to Pilot Shortage," *New York Times*, July 31, 2000.

50. Associated Press, "Dozens Accuse Army Officer of Proposing," *Tri City Herald* (Washington), June 14, 2003.

51. Ibid.

52. P. O'Neill, Irish Republican Publicity Bureau, Dublin, in a public statement released by the Irish Republican Army on July 16, 2002, to mark the thirtieth anniversary of an IRA operation in Belfast that resulted in nine people being killed and many more injured, as reported by Cable News Network.

53. Associated Press, "Mondale Joins Rites for Dead in '45 Tokyo Raid," *Boston Globe*, March 11, 1995.

54. Elaine Sciolino, "Sub's Commander Expresses Regret to Victims' Families," *New York Times*, February 26, 2001.

55. "Sub Captain Raises Anger," *New Zealand Herald*, February 27, 2001.

56. Dean Young and Stan Drake, *Blondie*, King Feature Syndicate, July 26, 1996, reprints available through King Features Licensing: http://www.kingfeatures.com/reprint/index.htm

57. David Barstow, "Hoping to Escape Life Term, Officer Admits Man's Torture," *New York Times*, May 26, 1999.

58. Ibid.

59. Ibid.

60. Robert S. McNamara, *In Retrospect* (New York: Vintage Books, 1995).

61. Paul Hendrickson, *The Living and the Dead* (New York: Alfred A. Knopf: 1996), 376.

62. Editorial, "Mr. McNamara's War," *New York Times*, April 12, 1995.

63. McNamara, *In Retrospect*, preface, p. xx.

64. Ibid., 321.

65. Hendrickson, *The Living and the Dead,* 361. According to Hendrickson, this is a quote by David Halberstam in his letter to the editor of the *New York Times*, June 10, 1979.

FIVE: REMORSE, EXPLANATIONS, AND REPARATION

1. Thomas Moore, "Re-Morse: An Initiatory Disturbance of the Soul," in *Psychotherapy and the Remorseful Patient*, ed. E. Mark Stern (New York: Haworth Press, 1989), 83–93.

2. David Weber, "Killer Surgeon Sentenced: Kartell Gets Minimum 5 Years in Jail," *Boston Herald*, July 20, 2000.

3. F. W. de Klerk, Remarks of South African President de Klerk at a news conference held in South Africa to launch a new logo for the governing National Party, April 29, 1993.

4. Ibid.

5. Ibid.

6. Kevin Gover, September 8, 2000.

7. Ibid.

8. Murray Chass, "Baseball Roundup; Bonds Defends Clemens after Piazza Beanball," *New York Times*, July 11, 2000.

9. "20 Years for Woman in Husband's Killing," *New York Times*, May 31, 1995.

10. Adam Nossiter, "Lack of Regret in Confessions by the Suspect in 4 Beatings," *New York Times*, July 17, 1996.

11. Associated Press, "Man Sentenced for Sex Assault Blames Victim," *Bangor Daily News*, August 19–20, 2000.

12. Ibid.

13. Carolyn Thompson, "No Remorse From McVeigh," *Boston Herald*, March 29, 2001.

14. Ibid.

15. Rex W. Huppke, Associated Press, "McVeigh Executed for Oklahoma City Bombing; Dies with No Trace of Remorse," June 11, 2001.

16. Tony Czucka, Associated Press, "Immigrant Slaying Trial Opens in Germany," *Boston Globe*, August 23, 2000.

17. Ibid.

18. Ibid.

19. Associated Press, "Man Admits Shooting Half-Brother," *Maine Sunday Telegram*, July 31, 1994.

20. Ibid.

21. Ibid.

22. Scot Lehigh, "A Massive Murderer's Final Insult," *Boston Globe*, April 26, 2002.

23. Ibid.

24. Samuel Sewall, *The Diary and Life of Samuel Sewall*, Melvin Yazawa, ed. (Bedford Books: 1998), 2.

25. Ibid.

26. T. R. Reid, "Japan's Shame Brings Apology for Dec. 7, 1941," *Boston Globe*, November 22, 1994.

27. Editorial, David Brooks, "Prime-Time Monica," *New York Times*, March 5, 1999.

28. Ellen Goodman, "Say You're Sorry, Monica," *Boston Globe*, February 18, 1999.

29. Patrick Healy and Walter V. Robinson, "Professor Apologizes for Fabrications," *Boston Globe*, June 19, 2001

30. Sabrina Tavernise with Sophia Kishkovsky, "For the Families, Anger Mixes with Mourning," *New York Times*, August 18, 2000.

31. Ibid.

32. Judith Gaines, "Frank Sees Nation 'Upset' by Slur," *Boston Sunday Globe*, January 29, 1995.

33. Jill Zuckman, "GOP Leader Uses Slur to Refer to Frank," *Boston Globe*, January 28, 1995.

34. Ibid.

35. Editorial, "Hate Speech Comes to Congress," *New York Times*, January 29, 1995.

36. Ibid.

37. "Driver Who Hit Writer Wants to Apologize Personally," *Times Union*, (Albany, NY), September 3, 1999.

38. Kris Banvard, "The Prince and the Apology, *Columbus Dispatch*, July 1, 2002.

39. Selena Roberts, "Lights, Camera, Apology: Sprewell Takes the Stage," *New York Times*, January 23, 1999.

40. Ibid.

41. Associated Press, "Montana Senator Apologizes for Description of Arabs," Cable News Network, CNN.com, March 12, 1999.

42. Ibid.

43. James Sterngold, "Sailor Gets Life for Killing Gay Shipmate," *New York Times*, May 27, 1993.

44. Personal communication to the author in 1995.

45. Personal communication to the author in 1979.

46. Reuters, "Car Thief Sends Apologies," May 27, 1998.

47. Marc Fisher, "Glass's Actions Shout Volumes, Words Whisper," *Washington Post*, November 11, 2003.

48. Ibid.

49. Usha Lee McFarling, "In Tobacco War, Lobbyist Switches Allegiance; Ex-lawmaker Fights Cancer, Industry," *Boston Globe*, March 6, 1995.

50. Homer, *The Iliad*, trans. Robert Fitzgerald (New York: International Collectors Library, 1974), 207–8.

51. Ibid.

52. Ibid.

53. Ibid.

54. Ibid., 211.

55. Ibid., 215.

56. Associated Press, "Dodgers Apologize to Lesbian Couple," *New York Times*, August 23, 2000.

57. Ibid.

58. Personal communication to the author in 1997.

59. Eric Convey, "Payout Is No Relief for Abuse Victims," *Boston Sunday Herald*, December 21, 2003.

60. Lincoln's second inaugural speech, delivered on March 4, 1865.

SIX: WHY PEOPLE APOLOGIZE

1. Martin L. Hoffman, "Varieties of Empathy-Based Guilt," in *Guilt and Children*, ed. Jane Bybee (San Diego: Academic Press, 1998), 91–109.
2. Ibid.
3. June Price Tangney and Kurt W. Fischer, *Self-Conscious Emotions: The Psychology of Shame, Guilt, Embarrassment and Pride* (New York: Guilford Press, 1995).
4. This is a personal story generously related to me by a friend, November 25, 2003.
5. Foote, *The Civil War, A Narrative*, 567.
6. Ibid., 568.
7. Ibid.
8. Ibid., 569.
9. Ibid.
10. Ibid., 568.
11. Personal communication to the author in 1995.
12. This is a personal story generously related to me following my lecture by someone in the audience.
13. John Carmody, "Brinkley's Parting Shots at Clinton; On-Air Remarks May Jeopardize Interview," *Washington Post*, November 7, 1996.
14. Ibid.
15. David Bauder, "Brinkley Bows out with Apology, Little Sentiment," Associated Press wire, November 10, 1996.
16. "Brinkley Apologizes, Clinton Accepts," *This Week with David Brinkley*, November 10, 1996.
17. United Press International, "Clinton Accepts Brinkley Apology," November 10, 1996.
18. This is a personal story generously related to me by a friend on November 18, 2003.
19. Ibid.
20. This is a personal story generously related to me by a friend in 1997.
21. Rick Bragg, "Just a Grave for a Baby, but Anguish for a Town," *New York Times*, March 31, 1996.
22. Ibid.
23. Ibid.
24. Ibid.
25. Ibid.
26. Gustav Niebuhr, "Falwell Apologies for Saying an Angry God Allowed Attacks," *New York Times*, September 18, 2001.

27. Press release from the Jerry Falwell Ministries newsroom, September 17, 2001, originally posted on http://www.falwell.com. See also http://www.justice-respect.org/bkg/falwell_statement_2001.html. (last accessed March 12, 2004).

28. Ibid.

29. Ibid.

30. Ibid.

31. Lincoln's second inaugural speech, delivered on March 4, 1865.

32. Ellen Goodman, "Apology Not Accepted," *Boston Globe* as it appeared in the *Buffalo News*, September 21, 2001.

33. Ron Borges, "Tyson Apologizes for Biting; Asks for Chance to Box Again," *Boston Globe*, July 1, 1997.

34. Tim Graham, "Tyson Apologizes, Ex-Champ Chews to Make Amends," *Boston Herald*, July 1, 1997.

35. Ron Borges, "Tyson Apologizes for Biting; Asks for Chance to Box Again," *Boston Globe*, July 1, 1997.

36. Ibid.

37. Ibid., and Associated Press, "Contrite Tyson Says He Snapped," *Telegram & Gazette* (Worcester, MA), July 1, 1997.

38. Charlie Kenny, Barbara Kenny, and Ken Fowler, "Breaking the Curse of the Babe," letter to the editor, *Boston Globe*, October 4, 1995.

39. Ibid.

40. Samisoni Pareti, Associated Press, "Cannibals' Descendants Offer Apology in 1867 Death," *Boston Globe*, November 14, 2003.

41. Ibid.

EIGHT: THE TIMING OF APOLOGIES

1. Michael Kranish, "Thompson Apologizes to Clinton," *Boston Globe*, October 9, 1997.

2. Personal communication to the author in 1999.

3. Robeznieks, "The Power of an Apology."

4. Katharine Q. Seelye, "Chinese Finally Allow Clinton Time for a Telephone Apology," *New York Times*, May 15, 1999.

NINE: DELAYED APOLOGIES

1. Peter Pae, "At Long Last, a Conflict Ends for Minister; Decades after Napalm Bombing, U.S. Commander, Vietnamese Woman Make Their

Peace," *Washington Post*, February 20, 1997. (Some controversy followed the publication of John Plummer's story as first published in a religious magazine. While he acknowledged that he did not in fact "order" the strikes, it appears that he felt remorse and responsibility on behalf of the U.S. military, of which he was a part.)

2. Anne Gearan, Associated Press, "A Haunting Picture of Vietnam: Forgiven: Pilot Whose Napalm Burned Kim Phuc Finds Redemption," *Ottawa Citizen*, April 13, 1997.

3. Denise Chong, *The Girl in the Picture: The Story of Kim Phuc, the Photograph, and the Vietnam War* (New York: Penguin Books, 1999), 361.

4. Ibid., 360.

5. Gearan, "A Haunting Picture of Vietnam."

6. Ibid.

7. Eric Lomax, *The Railway Man: A POW's Searing Account of War, Brutality and Forgiveness* (New York: W. W. Norton, 1995).

8. Leonard Greene, "Attacker's Confession Stirs Long-Forgotten Memories of Racial Strife," *Boston Herald*, March 18, 1994.

9. Ibid.

10. Ibid.

11. Ibid.

12. Alcoholics Anonymous®, *Twelve Steps and Twelve Traditions* (New York: Alcoholics Anonymous World Services, 1953), 77.

13. Ibid.

14. Ibid.

15. Ibid., 83.

16. George F. Mahl, "A Personal Encounter with Scientific Deviance" (editorial), *American Psychologist*, 50, no. 10, (1995): 882–883. Copyright©1995 by the American Psychological Association. Reprinted with permission.

17. Ibid.

18. Ibid.

19. Ibid.

20. Ibid.

21. Harvey Araton, "Yogi and the Boss Complete Makeup Game," *New York Times*, January 6, 1999.

22. Ibid.

23. Ibid.

24. Ibid.

25. Richard Sandomir, "No Floating, No Stinging: Ali Extends Hand to Frazier," *New York Times*, March 15, 2001.

26. Ibid.

27. Ibid.

28. Ibid.

29. Associated Press, "Ali Apologizes for Frazier Remarks," *Times Union* (Albany, N.Y.), March 16, 2001.

30. Press Association Limited, "Stolen Flag Returned After 49 Years," February 2, 1994.

31. Ibid.

32. Ibid.

33. Reverend Billy Graham, in a transcript of an Oval Office conversation with Richard M. Nixon from 1972, made public by the National Archives in 2002. Third chronological release made on February 28, 2002. Available from the Nixon Presidential Materials Staff at the National Archives and Records Administration. Reported by David Firestone, "Billy Graham Responds to Lingering Anger over 1972 Remarks on Jews," *New York Times*, March 17, 2002.

34. Statement by Billy Graham released by his public relations firm (A. Larry Ross Communications, Dallas, Texas) on Friday, March 1, 2002.

35. Associated Press, "Romance Novelist Admits Plagerism," *St. Louis Post Dispatch,* July 30, 1997. Reprinted with the permission of the Associated Press.

36. "More Swiss Secrets," *Intelligencer Journal,* July 26, 1997.

37. Dan T. Carter, *The Politics of Rage: George Wallace, the Origins of the New Conservatism, and the Transformation of American Politics* (Baton Rouge: Louisiana State University Press, 1995), 415.

38. Ibid.

39. Ibid.

40. Ibid.

41. Howard Kurtz, "Author Says He Lied in Book on Anita Hill," *Washington Post,* June 27, 2001.

42. Ibid.

43. Robert Siegel and Noah Adams, anchors; Nina Totenberg, reporter, on *"All Things Considered,"* David Brock's Forthcoming Book *Blinded by the Right*, National Public Radio, July 2, 2001.

44. Ibid.

45. Personal communication with the author in 2003.

46. Martin F. Nolan, "An Apology to Gerald Ford," *Boston Globe*, December 18, 1996.

47. Richard Reeves, "I'm Sorry, Mr. President," *American Heritage* 47, no. 8 (December 1996): 52–55.

48. Ibid.

49. Ibid.

50. Luigi Accattoli, *When a Pope Asks Forgiveness: The Mea Culpas of John Paul II*, trans. Jordan Aumann (Boston: Pauline Books, 1998).

51. Ibid., 69.

52. Ibid.

53. Ibid.

54. Alison Mitchell, "Clinton Regrets 'Clearly Racist' U.S. Study," *New York Times*, May 17, 1997.

55. "Report of the Tuskegee Syphilis Study Legacy Committee Final Report," May 20, 1996. Available at http://hsc.virginia.edu/hs-library/historical/apology/report.html

56. On May 16, 1997, the surviving participants of the Tuskegee Syphilis Study and the members of the Tuskegee Syphilis Study Legacy Committee gathered at the White House and witnessed the president's apology on behalf of the U.S. government. Remarks of William Jefferson Clinton are available in the national archives at http://clinton4.nara.gov/textonly/new/remarks/Fri/19970516-898.html

57. The statement attributed to Adolph Hitler is the subject of scholarly debate. Kevork B. Bardakjian, in his book *Hitler and the Armenian Genocide* (Cambridge, MA: The Zoryan Institute, 1985), presents the quote as an English version of the German document handed to Louis P. Lochner in Berlin, which first appeared in Lochner's *What about Germany?* (New York: Dodd, Mead, 1942), 1–4. He indicates that the document was later presented at the Nuremberg Tribunal and identified as L-3 or Exhibit USA-28. For the German original see *Akten zur Deutschen Auswartigen Politik 1918–1945*, Serie D, Band VII, (Baden-Baden, 1956): 171–2. For a detailed analysis of the Nuremberg Trial's records indicating that this statement is falsely attributed to Hitler, refer to Heath W. Lowry, "The U.S. Congress and Adolf Hitler on the Armenians," *Political Communication and Persuasion 3*, no. 2 (1985).

58. Peter Balakian, *The Burning Tigris: The Armenian Genocide and America's Response* (New York: HarperCollins, 2003), xix.

59. "Regret but No Apology for Aborigines," BBC News Network, August 25, 1999.

60. Ibid.

61. *Declaration on the Relation of the Church to Non-Christian Religions (Nostra Aetate)*, October 28, 1965.

62. Ibid.

63. At a press conference on March 16, 1998, Cardinal Cassidy, president of the Holy See's Commission for Religious Relations with the Jews, presented for publication the document *We Remember: A Reflection on*

the Shoah. Joining him in the presentation were Bishop Pierre Duprey, vice president of the commission, and Father Remi Hoeckmann, O.P., its secretary. In the letter from Pope John Paul II to Cardinal Cassidy dated March 12, 1998, he wrote "it is my fervent hope that the document: *We Remember: A Reflection on the Shoah,* which the Commission for Religious Relations with the Jews has prepared under your direction, will indeed help to heal the wounds of past misunderstandings and injustices.

64. "A Great Leap backwards? Dialogue has not prevented a slide in Catholic-Jewish relations over Catholicism's narrative and symbolization of the Shoah," World Jewish Congress, *Policy Dispatches* no. 36 (November 1998), available at http://www.wjc.org.il/publications/policy_dispatches/pub_dis36.html

65. "Towards Renovation of the Relationship of Christians and Jews," Synod of the Evangelical Church of the Rhineland (FRG), 1980, http://www.bc.edu/research/cjl/meta-elements/texts/documents/protestant/EvChFRG1980.htm

66. See Brooks, "The Age of Apology," 309–374; and Eric K. Yamamoto, *Interracial Justice: Conflict and Reconciliation in Post-Civil Rights America* (New York: New York University Press, 1999).

TEN: NEGOTIATING APOLOGIES

1. Aaron Lazare, "The Interview as a Clinical Negotiation," in *The Medical Interview: Clinical Care, Education, and Research,* ed. Mack Lipkin, Jr., Samuel M. Putnam, and Aaron Lazare (New York: Springer-Verlag, 1995), 60–62.

2. Aaron Lazare, "Clinician/Patient Relations II: Conflict and Negotiation" in *Outpatient Psychiatry: Diagnosis and Treatment* (Baltimore: Williams & Wilkins, 1989), 137–152.

3. Personal communication to the author on May 27, 2003.

4. "Judge Cites Prosecutor, Then Relents in O. J. Case," *St. Louis Post-Dispatch,* February 24, 1995.

5. Ibid.

6. Scott Waddle with Ken Abraham, *The Right Thing* (Nashville, TN: Integrity, 2002).

7. Doug Struck, "In Japan, Victims' Families Expect a Personal Apology," *Washington Post,* February 27, 2001.

8. "Waddle, Facing End of Navy Career, Wants to Apologize to Families in Japan," *The Stars and Stripes,* April 21, 2001, available at

http://www.estripes.com/article.asp?section=104&article=1676&archive=true

9. Text of the letter released by Commander Scott Waddle's civilian lawyer, Charles W. Gittins, as it appeared in "Skipper of Sub Sends Regrets to Japanese," *St. Petersburg Times*, February 26, 2001.

10. Struck, "In Japan, Victims' Families Expect a Personal Apology."

11. John Kifner, "Captain of Sub is Reprimanded and Will Quit," *New York Times*, April 24, 2001.

12. Ibid.

13. Elaine Sciolino, "Sub Commander Apologizes More Directly to Families," *New York Times*, March 1, 2001.

14. "Tearful Ex-US Navy Skipper Prays for Japanese Collision Victims," *Spacewire*, December 15, 2002.

15. Ryan Kawailani, "Waddle Revisits Sub Accident, Slams Navy," Hawaiinews.com, January 24, 2003.

16. Paul Alexander, Associated Press, "Helicopter Pilot Bobby Hall Released by North Korea," AP Wire, Panmunjon, South Korea, December 30, 1994. Reprinted with Permission of the Associated Press.

17. Paul Alexander, Associated Press, "North Korea Releases Statement from Captive Pilot," AP Wire, Seoul, South Korea, December 29, 1994.

18. "Collision With China," *New York Times*, April 12, 2001.

19. Letter from Ambassador Prueher to Chinese Minister of Foreign Affairs Tang, Office of the Press Secretary, April 11, 2001, http://www.pbs.org/newshour/bb/asia/china/plane/letter_4-11.html

20. Helen Kennedy, "Crises Ends as China Frees Yanks, U.S. Says It's 'Very Sorry' —Twice," *Daily News* (New York), April 12, 2001.

21. Ibid.

22. Norman B. Ferris, *The Trent Affair: A Diplomatic Crisis* (Nashville, TN: University of Tennessee Press, 1977), 18.

23. Gordon H. Warren, *Fountain of Discontent: The Trent Affair and Freedom of the Seas* (Boston: Northeastern University Press, 1981), 104.

24. Ibid., 105.

25. Ferris, *The Trent Affair*, 51.

26. Ibid., 183–91.

27. Patrick Healy, "Professor Apologizes for Fabrications," *Boston Globe*, June 19, 2001.

28. Joseph J. Ellis, further statement issued through his attorney, John Taylor Williams, Esq., and published on the Mt. Holyoke website, August 17, 2001.

29. Associated Press, "Lott Apologies for Terrible Words," *Telegram & Gazette* (Worcester, MA), December 12, 2002.

30. Ibid.

31. Scott Shepard, "As Furor Grows, Lott Expands his Apology," *Atlanta Journal-Constitution*, December 12, 2002.

32. Adam Nagourney and Carl Hulse, "Bush Rebukes Lott over Remarks on Thurmond," *New York Times*, December 13, 2002.

33. David M. Halbfinger, "Lott Apologizes but Won't Yield Leadership Post," *New York Times*, December 14, 2002.

34. D'Este, *Patton*, 521–46.

35. Martin Blumenson, *The Patton Papers, 1940–1945* (Boston: Houghton-Mifflin, 1974) 330–31.

36. D'Este, *Patton*, 521–46.

37. Ibid.

38. Barkan, *The Guilt of Nations*, xxix.

ELEVEN: APOLOGY AND FORGIVENESS

1. Loren L. Toussaint, David R. Williams, Marc A Musick, and Susan A. Everson, *Forgiveness and Health: Age Differences in a U.S. Probability Sample, Journal of Adult Development*, 8, no. 4 (2001): 249–57.

2. See Adin Steinsaltz, *Teshuvah: A Guide for the Newly Observant Jew* (Northvale, NJ: Jason Aronson, 1996); and Pinchus H. Peli, *On Repentance: The Thoughts and Oral Discourses of Rabbi Joseph Dov Soloveitchik* (Northvale, NJ: Jason Aronson, 2000).

3. Steinsaltz, *Teshuvah*.

4. Rabbi Eliyahu Touger, *Maimonides Mishneh Torah: The Laws of Repentance* (New York: Moznaim, 1990).

5. Harvey Cox, "The Roots of Repentance: Some Thoughts on Forgiveness for a Nation in the Midst of Apologies," *Religion and Values in Public Life*, The Center for the Study of Values in Public Life at Harvard Divinity School, 5, no. 4 (Summer 1997).

6. Robert D. Enright and Joanna North, eds., *Exploring Forgiveness* (Madison: University of Wisconsin Press, 1998), 47.

7. L. Gregory Jones, *Embodying Forgiveness: A Theological Analysis* (Grand Rapids, MI: Eerdmans, 1995), 159.

8. Ibid.

9. Donald W. Shriver, Jr., "Is There Forgiveness in Politics?" in *Exploring Forgiveness*, eds. Robert D. Enright and Joanna North (Madison: University of Wisconsin Press, 1998), 136.

10. John H. White, "Bernardin's Accuser Dies: Cook, 36, Was Forgiven by Cardinal after Dropping Sex Abuse Charges," *Chicago Sun Times*, September 23, 1995.

11. Gustav Niebuhr, "For Cardinal and Accuser, a Profound Reconciliation," *New York Times*, January 7, 1995.

12. Edward Walsh, "Cardinal Describes 'Profound Reconciliation' with Former Accuser," *Washington Post*, January 5, 1995.

13. Brian Jackson, "Bernardin, Ex-accuser Find Peace," *Chicago Sun-Times*, January 4, 1995.

14. Gustav Niebuhr, "For Cardinal and Accuser, Profound Reconciliation," *New York Times*, January 7, 1995.

15. Edward Walsh, "Cardinal Describes 'Profound Reconciliation.'"

16. George Herald, "My Favorite Assassin," *Harper's* (April 1943): 449–451.

17. Ibid.

18. Ibid.

19. Victor Hugo, *Les Misérables* (New York: Modern Library, 1992).

20. Ibid., 92.

21. Dietrich Bonhoeffer, *The Cost of Discipleship* (New York: Macmillan, 1963), 47.

22. Ibid.

23. Eric Lomax, *The Railway Man: A POW's Searing Account of War, Brutality and Forgiveness* (New York: W. W. Norton, 1995).

24. Ibid., 206.

25. Ibid., 256.

26. Ibid., 225.

27. Ibid., 226.

28. Ibid., 233.

29. Ibid., 241.

30. Ibid., 240

31. Ibid., 252.

32. Ibid., 253.

33. Ibid., 254–55.

34. Ibid., 263.

35. Ibid., 264.

36. Ibid., 266.

37. Ibid., 268.

38. Ibid., 271.

39. Ibid., 274.

40. Ibid., 275.

41. Ibid., 276.

TWELVE: AFTERWORD: THE FUTURE OF APOLOGIES

1. Michael Henderson, *The Forgiveness Factor: Stories of Hope in a World of Conflict* (Salem, OR: Grosvenor Books, 1996).

2. Barkan, *The Guilt of Nations*, xxiv–xxv.

3. Michael Phayer, *The Catholic Church and the Holocaust, 1930–1965* (Bloomington: Indiana University Press, 2000).

4. *Declaration on the Relation of the Church to Non-Christian Religions (Nostra Aetate)*, October 28, 1965.

5. Ibid.

6. Michael Phayer, *The Catholic Church and the Holocaust*, 203.

7. *Declaration on the Relation of the Church to Non-Christian Religions (Nostra Aetate)*, October 28, 1965.

8. Ibid.

9. Michael Phayer, *The Catholic Church and the Holocaust*, 214.

10. Richard von Weizsacker, May 8, 1985.

11. Ibid.

12. Anthony Lewis, *New York Times*, Editorial, May 1, 1986.

13. Jeffrey Herf, *Divided Memory: The Nazi Past in the Two Germanys* (Cambridge: Harvard University Press, 1997), 355.

14. Eric K. Yamamoto, Margaret Chon, Carol L. Izumi, Jerry Kang, and Frank H. Wu, *Race, Rights and Reparation: Law and the Japanese American Internment* (New York: Aspen Law, 2001).

15. Barkan, *The Guilt of Nations*, 30.

16. Ibid., 31.

17. Wills, *Lincoln at Gettysburg*, 17–19.

18. President Ulysses S. Grant, Eighth Annual Message to Congress, December 5, 1876, http://www.geocities.com/presidentialspeeches/1876.htm

19. See, e.g., Erving Goffman, *Relations in Public: Microstudies of the Public Order* (New York: Basic Books, 1971); Shoshana Blum-Kulka, Juliane House, and Gabriele Kasper, eds., *Cross Cultural Pragmatics: Requests and Apologies*, vol. 31 (New Jersey: Ablex, 1989); and William L. Benoit, *Accounts, Excuses, and Apologies: A Theory of Image Restoration Strategies* (New York: State University of New York Press, 1995).

20. See, e.g., Tavuchis, *Mea Culpa*; Engel, *The Power of Apology*; Blanchard and McBride, *The One Minute Apology*; and Brooks, "The Age of Apology."

21. Babylonian Talmud, Pes. 54a.

22. A summary of this talk was published in "What makes for a good apology," *For a Change* 16, no. 1 (February/March 2003); see also my

unpublished essay on my experience at Caux, copy available from author.

23. Robert Jay Lifton, *Super Power Syndrome: America's Apocalyptic Confrontation with the World* (New York: Thunder's Mouth Press, 2003).

24. Lifton, *Super Power Syndrome;* Jessica Stern, *Terror in the Name of God: Why Religious Militants Kill* (New York: HarperCollins, 2003); Editorial, Thomas L. Friedman, "The Humiliation Factor," *New York Times*, November 9, 2003; and for Thucydides, see Donald Kagan, *On the Origins of War and the Preservation of Peace* (New York: Doubleday, 1995).

25. Thomas J. Scheff, *Bloody Revenge: Emotions, Nationalism, and War* (Boulder, CO: Westview Press, 1994).

Bibliography

Accattoli, Luigi. *When a Pope Asks Forgiveness: The* Mea Culpas *of John Paul II*, translated by Jordan Aumann. Boston: Pauline Books, 1998.

Alcoholics Anonymous, *Twelve Steps and Twelve Traditions*. New York: Alcoholics Anonymous World Services, 1953.

Balakian, Peter. *The Burning Tigris: The Armenian Genocide and America's Response*. New York: HarperCollins, 2003.

Bardakjian, Kevork B. *Hitler and the Armenian Genocide*. Cambridge, MA: The Zoryan Institute, 1985.

Barkan, Elazar. *The Guilt of Nations: Restitution and Negotiating Historical Injustices*. New York: W. W. Norton, 2000.

Benoit, William L. *Accounts, Excuses, and Apologies: A Theory of Image Restoration Strategies*. New York: State University of New York Press, 1995.

Blanchard, Ken and Margaret McBride. *The One Minute Apology: A Powerful Way to Make Things Better*. New York: William Morrow, 2003.

Blum-Kulka, Shoshana, Julian House and Gabreile Kasper, ed. *Cross Cultural Pragmatics: Requests and Apologies*, vol. 31. New Jersey: Ablex, 1989.

Bonhoeffer, Dietrich. *The Cost of Discipleship*. New York: MacMillan, 1963.

Brooks, Roy L. "The Age of Apology." In *When Sorry Isn't Enough*, ed. Roy L. Brooks. New York: New York University Press, 1999.

Bybee, Jane. "The Emergence of Gender Differences in Guilt during Adolescence." In *Guilt and Children*, ed. Jane Bybee. San Diego: Academic Press, 1998, 113–22.

Carroll, James. *Constantine's Sword: The Church and the Jews*. Boston, MA: Houghton Mifflin, 2001.

Carter, Dan T. *The Politics of Rage: George Wallace, the Origins of the New Conservatism, and the Transformation of American Politics*. Baton Rouge: Louisiana State University Press, 1995.

Chong, Denise. *The Girl in the Picture: The Story of Kim Phuc, the Photograph, and the Vietnam War*. New York: Penguin Books, 1999.

Cox, Harvey. "The Roots of Repentance: Some Thoughts on Forgiveness for a Nation in the Midst of Apologies." In *Religion and Values in Public*

Life, The Center for the Study of Values in Public Life at Harvard Divinity School, 5, no. 4, Summer 1975.

D'Este, Carlo. *Patton: A Genius for War.* New York: HarperCollins, 1995.

Eisenhower, John S. D. *General Ike: A Personal Reminiscence.* New York: Free Press, 2003.

Engel, Beverly. *The Power of Apology: Healing Steps to Transform All Your Relationships.* New York: JohnWiley, 2001.

Enright, Robert D., and Joanna North, eds. *Exploring Forgiveness.* Madison: The University of Wisconsin Press, 1998.

Ferris, Norman B. *The Trent Affair: A Diplomatic Crisis.* Knoxville, TN: University of Tennessee Press, 1977.

Foote, Shelby. *The Civil War, A Narrative: Fredericksburg to Meridian.* New York, Random House, 1986.

Gilligan, Carol. *In a Different Voice: Psychological Theory and Women's Development.* Cambridge: Harvard University Press, 1982.

Gobodo-Madikizela, Pumla. *A Human Being Died That Night: A South African Story of Forgiveness.* New York: Houghton Mifflin, 2003.

Goffman, Erving. *Relations in Public: Microstudies of the Public Order.* New York: Basic Books, 1971.

Gomes, Peter. *The Good Book: Reading the Bible with Mind and Heart.* New York: William Morrow, 1996.

Goodspeed, D. J. *The German Wars: 1914–1915.* Boston: Houghton Mifflin, 1977.

Helmick, Raymond, S. J., and Rodney L. Petersen, eds. *Forgiveness and Reconciliation: Religion, Public Policy, and Conflict Transformation.* Radnor, PA: Templeton Foundation Press, 2001.

Henderson, Michael. *The Forgiveness Factor: Stories of Hope in a World of Conflict.* Salem, OR: Grosvenor Books, 1996.

Hendrickson, Paul. *The Living and the Dead.* New York: Alfred A. Knopf, 1996.

Herf, Jeffrey. *Divided Memory: The Nazi Past in the Two Germanys.* Cambridge: Harvard University Press, 1997.

Hoffman, Martin L. "Varieties of Empathy-Based Guilt." In *Guilt and Children,* ed. Jane Bybee. San Diego: Academic Press, 1998, 91–109.

Homer. *The Iliad.* Translated by Robert Fitzgerald. New York: International Collectors Library, 1974.

Hugo, Victor. *Les Misérables.* New York: Random House, 1992.

Jones, L. Gregory. *Embodying Forgiveness: A Theological Analysis.* Grand Rapids, MI: Eerdmans, 1995.

Kagan, Donald. *On the Origins of War and the Preservation of Peace.* New York: Doubleday, 1995.

Lazare, Aaron. *"The Interview as a Clinical Negotiation."* In *The Medical Interview: Clinical Care, Education, and Research,* ed. Mack Lipkin, Jr., Samuel M. Putnam, and Aaron Lazare. New York: Springer-Verlag, 1995.

Lazare, Aaron. *"Clinician/Patient Relations II: Conflict and Negotiation."* In *Outpatient Psychiatry: Diagnosis and Treatment.* Baltimore: Williams and Wilkins, 1989.

Lifton, Robert Jay. *Super Power Syndrome: America's Apocalyptic Confrontation with the World.* New York: Thunder's Mouth Press, 2003.

Lipkin, Mack, Jr., Samuel M. Putnam, and Aaron Lazare, eds. *The Medical Interview: Clinical Care, Education, and Research.* New York: Springer-Verlag, 1995.

Lochner, Louis P. *What about Germany?* New York: Dodd, Mead, 1942.

Lomax, Eric. *The Railway Man: A POW's Searing Account of War, Brutality and Forgiveness.* New York: W. W. Norton, 1995.

McCullough, David. *Truman.* New York: Simon & Schuster, 1992.

McLuhan, Marshall and Quentin Fiore. *The Medium is the Massage.* Coordinated by Jerome Agel. New York: Bantam Books, 1967.

McNamara, Robert S. *In Retrospect.* New York: Vintage Books, 1995.

Meyer, Christopher, and Stan Davis. *It's Alive: The Coming Convergence of Information, Biology, and Business.* New York: Crown Business, 2003.

Minow, Martha. "Truth Commissions." In *Between Vengeance and Forgiveness.* Boston: Beacon Press, 1998.

Moore, Thomas. "Re-Morse: An Initiatory Disturbance of the Soul." In *Psychotherapy and the Remorseful Patient,* ed. E. Mark Stern. New York: Haworth Press, 1989, 83–93.

Murphy, Jeffrie G. and Jean Hampton. *Forgiveness and Mercy.* New York: Cambridge University Press, 1988.

Newman, Louis J., ed. *The Talmudic Anthology.* New York: Behrman House, 1947.

Olshtain, Elite. "Apologies across Languages." In *Cross-Cultural Pragmatics: Requests and Apologies,* ed. by Shoshana Blum-Kulka, Juliane House, and Gabriele Kasper. New Jersey: Ablex, 1989, 157.

Oxford English Dictionary. Vol. 1. New York: Oxford University Press, 1989.

Peli, Pinchus. *On Repentance: The Thought and Oral Discourses of Rabbi Joseph Dov Soloveitchik.* Northvale, N J: Jason Aronson, 2000.

Phayer, Michael. *The Catholic Church and the Holocaust: 1930–1965.* Bloomington: Indiana University Press, 2000.

Rice, Allen Thorndike. "Frederick Douglass." In *Reminiscences of Abraham Lincoln.* New York: The North American Review, 1888, 192–93.

Scheff, Thomas J. *Bloody Revenge: Emotions, Nationalism, and War.* Boulder, CO: Westview Press, 1994.

Schimmel, Solomon. *Wounds Not Healed by Time: The Power of Repentance and Forgiveness*. New York: Oxford University Press, 2002.

Sewall, Samuel. *The Diary and Life of Samuel Sewall*, ed. Melvin Yazawa. Bedford, MA: St. Martin's, 1998.

Shriver, Donald W., Jr. *An Ethic for Enemies: Forgiveness in Politics*. New York: Oxford University Press, 1995.

Steinsaltz, Adin. *Teshuvah: A Guide for the Newly Observant Jew*. Northvale, NJ: Jason Aronson, 1996.

Stern, Jessica. *Terror in the Name of God: Why Religious Militants Kill*. New York: HarperCollins, 2003.

Sugimoto, Naomi, ed. *Japanese Apology across Disciplines*. Commack, NY: Nova Science, 1999.

Tangney, June Price and Kurt W. Fischer. *Self-Conscious Emotions: The Psychology of Shame, Guilt, Embarrassment and Pride*. New York: Guilford Press, 1995.

Tannen, Deborah. *Talking from 9–5: How Women's and Men's Conversational Styles Affect Who Gets Heard, Who Gets Credit, and What Gets Done at Work*. New York: William Morrow, 1994.

Tavuchis, Nicholas. *Mea Culpa: A Sociology of Apology and Reconciliation*. Stanford: Stanford University Press, 1991.

Touger, Rabbi Eliyahu. *Maimonides Mishneh Torah: The Laws of Repentance*. New York: Moznaim, 1990.

Tutu, Desmond Mpilo. *No Future without Forgiveness*. New York: Doubleday, 1999.

Waddle, Scott, with Ken Abraham. *"The Right Thing."* Nashville, TN: Integrity, 2002.

Warren, Gordon H. *Fountain of Discontent: The Trent Affair and Freedom of the Seas*. Boston: Northeastern University Press, 1981.

White, Ronald C. Jr. *Lincoln's Greatest Speech: The Second Inaugural*. New York: Simon and Schuster, 2002.

Wills, Garry. *Lincoln at Gettysburg: the Words That Remade America*. New York: Simon and Schuster, 1992.

Worthington, Everett L., Jr., ed. *Dimensions of Forgiveness: Psychological Research & Theological Perspectives*. Philadelphia, PA: Templeton Foundation Press, 1998.

Wright, Robert. *Nonzero: The Logic of Human Destiny*. New York: Vintage Books, 2000.

Yamamoto, Eric K. *Interracial Justice: Conflict and Reconciliation in Post–Civil Rights America*. New York: New York University Press, 1999.

Yamamoto, Eric K., Margaret Chon, Carol L. Izumi, Jerry Kang, and Frank H. Wu. *Race, Rights and Reparation: Law and the Japanese American Internment*. New York: Aspen Law, 2001.

Index

Note: Page numbers in *italics* indicate tables. Page numbers in **bold** indicate entire chapter ranges.

Discussion Group Guide for
Aaron Lazare's *On Apology*

What role does sincerity play in the effectiveness of an apology?

Is it meaningful for citizens of a country to apologize for national offenses committed before they were born?

Should the American government make an apology to African Americans for slavery? If so, why has it not happened?

Why do so many apologies seem to be inadequate or even offensive?

What is the relationship of apology to forgiveness?

What relevance do apologies have to the following groups: law enforcement officials, religious organizations, attorneys, physicians, sick or dying individuals?

Select an apology that appeared in the news during the last year and discuss the motives for offering the apology and the effectiveness of the apology.

From your own personal life, discuss an apology that you received and the reasons for its effectiveness or lack thereof.

Distinguish between apologies in everyday life, repentance in religious practice, and apologies in jurisprudence.